LAKELAND WATERWAYS

A history of travel along the English Lakes

Robert Beale & Richard Kirkman

Lily Publications

Previous page: **Raven** pictured
en-route from Howtown to
Glenridding, with Birk Crag
behind.

ISBN 978-1-907945-86-1

The rights of Robert Beale and
Richard Kirkman to be identified
as the authors of this work have
been asserted in accordance with
the Copyright Act 1991.

Produced in the Isle of Man by
Lily Publications Ltd.

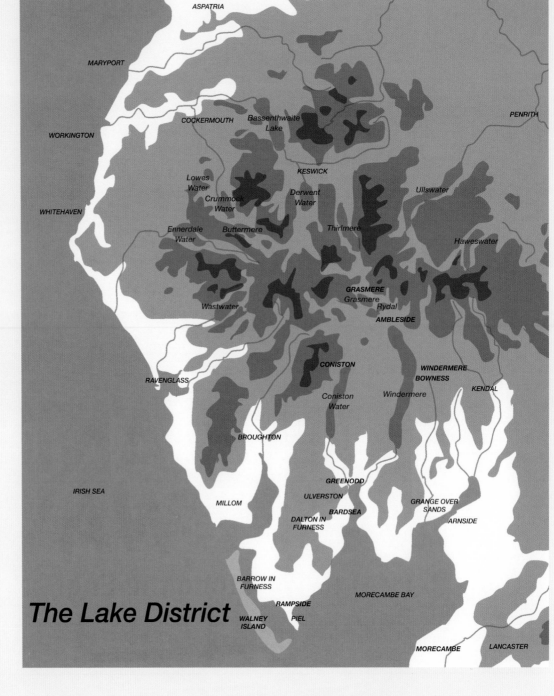

The Lake District

Contents

Foreword

The Lake District has long been a magnet for visitors, drawn to England's largest and most popular National Park to enjoy spectacular scenery, the country's highest mountains and it's longest and deepest lakes. Today, no visit is complete without taking advantage of a trip aboard one of the extensive fleets of historic ships.

The lakes radiate from the centre of the region, betraying their glacial origin. Long before they became tourist attractions in their own right, these Lakeland waterways played a significant role in allowing the earliest settlers to travel around what was initially a heavily wooded region. They aided the development of local industries by becoming a crucial transport artery, facilitating the growth of lake-side woodland trades, mining and quarrying, as local roads were primitive and often impassable. For generations the lakes provided a communications lifeline to the communities bordering their shores, and ferries offered more direct links across the region.

The scenic beauty of Lakeland took time to be appreciated, as the rugged splendour did not initially appeal to the sensibilities of the few who could afford to visit this remote region. Although access was difficult, a handful of 18th century pioneers produced guide books to publicise itineraries and encourage visitors by establishing 'viewing stations' to see the best of the scenery; Wordsworth published his own 'Guide to the Lakes' in 1810.

Lakeland remained remote until the coming of the railways transformed access from the main population centres and acted as a catalyst to a significant expansion in tourism. By the mid-Victorian era, Windermere, Coniston, Keswick and Lakeside has successively been added to the network, supplementing the cross-Morecambe Bay steamers that brought visitors from Fleetwood and Blackpool. The parallel development of tourist facilities saw steamer services established on Windermere, Coniston Water, Derwentwater and Ullswater, strongly encouraged or owned by the railway companies, who developed tour programmes to offer attractive packages to the potential traveller.

The story of the Lakeland Waterways is one of intense Victorian competition, of triumph, severe weather, fires, speed records, accidents and tragic sinkings, of opulence and of innovation, as successive fleets raised the quality standards. From the smallest rowing boat to the most substantial steamer, the history of the Lake services reflects the wider tale of the development and growth of the Lake District economy.

Today tourism is the major industry in the National Park, and the Lakeland Waterways play a key role in attracting visitors; Windermere Lake Cruises is consistently one of the top 10 paid visitor attractions in England, with over 1.4 million trips annually. The Lakes still offer a rich variety of sailings on fleets ranging from traditional historic steamers to more modern vessels or a variety of 'self-hire' options, repeating the journeys appreciated by generations of visitors since Victorian times. And they remain the home to thousands of registered small boats. The authors hope this book will encourage many more to enjoy this experience.

Robert Beale and Richard Kirkman
May 2015

Opposite: **Raven** rests at Glenridding Pier.

Left: **Mallard** in her present condition.

Above: Windermere Ferry by William Anderson (1757 – 1837). Below: Engraving from 1784 showing Belle Isle, the newly built roundhouse and the Nab Ferry.

Excursions to the Lake District

The Lake District in the eighteenth century was an inaccessible, little visited and forbidding place. Early observers had mixed views as to the region's attractiveness. In 1772, Daniel Defoe observed scenery *'the wildest, most barren and frightful of any that I have passed over in England'*, but William Gilpin, who thought lakes should have irregular shorelines with islands dotted about, found much to his pleasure. Thomas West's 1778 Guide outlined tours with 'viewing stations', and itineraries incorporating up to half a dozen stations. His tour of Windermere included stops at Station Scar above the Ferry, Belle Isle and Rawlinson Nab, and recommended a stop in Bowness Bay. In 1783 Keswick cartographer Peter Crosthwaite published the first quality maps of the area, marking West's stations as well as others at locations of his choosing. Wordsworth did more than any other to promote Windermere when his 'Guide to the Lakes' was published – initially anonymously – in 1810. He celebrated the mountains and lakes for their natural beauty, not conforming to Gilpin's ideal, or framed within one of West's stations.

Thomas Gray was one of the earliest Lake District tourists. He travelled in the Romantic style with notebook and mirror, observing the landscape 'in reverse', by framing a scene to optimise its picturesque qualities. A growing stream of visitors – known as Lakers – followed, prompted further by Ackermann's 'A Picturesque Tour of the English Lakes' of 1821 which described Windermere as *'a bold foreground, a fine transparent sheet of water, with islands, rich woods, and wavy mountains'*. The remoteness of the district limited the number of visitors as the only way to cross the area was on foot or horseback, on roads of such poor quality that Gilpin observed of Derwentwater *'it seems to have been so little frequented, that... we had some difficulty in finding a bridle road'* and; *'were the roads better, the tour of the lake of Keswick would perhaps be one of the grandest and most beautiful rides in England'*.

The state of the roads ensured that only essential travel was undertaken. Whilst horses and carts gradually enabled trade routes elsewhere, packhorses remained necessary in the Lake District. A network linked Ulverston, Hawkshead, Kendal, and Cockermouth to the west coast; Kendal becoming an important hub on the main route to Scotland, with up to 350 packhorses frequenting the town each week. Wheeled vehicles reached Ambleside from the south, but thereafter roads deteriorated making horseback the only practical proposition.

Road improvements came with the turnpikes, which reached Whitehaven in 1739. A Kendal turnpike trust was formed in 1761, which upgraded the main route to Keswick via Ambleside and Grasmere. This brought wheeled transport to the central lakes, with the first stagecoaches arriving in the 1760s, but private carriages only reached Rydal as late as 1801 – a noteworthy event diarised by Dorothy Wordsworth. The growing tourist trade further increased road traffic with 15,240 carriages passing Rydal in 1855.

From 1819, passengers from the south completed their journey from Preston and Lancaster by swift horse-drawn packet boats on the Kendal Canal. Timetabled

The Furness Railway was an enthusiastic promoter of tourist business – this hand cart took the message onto the streets for the Barrow Hospital parade in 1909. (Sankey collection)

Gwalia approached Fleetwood with a heavily laden inbound sailing.

Above: The FR made strenuous efforts to promote tourism.

Right: A heavily laden **Lady Evelyn** prepares to head across Morecambe Bay. (Sankey collection)

coach routes were advertised, and were available from Kendal for onward travel to Windermere.

Early railway promoters saw the Lake District more as a barrier to direct links to Scotland than a source of potential business. By 1835 construction was under way of a trunk route from London to Preston, with the Preston & Wyre Railway preparing to provide a link to Fleetwood, whence steamer services would reach Ardrossan, for Glasgow. Little traffic was foreseen from the country between Preston and Glasgow.

Regular steamer services were soon established across Morecambe Bay. A network of sailings from Ulverston, Bardsea, Piel and Barrow linked to Liverpool, Blackpool, Fleetwood, Lancaster and Morecambe. The steamer *Windermere* inaugurated services between Liverpool and Ulverston (Canal Foot) via Blackpool in 1835; by July 1843 twice-weekly sailings were advertised on the route. Later she made the return trip three times a week, leaving each port on alternate days, with Sundays off. Other services were operated daily between Morecambe and Piel by the Fleetwood built steamer *Albion,* and by the *Rose,* which traded between Blackpool and Ulverston.

On 30th July 1844 the Cumberland Pacquet reported *'the great number of tourists constantly arriving and departing by the steamer from Fleetwood and the Windermere from Liverpool'* and noted that *'Ulverston may be ranked among the various points from which tourists set out on their excursion among the Lakes'*.

Rails to Windermere

The railway reached Lancaster and Fleetwood in 1840 and construction of the 69 miles northwards from Lancaster to Carlisle followed; the first section opened to Kendal on 22nd September 1846, with a connecting coach from the Kings Arms to the piers at Bowness. This marked the end of the fast packet boat canal service from Preston.

In August 1844, the Kendal & Windermere Railway Company announced plans to extend the railway from Kendal to Low Wood, a natural lake-side destination with a popular hotel. The idea provoked protest from William Wordsworth. In October 1844 he published his celebrated sonnet *'Is there no nook of English ground secure from rash assault…'* Further opposition came from landowners and Wordsworth's literary friends, but they were appeased when the line was cut back to Birthwaite – a small hamlet a mile from the lake at Bowness – thereby avoiding land conflicts and reducing construction costs. The new alignment made passive provision for a future northwards extension.

The line opened to Birthwaite on 20th April 1847. There was little to entertain passengers at the terminus on opening day, so they headed to Bowness to promenade or take a steamer trip. The Directors retired for a celebratory lunch at the Royal Hotel in Bowness, followed by dinner at the Crown Hotel. Cornelius Nicholson envisaged that the railway would *'give the dwellers of the great hives of manufacturing industry an opportunity of exchanging their murky atmosphere*

for the silvery mists of the mountains in perhaps two hours and a half'.

The railway shareholders provided finance to build an hotel adjacent to the station, which opened on 12th May 1847. The 1849 Mannex & Co Directory refers to *'a splendid hotel, denominated the Windermere Hotel'*. By 1854 it was advertised as 'Rigg's Windermere Hotel', reflecting the contemporary practice of incorporating the proprietor's name.

The first excursion took place in July 1847, and the settlement grew with ribbon development down the road to Bowness. In 1858 it was named Windermere by the Post Office. The railway appealed to both the working class day-tripper and the cotton magnates, who developed exclusive lake-shore residences and accessed their offices in Liverpool and Manchester by rail.

The railway soon carried gunpowder traffic, brought by road from Langdale instead of sailing to Newby Bridge, and new businesses opened up to get local fish to market in Manchester.

The tourist business expanded, with up to 17 excursion trains timetabled to Windermere on peak weekends. In 1869 there were reports of large numbers of visitors from Yorkshire and Lancashire; on Whit Monday 1883 around 8,000 arrived by train. The platforms were extended and two bays added. In 1875 there were nine weekday services scheduled on the branch, but the Sunday service was extremely limited. By the First World War the service had grown to eleven weekday departures.

The growth of wealthy residences on the lake-shore was sufficient to justify the establishment in 1912 of a daily 'Club Train' whose members paid a supplement to the First Class fare to ride in an exclusive special saloon to Preston, Wigan and Manchester.

Further routes were promoted within the Lake District, particularly after 1875, but opposition was much stronger than for the earlier schemes, and Ruskin was particularly prominent in voicing his concerns. He remarked: *'The stupid herds of modern tourists let themselves be emptied, like coals from a sack, at Windermere and Keswick. Having got there, what the new railway has to do is to shovel those who have come to Keswick, to Windermere – and to shovel those who have come to Windermere, to Keswick…'*

In 1899 the British Electric Traction Company contemplated a 3ft 6in gauge electric tramway along

the eastern shore from Bowness to Ambleside, but local landowners and residents strongly opposed the idea and it came to naught.

Opening up the Furness district

The first railway in Furness was a more domestic affair. The Furness Railway Company (FR) sought to exploit potential slate traffic (from Kirkby) and ore (from Lindal) to the fledgling port of Barrow. These initial routes opened from Millwood to Kirkby on 3rd May 1846 (with coach connections offered from Kirkby to Coniston from August 1846) and from Crooklands (near Dalton) to Barrow on 3rd June 1846.

Tourist potential was not completely ignored; in February 1846 the company formalised agreement with John Abel Smith and Mr Laidlaw of Fleetwood to coordinate rail and twice-daily steamer services between Fleetwood and Piel. Through ticketing was to be offered from stations in Lancashire, with a series of onward omnibus connections to the Lakes from Dalton and Kirkby.

The Westmorland Gazette of 22nd August published the timetable: -

NOTICE: The 'Ayrshire Lassie' plies daily, weather permitting. Fleetwood depart 11am and 2pm; Piel depart 1pm and 4pm; Dalton depart 12.30pm and 3.30pm in connexion with the 6.45pm Fleetwood Mail Train to Preston. Conveyances connect with the steam yachts 'Lord of the Isles' and 'Lady of the Lake' to Bowness and Ambleside.

In March 1847 the FR agreed to charter the steamer *Lochlong* – which had served the Glasgow-Loch Long route since 1842 – for the service to Piel. Renamed *Helvellyn* she operated between Fleetwood and Piel from 24th May. The Liverpool, Fleetwood and Furness Steam Packet Company placed *Zephyr* on the route from Liverpool via Fleetwood to Piel in 1848, but she was withdrawn at the end of the 1849 season.

Meanwhile the FR was extending to Piel Pier along an embankment constructed by Abel Smith, but the parties failed to reach agreement on terms for using the pier. Fleetwood services transferred to Barrow from 1847, with the season continuing until 31st October and the timetable became tidal dependent. Departure times from Fleetwood varied between 06.00 am and 3.30 pm, making it an unattractive prospect. For the 1848 season the service operated to a fixed schedule to Piel but the two parties still differed and the FR built a 'steamboat wharf' at Barrow, opening in 1849. In 1852 the FR agreed to lease the Piel operation, but before the transaction was completed much of the pier was destroyed in a storm. The railway purchased Abel Smith's interest for £15,000 and repaired the facility.

The opening of the Ulverstone & Lancaster Railway in 1857 gave the FR a link to the main line at Carnforth and the Fleetwood link became seasonal. The *Helvellyn* continued on the Fleetwood to Piel service until the end of the 1867 season, when the replacement *Walney* (I) was secured from McNab & Co of Greenock. Entering service on 1st June 1868, she also operated as a tug in the expanding Barrow Docks. The increasing volume of dock traffic prompted the FR to close the Fleetwood link at the end of the 1869 season.

The Morecambe link to Piel was worked by the Midland Railway from the opening of Morecambe harbour in 1851. The *Albion*, already operating on the route, was purchased and supplemented by a new build – the *Plover* – from Denny Bros of Dumbarton in 1852. Traffic was sufficiently strong by the end of the season to justify placing a further order.

The limitations of Piel Harbour for the more intensive services resulted in the development of Ramsden Dock as a new steamboat quay and station facility, and services transferred there from 1st June 1881.

A link to Coniston

In 1848 the FR extended from Kirkby to Broughton-in-Furness, tapping into copper ore traffic, and linking up at Foxfield with the Whitehaven and Furness Junction Railway from November 1850.

The Furness Railway exhibition stand at the International Exhibition at White City in 1908.

Map showing the Furness Railway network with connecting services.

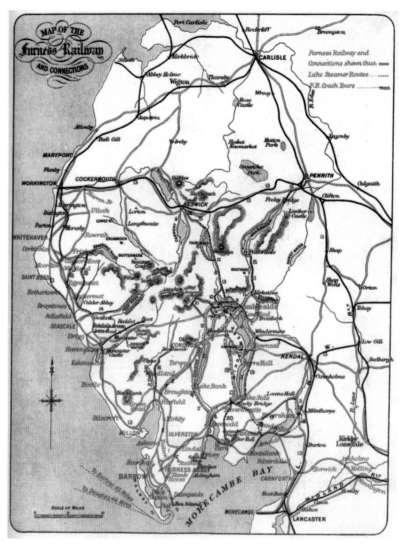

The potential for mineral traffic from Coniston was recognised by the FR Board, which authorised £500 for road improvements between Broughton and Coniston in December 1850. John Barraclough Fell mooted plans for a narrow gauge mineral railway to serve the copper mines and slate quarries at Coniston in 1849, but the financial climate was unsupportive. On 10th August 1857 a standard gauge extension from Broughton to Coniston received the Royal Assent, under the nominally independent guise of the Coniston Railway Company, satisfying an FR requirement for local interests to participate in the funding of the line. The FR oversaw completion of the line after the original contractor suffered bankruptcy and it opened on 18th June 1859; a short extension towards the copper mines following in 1860.

The Coniston Railway remained independent until 1862, when it amalgamated with the FR. The opening coincided with a peak in copper trade before a prolonged downturn in traffic, so tourist traffic rapidly became important, even though the branch was remote from main centres of population.

From the beginning Broughton trains were scheduled to serve the steamer services between Piel and Fleetwood; from spring 1848 a twice-daily service was in operation, connecting with steamers. This expanded to four round trips during the summer, with two northbound and one southbound train connecting with the Fleetwood steamer. The pattern of four trains was expanded to five to Coniston by 1908, with the 5.45 pm departure from Coniston running through to Barrow Ramsden Dock.

The terminus at Coniston was situated away from, and high above the village with panoramic views, and the FR had to build a steep connecting road to the village and pier. The station and platforms were extended by 1892 and a refreshment room added in 1905. Excursion traffic was more limited than other Lake District lines, but on 1st July 1905 the Barrow News noted that 2,000 Catholics took two trains to Coniston the previous Saturday, with a further 700 from Workington following on the Sunday. They spent time boating on and driving round the lake, as well as rambling and visiting waterfalls.

Coniston station c1890 with FR 2-4-2 tank about to depart for Foxfield.

Rails to Lakeside

As steamer services on Windermere developed, so tapping into this tourist trade at Newby Bridge looked attractive. Year round gunpowder, cotton and ironworks industries could supplement a seasonal passenger business. In 1845 the Furness & Windermere Railway Company (F&W) proposed a link from the FR at Ulverston, along the eastern shore of Windermere to join the Kendal & Windermere Railway. The company secretary was John Barraclough Fell of Spark Bridge, also secretary of the Windermere Steam Yacht Company. Chairman of the Steam Yacht Company Thomas Roper (of Newlands Ironworks) was also a director of the F&W, so the interests of the two were clearly inter-twined. The Lancaster & Carlisle Railway also proposed an 'Ulverston & Furness and Lancaster & Carlisle Railway' from Milnthorpe to Ulverston via Newby Bridge.

In 1865 the FR proposed a branch from Plumpton, two miles east of Ulverston, to Greenodd, with the intention of extending to Newby Bridge via Backbarrow. FR General Manager, James Ramsden, cut the first sod at Haverthwaite on 22nd November 1866. Whilst construction was underway, the Directors agreed to extend the route northwards to a new terminus at the southern end of Windermere, thereby overcoming the difficulties of navigating the River Leven. This extended the branch by a further mile and it was formally opened on Tuesday 1st June 1869.

The railway quickly developed freight traffic, bringing in coal for the steamers, ore for Backbarrow Ironworks, saltpetre and sulphur for the gunpowder works and building materials for the growing number of lake-side residences. Return traffic included bobbins from Stott Park, pig iron, gunpowder, pit props, and dye from the ultramarine works at Backbarrow.

The April 1910 timetable shows six daily trains making the 25-minute journey from Ulverston to Lakeside. This was later increased to eight services, with one operating directly from Carnforth via the Leven curve.

The Midland Railway introduced a 'Windermere Cruise Train', leaving London St Pancras at 10.30 am and arriving at Lakeside by 5.15 pm in time for the boat up the lake to Waterhead, reached at 6.30 pm. Onward coaches conveyed tourists to hotels in Ambleside and Grasmere.

Promoting the lake services

The passenger business was a secondary activity for the FR for much of the 19th century, but a lengthy depression precipitated a slump in freight carryings. The company sought to compensate by exploiting the growing opportunity of tourist traffic. With branches to Coniston and Lakeside and ownership of steamers on Coniston and Windermere, the Company had the ingredients to create a tour programme. Whilst there had been no (FR) cross-bay service since 1869, the growth of the Lancashire Coast resorts – especially Blackpool – placed substantial numbers of holidaymakers within reach of the FR. They could be enticed to the Lake District using the company's steamers and rail services, and there was potential for traffic in the opposite direction for trips to Fleetwood and Blackpool. Operating Superintendent Henry Cook introduced a programme of four circular tours in 1870, which included steamer travel:

Outer Circle – Train to Lakeside for a steamer to Ambleside. Coach to Coniston for a train home. (A Coniston cruise was an optional extra.)

Inner Circle – Train to Coniston, walk to Waterhead pier, for the *Gondola* to Lake Bank pier. Coach to Greenodd for a train home.

Middle Circle – Train to Lakeside, for steamer to Ambleside. Coach connection to the *Gondola* at Coniston to Lake Bank pier. Coach to Greenodd station for a train home.

Grange Circular – Train to Grange over Sands, thence to Kendal and Windermere, for steamer to Lakeside for a train home.

On retirement in 1895, Cook was followed by Alfred Aslett, who was promoted to Secretary and General Manager in 1896 when James Ramsden died. He brought passenger railway experience and immediately set about improvements. The programme expanded to 20 tours, with the original four at the core. Cheaper excursion fares stimulated traffic, offering return day excursions at the equivalent of the single fare.

By the 1890s tours were being offered from Belfast in conjunction with the Barrow Steam Navigation Company (a consortium of the Furness and Midland Railway companies) sailings between Belfast and Barrow (Ramsden Dock). *'Sailing at 8 p.m. every evening... the tour involves one day's absence. Including Furness Abbey, Lakeside, steamer on Windermere Lake, Ambleside to Coniston (by coach), and rail to Barrow, Fares – Saloon and 1st class, 22s 3d; saloon and 2nd class, 11s....'*

Some circular tours took more than a day; others just a few hours, but they proved popular and increased trade considerably. Colourful brochures were produced with posters displayed across FR stations, and on the Lancashire coast – a key market for cross-bay steamers from Fleetwood. The first decade of the twentieth century was the heyday of this tour programme.

The twenty-tour programme remained largely unchanged, with the May – September 1907 offer being typical:

1. **Outer Circular Tour** – Windermere Lake, Furness Abbey, Coniston – Fare from 5/3 (including sailing on Windermere, Lakeside – Waterhead)
2. **Inner Circular Tour** – Furness Abbey, Coniston Lake, Crake Valley – Fare from 3/3 (including sailing Lake Bank – Coniston)
3. **Grange and Windermere Circular Tour** – Grange, Arnside, Kendal, Windermere Lake – Fare from 2/- (including sailing on Windermere, Bowness – Lakeside)
4. **Middle Circular Tour** – Windermere Lake, Crake Valley, Coniston Lake – Fare from 5/9 (including sailing on Windermere, Lakeside – Waterhead and on Coniston, Coniston to Lake Bank)
5. **Red Bank and Grasmere Tour** – via Ambleside and Skelwith Force, returning via Rydal Water – Fare from 2/9 (including return sailing on Windermere, Lakeside – Waterhead)
6. **Thirlmere, Grasmere and Windermere Tour** – via Ambleside, Clappersgate and Red Bank, and round Thirlmere Lake – Fare from 5/- (including return sailing on Windermere, Lakeside – Waterhead)
7. **The Four Lakes Circular Tour** – Coniston, Grasmere, Rydal, Windermere – Fare from 5/9 (including sailing on Windermere, Lakeside – Waterhead)
8. **Coniston to Coniston Tour** – via Red Bank, Grasmere and Ambleside, returning by Coach to Coniston – Fare from 4/6
9. **Tarn Hows Tour** – via Ambleside and Coniston, returning via Tilberthwaite and Elterwater – Fare from 4/6 (including return sailing on Windermere, Lakeside – Waterhead)
10. **Round the Langdales and Dungeon Ghyll Tour** – via Ambleside, Colwith Force, Grasmere and Rydal – Fare from 5/- (including return sailing on Windermere, Lakeside – Waterhead)
11. **Ullswater Tour** via Ambleside, Kirkstone Pass and Brothers Water, returning via the Vale of Troutbeck and Lowwood – Fare from 5/6 (including return sailing on Windermere, Lakeside – Waterhead)
12. **Derwentwater (Keswick) Tour** via Ambleside, Grasmere and Thirlmere – Fare from 6/- (including return sailing on Windermere, Lakeside – Waterhead)
13. **The Five Lakes Circular Tour** – Windermere, Rydal, Grasmere, Thirlmere and Derwentwater – Fare from 11/6 (including return sailing on Windermere, Lakeside – Waterhead)
14. **Wastwater Tour** via Seascale and Gosforth Churchyard Cross, ad 680 – Fare from 4/6
15. **The Six Lakes Circular Tour** – Windermere, Rydal, Grasmere, Thirlmere, Derwentwater and Ullswater – Fare from 11/3 (including return sailing

Bottom – Lakeside Station in July 1959. Note the dilapidated state of the platform. **Swift** and **Swan (II)** are alongside, the latter loading for departure.

The Furness Railway produced comprehensive guide books to encourage use of the railway and steamer services.

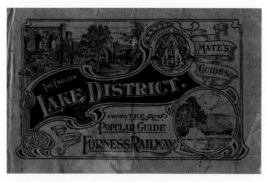

on Windermere, Lakeside – Waterhead and sailing from Pooley Bridge – Glenridding)

16. ***The Duddon Valley Tour*** via Broughton in Furness, Ulpha and Seathwaite – Fare from 3/9

17. ***The Three Waterfalls Tour*** Colwith, Dungeon Ghyll and Skelwith via Coniston and the Langdales – Fare from 4/9 [not operated in June]

18. ***Ennerdale Lake and Calder Abbey Tour*** via Seascale, Gosforth and Cold Fell – Fare from 4/6 [not operated in June]

19. ***Across the Ferry Tour*** via Lakeside, Esthwaite Water, Hawkshead, Ferry and Storrs Hall – Fare from 3/6 (including return sailing on Windermere, Lakeside – Storrs Hall)

20. ***Cartmel Priory and Newby Bridge Tour*** via Windermere (Lakeside), Backbarrow Falls, Holker Park and Grange – Fare from 2/9

Further particulars were published in 'Tours through English Lakeland' pamphlets priced at 1/2d and distributed through stations, Thomas Cook offices, WH Smith and Wyman & Sons. A Palette Album with colour illustrations of the tours could be obtained from bookstalls, priced 6d, with sets of six postcards available for 3d. Aslett borrowed the idea of selling postcards from Switzerland, and in 1902 the FR boasted it was the first railway in England to sell its own range of postcards. An annual 'Illustrated Guide' helped promote the resorts reached by the railway.

The Outer Circular tour was particularly popular with trippers from Blackpool, because it could be encompassed in one day. For 8s (3rd class), tourists joined the 10.05 am departure from Blackpool Talbot Road to Fleetwood, boarding the paddle steamer on the adjacent landing stage for the 10.30 am crossing to Barrow. Sailings were often heavily loaded on the open decks, but entertainment was frequently provided by a

An advert for cross bay steamers dating from 1911.

resident band, and photographer Edward Sankey was usually in attendance. The vessel berthed at Ramsden Dock at 11.45 am for transfer to a FR train to Lakeside, leaving at 11.55 am.

There was time to enjoy the refreshment pavilion at the Lakeside terminus – lunch could be booked for an additional 2s – before boarding the steamer for the 1.35 pm sailing to Waterhead. On arrival at 2.45 pm, the party transferred to horse drawn charabancs – as numbers on the tour could reach 300 there could be up to 15 four or six horse-drawn vehicles. Coniston was reached via Skelwith Bridge in 90 minutes, with time for refreshments at the station before the 6.00 pm departure for Ramsden Dock via Foxfield. Here the steamer left at 7.00 pm with time to purchase photographic souvenirs from the enterprising Mr Sankey. A crisp transfer at Fleetwood would take the trippers back to Talbot Road by 8.45 pm after an intensive but rewarding excursion.

The most extensive of the FR Tours was No 15, the 'Six Lakes Circular Tour'. Although potentially a day excursion, this required an early start on the 8.35 am steamer from Lakeside; so many participants took a later departure. It was possible to leave Whitehaven at 6.40 am, or Barrow at 8.40 am and connect with the sailing from Lakeside at 9.50 am. Arriving at Ambleside at 11.00 am, tourists quickly boarded one of Taylor's coaches at 11.05 am to travel along the shores of Rydal, Grasmere, and Thirlmere to Keswick, arriving at 1.45 pm. This left time to explore the town and take a stroll to Derwentwater, before catching the 6.29 pm Cockermouth, Keswick and Penrith Railway service to Penrith for an overnight stay.

The return journey began with a 30-minute trip by motorcar at 9.00 am to Pooley Bridge. Ullswater was enjoyed on the 9.35 am to Glenridding, whence passengers boarded Taylor's coach to Ambleside for the 2.40 pm sailing along Windermere for the train home from Lakeside. Barrow could be reached by 4.52 pm and Whitehaven by 6.30 pm. This excursion could be taken in either direction and the ticket lasted a week, giving participants the opportunity to break their journey.

From 1908-10 the FR participated in a series of International Exhibitions at London's White City, exhibiting local photographs and outlining the Tour itineraries in an extravagant walk-through stand. Shipping operations were publicised by models of *Lady of the Lake* (Coniston), *Swift* and *Lady Evelyn*. In 1908 visitors bought 51,954 guidebooks and 3,004 postcard sets. The exhibit was destroyed in a fire at an exhibition in Brussels on 14th August 1910, but the model of *Lady Evelyn* survives in the Dock Museum in Barrow.

The cross-bay steamers

The FR ordered the *Lady Evelyn* (named after the wife of Victor Cavendish a Director of the FR) from John Scott of Kinghorn, Kirkcaldy, and she commenced service on the Fleetwood to Barrow service on 26th May 1901. Response to the new service was positive; 29,165 passengers were carried in her first year and on occasion the FR tug *Furness* provided additional capacity. Demand was sufficient for *Lady Evelyn* to be lengthened by 30ft in1904 by Vickers in Barrow.

The 1895 built *Lady Margaret* was added to the fleet on 30th May 1903. By 1906 passenger numbers had risen to 120,115. *Lady Margaret* operated for five seasons, before being sold to the Admiralty in 1908 for £14,000. Her replacement was the 1889 *Philomel*, purchased through James Little & Co from the General Steam Navigation Co for £5,250. *Philomel* proved an unwise purchase requiring a prohibitively expensive new boiler after just two seasons work. She was sold for scrap in 1913.

Finding a replacement vessel for the 1910 season proved difficult but eventually the FR acquired the Barry Railway Company's *Gwalia* for £21,750. Renamed *Lady Moyra*, after the wife of FR director Lord Richard Cavendish, she entered service in June 1910. This season saw 127,617 passengers carried and this increased further to 179,000 in 1913.

Lady Evelyn and *Lady Moyra* maintained the cross-bay service until summer 1914, supplemented by the paddle-tug/tender *Walney* (II), which entered service in 1904. Services continued despite the outbreak of war in 1914, and a full season was planned for 1915, but the Admiralty had other ideas.

Lady Moyra was requisitioned as a minesweeper in 1915 before being sold to W. H. Tucker of Cardiff for £30,000 in 1919. *Lady Evelyn* was withdrawn at the end of August 1914, and followed a similar path to her sister, heading to the Admiralty in 1916 before being sold to W. H. Tucker of Cardiff for £20,000 in 1919. *Lady Margaret* completed fifteen years service with the Admiralty as a tender before being scrapped in 1923. *Walney* (II) worked through the FR era and transferred to both the LMS and British Railways.

Sailings ceased after the 1914 season, but hopes were raised that the Blackpool Passenger Steamboat Company would recommence the service after the conflict, although they only offered a few Sunday and Bank Holiday sailings in 1919. The post-war era saw many army surplus vehicles converted into primitive motor charabancs, and these took over from the declining steamer market by offering a diversified day trip market for visitors to Blackpool.

A further attempt to resurrect a cross-bay service was made by the FR in 1922, when the *Robina* was chartered between 12th August and 22nd September. However the sailings made a small loss and were not continued.

Keswick

Although railways through Keswick were proposed as early as 1846, it was not until the late 1850s when routes breached the Pennines that an alternative route to West Cumberland was considered practical. The Cockermouth, Keswick and Penrith Railway (CK&P) eyed freight traffic between the mines and blast furnaces of Furness and west Cumberland, and the iron and coke districts of Middlesbrough and South Durham. Whilst there was some anxiety about the potential 'invasion'

Top: **Lady Moyra** arriving at Fleetwood.

Middle: The **Lady Margaret** at Fleetwood.

Bottom: **Swift** at Waterhead with horse drawn coaches ready to head to Coniston, Glenridding, Grasmere and Keswick.

Top left: **Lady Moyra**.

Top right: **Lady Evelyn**.

Middle: LNWR luggage coach which operated from Windermere railway station.

Bottom: The coach for Newby Bridge waits at Grange-over-Sands railway station.

by 'excursionists', the Penrith Observer countered: *'Well let them come. The contemplation of the beautiful scenery that was to be seen on all sides was the best education they could have, and must have a good effect: it would sooth the careworn, when escaped for a time from the labours of the shop and the turmoil of the town'.*

The CK&P route between Penrith and Cockermouth opened for passengers on 2nd January 1864. Early excursions brought 1,200 visitors from Carlisle, Penrith and West Cumberland, and the Carlisle Journal reported on 25th May 1866: *'On Tuesday the first railway excursion trip for the season, employing no fewer than 4 monster trains containing between 3,000-4,000 people, ran from Preston to Keswick'.*

The company largely avoided the use of excursions and concentrated on service trains, acknowledging that Keswick – remote from the main centres of population – was a resort for the more discerning visitor. The CK&P helped develop the flagship Keswick Hotel adjacent to the station, and maintained close working arrangements as they developed a tour programme.

Like the FR, the CK&P experienced a decline in freight traffic during the latter years of the nineteenth century, so focused on building passenger business. 'Circular tour tickets' were introduced with the London & North Western Railway (LNWR) with tourist fares offered from stations south of Preston. Passengers could take a round trip via Keswick, with coach transfer for the homeward journey via Windermere, or vice versa.

The CK&P established links with hoteliers to provide

coach connections from Troutbeck to Patterdale, and this formed the core of their tour programme. These were generally operated in conjunction with service trains, although excursions were provided from the northeast and Yorkshire. Whilst more limited than the FR programme, the CK&P did compile its own tours based around local attractions. For the 1907 season these comprised:

Ullswater: Rail from Keswick to Troutbeck, for coach to Patterdale, or Penrith for coach to Pooley Bridge, Thence by steamer along Ullswater before returning to Keswick by the opposite route.

Early motorised road transport formed an integral part of the FR tour network – a party prepares to leave Windermere station.

Even individual tours were promoted by the Furness Railway, here seeking to attract traffic from Blackpool.

Cockermouth, Keswick & Penrith Railway.

CIRCULAR TOURS, BY RAIL, COACH AND STEAMER.

Glenridding Valley from Blowick.

For further particulars as to Trains &c., see Company's Time Table.

CIRCULAR TOUR TO ULLSWATER.
From Keswick by Rail to Troutbeck and Coach to Patterdale, or Rail to Penrith, Coach to Pooley Bridge, and Steamboat the full length of Ullswater Lake to Patterdale, returning by the alternative route. The journey may be completed on the same or following day.

CIRCULAR TOUR TO PATTERDALE AND WINDERMERE.
By Rail to Penrith—Coach to Pooley Bridge—Steamboat the full length of Ulswater Lake to Patterdale—or Rail to Troutbeck and Coach to Patterdale—thence by Coach to Windermere and Keswick.
These Tickets are available for seven days and may also be had for the same tour in the opposite direction at Mr. Rigg's Coach Offices at Keswick and Windermere.

CIRCULAR TOUR KESWICK TO PENRITH, PATTERDALE, AND AMBLESIDE.
During the Summer Months, tickets are issued by the 7.30 a.m. Train from Keswick to Penrith, thence by Coach to Pooley Bridge, Steamer to Patterdale, and Coach over Kirkstone Pass to Ambleside, and thence by Rigg's Coach to Keswick.

P. THOMPSON, *Secretary and General Manager,*
Keswick Station.

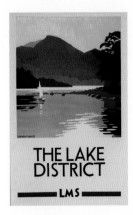

A typical LMS era advert dating from 1930, showing idyllic Ullswater.

Below: A Midland Railway map of 1903 ignores the competing west coast route from the south.

Bottom right: Scafell and Wastwater could be reached by motor vehicle services connecting with LMS services.

Patterdale and Windermere: Rail from Keswick to Troutbeck, for coach to Patterdale, or Penrith for coach to Pooley Bridge, and steamer along Ullswater to Patterdale. Then Rigg's coach from Patterdale to Windermere, and back to Keswick. Tickets were available for seven days and the tour could be completed in either direction.

Penrith, Patterdale and Ambleside: Taking the 7.30 am from Keswick to Penrith for coach to Pooley Bridge, and steamer along Ullswater to Patterdale. Then Rigg's coach from Patterdale to Ambleside, and back to Keswick.

The Maryport & Carlisle Railway also offered 'Coaching Tours to the Lake District' with combined rail and coach tickets to Keswick for coaching tours round Derwentwater, Bassenthwaite, Buttermere (via Honister, returning via Vale of Newlands), Scale Hill (via Lorton, returning via Newlands) and Grasmere. A more specific trip by rail was via Carlisle to Penrith for a coach connection to Pooley Bridge, and a round trip by steamer on Ullswater to Patterdale.

A programme of six circular tours was organised by the LNWR based on Penrith; three sample tours were: -

Penrith to Patterdale, and Troutbeck – Coach to Pooley Bridge, steamer to Patterdale, coach to Troutbeck (North) and thence by rail back to Penrith.

Penrith to Patterdale, Ambleside, and Keswick – Coach to Pooley Bridge, steamer to Patterdale, coach to Ambleside then a full Windermere cruise. Coach from Ambleside to Keswick via Rydal and Grasmere, returning to Penrith by rail.

Penrith to Shap, Kendal, Windermere, Kirkstone Pass, and Patterdale – Rail via Shap and Kendal to Windermere. Coach from Windermere over Kirkstone Pass to Patterdale, then steamer to Pooley Bridge and coach back to Penrith.

The three other tours were variations on the above. Aside from these the Midland Railway organised daily tours from the West Riding, which allowed 3 hours at the head of Ullswater, and returned the same day.

In 1921 Keswick was the destination for through coaches from Liverpool and Manchester operated by the LNWR, whilst the Midland Railway ran an express service from Leeds and Bradford via Ingleton and Shap, and the North Eastern Railway brought through coaches from York and Newcastle via Darlington and Penrith.

The LMS era

In 1923 the railways of the Lake District were brought together under the management of the London, Midland and Scottish Railway Company (LMS). Summer weekend services were introduced from London in 1927, with northbound departures on Fridays and Saturdays, returning on Saturdays and Sundays. The train maintained a fast 5hr 25min schedule to Windermere and operated with separate portions for Barrow (continuing up the coast to Maryport) and Keswick (and on to Workington). The train eventually became known as the 'Lakes Express'. The service continued through the Second World War, albeit to a slower schedule and combined with other services, but a dedicated service recommenced after the war.

At Coniston the branch line faced increasing competition when J Creighton established a bus service from Ulverston to Coniston in 1926, although bus services were incorporated into circular tours to make them a multi-modal experience. The rail motor service comprised ten daily departures, with extra services at weekends. Notable was the 6.00 pm from Coniston,

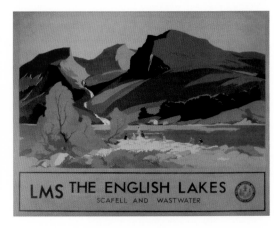

which ran through to Blackpool on weekdays and Morecambe on Saturdays.

The Blackpool Steam Navigation Company made one last attempt to operate the cross-bay service using *Atalanta*. Built for the Glasgow and South Western Railway, she passed into the hands of the LMS who sold her to the Blackpool Company. She sailed between Fleetwood and Barrow in 1937 to connect with the LMS Lake District tour programme. *Atalanta* also operated between Blackpool and Morecambe, but the Barrow experiment was abandoned after one season.

Winter services on the Lakeside branch were withdrawn in 1938, and the summer service followed after a limited operation in the 1941 season, not resuming until 1946.

The tour programme continued and more were added by the LMS. The 1939 timetable shows twenty-nine tours with eighteen including Windermere. Keswick was the destination for ambitious excursions from Blackpool and Morecambe, which headed around the Cumbrian Coast to Ravenglass, for a trip on the Ravenglass & Eskdale Railway, thence via Workington to Keswick where time was allowed for a walk to Derwentwater and a trip on the Lake. The return journey was via Penrith and Shap.

Nationalisation

From 1948 management passed to British Railways and the tours were replaced by rail excursions. Circular tours were resurrected in the 1950s; day trips from Manchester or Liverpool were advertised to Lakeside for the steamer to Ambleside, allowing time ashore. Steps were retraced as far as Bowness for a train home from Windermere. Others from Lancaster and Morecambe offered a train trip to Lakeside, a cruise on the lake and a return train from Windermere for 10s 6d (3d more from Morecambe).

Nationalisation made little immediate difference to train services. Initially petrol rationing suppressed car competition and the railway enjoyed a short period of good business. Nine daily services operated on the Coniston branch and the through service to Blackpool was maintained. The 1950s became a difficult time for the Coniston branch as carryings were hit by Ribble bus competition, and a 1957 British Railways survey noted just 18 passengers carried on each train. Despite strong local protests the last passenger train from Foxfield to Coniston ran on 4th October 1958, with freight services lingering until 30th April 1962. A subsidised replacement bus service operated by Ribble covered only 40% of the required subsidy in fares, and was withdrawn in 1968.

The Lake District Transport Report of 1961 commented that *'British Railways give the Lake District low priority, passengers to Windermere and Keswick being regarded as less important than the greater number going to Glasgow, where there is now keen air competition'*. Noting that railway facilities had changed little over the last half-century, the report also observed that long distance expresses were, on balance, slower than in 1910. The Windermere branch services

saw many winter trains carrying fewer than ten passengers, although the *'grim'* terminus was a hive of activity in the summer months. The closure of the Lakeside branch was argued against, on the basis that this *'would encourage the belief that to see the Lake District a car is necessary'*.

The Beeching Plan contemplated closure for lines carrying fewer than 10,000 passengers per week. The Lakeside branch with just 5,000 was a prime target. At the Ulverston inquiry into closure proposals on 13th January 1965, it was noted that 46,709 passengers had used the Lakeside branch in the 1964 season, with 49,569 making the return journey. Closure was announced for the end of the 1965 season and on 5th September the last passenger train left Lakeside, although freight operations between Ulverston and Haverthwaite continued until 1967.

The railway to Lakeside was severed by road improvements south of Haverthwaite, but not before the Lakeside Railway Society had moved rolling stock up the branch. This formed the nucleus of a new preserved railway operation between Lakeside and Haverthwaite, which opened on 2nd May 1973, with trains timed to connect with steamers.

Diesel Multiple Units took over operation of the Keswick services in 1955, precipitating the re-introduction of Sunday services but this optimism was short-lived. A brief reintroduction of Keswick 'circular tours', operated from Manchester, but heavy losses continued. The Friends of the Lake District expressed concern in their Annual Report for 1959: *'If official railway policy is to favour the virtual superseding by road transport of rural passenger services, then the prospect for the Lake District is very grim indeed'*.

The 'Lake District Transport Report' estimated that the line was losing £50,000 per year, and less than 20% of Keswick visitors used the train. Author David St John Thomas questioned *'what inconvenience would the withdrawal of trains cause?'* Services west of Keswick were withdrawn in 1966, whilst the rest of the route was reduced to an unmanned single-track from July 1968. This service survived until 6th March 1972.

The Windermere branch lost the exclusivity of the

Cat Bells, Derwentwater and Keswick seen from Latrigg. Keswick station lies in the foreground, a walk across town from the lake.

Club Coach during the Second World War, although First Class was still provided. The Lakes Express survived for a time, being withdrawn in 1965, but a single Windermere – London service survived until 1970. The last Club Train ran in 1966 and Preston became the furthest destination reached by direct train from Windermere. A gradual run down of infrastructure began with the withdrawal of freight services in 1969, although they continued at Kendal for a further year. Electrification and re-signalling of the main line forced singling of the branch in May 1973, when it became a long siding from Oxenholme, constraining the timetable and effectively eliminating excursion traffic.

The station building at Windermere was sold in 1980 to form part of a Booths supermarket, with the line cut back to a less prominent terminus. This precipitated the formation of the Lakes Line Action Group, which was successful in lobbying for a more substantial station structure, which opened in 1986.

After privatisation of the railway system, the operation of the Windermere branch services passed from North West Trains to First North Western and now First TransPennine Express. Services with modern rolling stock were introduced to Manchester Airport from May 1994, and the single line is now running close to capacity, having been completely rebuilt in 2002. Today this diesel-operated enclave survives and prospers, and confirmation in November 2014 of a workstream to electrify the branch reconfirmed its longevity. In 2012-13 around 375,000 passengers used Windermere station, a growth of 25% in five years.

Road services

The arrival of the railway improved access to the Lake District and created opportunities to provide onward coach services to tour more inaccessible parts of the region. The route of today's 555 bus from Lancaster to Keswick can trace its origins back to the 1840s, when a coach left Keswick at 6.00 am for Lancaster, with horses changed at staging posts, including the Low Wood Hotel. It returned to Keswick at 8.00 pm, after a round trip of fourteen hours, which today takes just over 5½!

The arrival of steamer services on Windermere in 1845 improved business for the Ambleside Turnpike

The optimism generated by the arrival of diesel multiple unit trains (above) failed to stem the tide of losses. By the end the CK&P was reduced to a single line from Penrith to Keswick; a two car unit waits to leave Keswick in summer 1971.

The Keswick coach, looking rather full, waits for the scheduled departure time from Windermere station before commencing the long trip north past the lakes of Windermere, Rydal, Grasmere, Thirlmere and Derwentwater.

Trust with receipts rising from £396 in 1846 to £570 in 1848 and £899 in 1865, helped by campaigns that resisted further incursion of railways beyond Windermere. Records of the Trust show 21,480 coaches crossing Troutbeck Bridge in 1855.

Many of the operators gave their coaches names, much like today's route numbering system. Some routes had coaches with more than one name, with each vehicle usually operating at a specific time. These included;

Cockermouth Mail – Windermere to Cockermouth
Broughton Mail – Windermere to Broughton
Defiance – Keswick to Windermere (From Keswick at 8.15 am, and Windermere at 11.50 am)
New Mail – Keswick to Windermere (at 2.00 pm)
New Day Mail – Windermere to Keswick (at 6.00 pm)
Jenny Lind – Windermere to Coniston via the Ferry and Hawkshead
Le Papillon – Windermere to Ambleside
Skiddaw – Keswick to Patterdale
Helvellyn – Ambleside to Penrith

Routes that surmounted Kirkstone Pass (and presumably Honister) required male occupants to get out and walk on the ascent, and charabancs were used instead of coaches. These had no inside seats at all. Fares were high; in 1884 a trip from Windermere to Keswick cost 7s, the average weekly pay of a Manchester mill worker.

Steamers on Windermere were met at Newby Bridge, the Ferry Hotel, Bowness and Waterhead. From the Ferry Hotel, a coach departed at 10.15 am for Coniston, and at Bowness every hotel had its own coach – the Old England Hotel's coach and driver was adorned in green and scarlet. Coaches from Bowness connected to Windermere station and Ullswater, whilst at Waterhead coaches departed for Coniston, Keswick, Grasmere and hotels in Ambleside.

Richard Rigg ran a successful coaching business alongside his hotel interests, in conjunction with the arrival of trains at Windermere. He provided a first class service in relative comfort inside the carriage, whilst up to sixteen-second class passengers sat outside. Huge padded waterproof sheets were provided as cover in the event of rainfall. Rigg held the mail contract and was known as the 'Coaching King'. His drivers, nicknamed 'Robin Redbreasts', wore scarlet coats and black top hats, contrasting with their yellow and black four-in-hand coaches. These ran daily on the three – four hour journey between Windermere and Keswick. In 1862 there were three daily departures with some extended to Cockermouth.

The link from Windermere over Kirkstone Pass to Ullswater was established in 1859 and it became possible to undertake unofficial circular tours by taking advantage of coaches from Patterdale to Keswick, or

An advert detailing Richard Rigg's coaching services throughout the Lakes.

The English Lakes

Perfect for an outdoor holiday amid lovely lake and mountain scenery. Cruises on Windermere and Ullswater and holiday runabout tickets during the season will add to your pleasure

GO IN COMFORT BY TRAIN   BRITISH RAILWAYS

A 1959 British Railways poster promoting holidays in the Lake District.

The innovative Mountain Goat minibus, Li'le Billy, waiting at Windermere railway station.

Pooley Bridge to Penrith. By the 1880s, Rigg's employed over 200 horses during the tourist season; their coach services continued until 1921. The Windermere Hotel is now in the hands of the Shearings group, retaining the link with a specialist coach operator.

Thomas Taylor, the proprietor of Ambleside's Salutation, Queen's and Waterhead hotels managed a fleet of four-in-hand and other 'well appointed' coaches and offered a programme of eight tours which left his hotels and steamer piers several times daily during the season. These replicated the FR tours and were effectively selling the shore elements as a separate trip. Around 100 horses were stabled at the Salutation Hotel.

The 1900 FR Holiday Resort brochure noted that Mr Robinson of the Lakeside Hotel offered charabancs to connect with train services during the season. Robinson had made his name as a coach operator, and built up enough capital to take over the hotel. He offered two specific tours; the Esthwaite and Ferry

circular, and Cartmel Priory and Newby Bridge. Further down the branch the Swan Hotel offered a bus to meet all trains.

In 1903 'The Engineer' Magazine noted that a motorcar service between Windermere and Keswick was under consideration and that experiments with a steam motor lorry had been successful. The following year the Lake District Road Traffic Company – run mainly by hoteliers – started a service between Bowness, Windermere and Grasmere using a steam bus. Growth in business after the First World War saw the company's distinctive 'Yellow Peril' chain-driven Thornycroft coaches become a familiar feature on the roads, with services operating at a sedate 12 mph between Windermere and Keswick, and Ambleside and Coniston. With solid tyres, this was perhaps as much as passengers could tolerate.

The Penrith and District Motor Company introduced a 24 seat charabanc service from Penrith to Pooley Bridge, but their initial vehicles were under-powered and for a while the horse coaches of Armstrong and Siddle had the last laugh. In the 1906 season, the fleet of three charabancs carried 7,400 passengers, but the service struggled and was eventually taken over by Armstrong and Siddle. By 1915 the Ullswater (Royal Mail) Motor Service were running twice daily between Penrith and Patterdale.

Lake Hotel Coaches Ltd. were established in 1909 and soon became one of Keswick's principal operators. Borrowdale was an early focus for road services, with a service between Seatoller and Keswick commencing before the First World War. Following road improvements in the valley five different services were to be offered by late 1920s, levels far superior to anything offered today. The Honister route was considered the most famous of the charabanc routes with the Ward Locke Guide noting that the steep descents take place 'at a walking pace, and nervous passengers may remember that the drivers attach considerable value to their own necks'.

After the First World War there was a rapid expansion of motor vehicles. In 1925 'Commercial Motor' noted that whilst horse coaches were still in service, the popularity of the motor coach was rapidly increasing. In the following year, their correspondent reported: – 'The Ullswater Royal Mail Motor Service have a working arrangement with the Ullswater Navigation and Transit Co., who operate steam yachts on Ullswater, and passengers may make the through journey from Penrith to Patterdale, changing from the road vehicle to steamer at Patterdale'.

With the explosion in private car ownership many of the more remote coaching routes were withdrawn, and by the mid-1920s only the main trunk routes received a year round service. A few summer-only services lingered on the old routes, such as that over Honister Pass. A year later one of the Lake District Road Traffic Company's drivers, Charles Head, formed his own bus company – The Magnet – operating between Windermere and Bowness using a converted Ford vehicle. By then James and Fred Airey were running between Ambleside, Hawkshead and the Windermere Ferry and by 1933 had grown sufficiently to justify operation of two vehicles. Ribble took over the Lancashire and Westmorland Motor Services Ltd in 1927 and the Kendal Motor Bus Company in 1930. This left a handful of independent operators in the South Lakes area, the largest of which was The Magnet, eventually taken over by Ribble in 1946.

The first motor vehicles on the 555 trunk route were introduced by Westmorland Motor Services Ltd on 15th July 1925. Formed by Henry Meageen of Cumberland Motor Services with the intention of linking Kendal and Keswick, the company was an amalgamation of the Lake District Road Traffic Company, Kendal based Rutters, and Feirn (Ambleside) Ltd who pooled their vehicles, with Meageen also supplying five vehicles. During 1925 the company took over operations around Lancaster, becoming Lancashire and Westmorland Motor Services Ltd. Single deck vehicles were compulsory on the route due to restrictions applied to Dunmail Raise. In the late 1940s this restriction was lifted and double-decker buses have since served the Kendal to Keswick route, new purpose built vehicles being introduced in 2011.

Brown's of Ambleside continued to operate horse charabancs until the Second World War and J Creighton established a bus service from Ulverston to Coniston in 1926.

In west Cumberland the Whitehaven Motor Service Company was formed in 1912, becoming Cumberland Motor Services (CMS) in 1921 to reflect their northern expansion. By 1930 services were operated to Carlisle, Keswick and Wigton creating a virtual monopoly in the north and west Lake District. On 8th November 1948 CMS became state owned but operations continued with little change.

The Lake District Transport Report recorded that residents accounted for 60% of summer bus journeys, with visitors making up the remaining 40%. The number of day-trippers visiting the area by bus was negligible. Rural bus services operated at a loss, estimated at around £120k per annum. The Lake District accounted for around 10% of Ribble's business making, on average, a 10% loss. The company offered a large number of stage and long distance express services, including double decker 'gay hostesses' on the London – Windermere – Keswick route. There was also some co-operation with British Railways through joint publication of tour booklets. The National Bus Company was formed on the 1st January 1969, both CMS and Ribble becoming part of its Northwest area.

As road traffic grew after the Second World War, the need for better road links was apparent. The northwest experienced early motorway construction with the Preston by-pass opening on 5 December 1958, the Lancaster by-pass in 1960 and the link between the two in 1965. The route northwards to Penrith was opened in 1970, following much of the alignment engineered by the Lancaster & Carlisle Railway over a century before, and the following year the motorway link from the M1 at Rugby through to Carlisle was complete. The

A591 Kendal bypass opened in August 1971, further speeding up access to the Lake District.

Road access to the northern Lake District was improved from the early 1970s when the A66 from Penrith to Cockermouth via Keswick was gradually upgraded. It was no coincidence that the railway had closed at the same time, and the trunk route utilised the trackbed west of Keswick. This relieved pressure on the A591 through the central lakes by encouraging Keswick traffic to take the M6 and A66.

The Mountain Goat bus company operated their first minibus from Bowness to Glenridding in 1972, re-establishing a withdrawn bus connection. The intimacy of the small vehicles proved popular with travellers, and the company expanded to operate a range of tours to more remote parts of the Lake District, exploiting the wider geographical capability of minibuses.

The 1985 Transport Act included provision to deregulate bus services, abolishing local operators protection from competition. Deregulation day was Sunday 26th October 1986 and new operators soon registered competing routes to both CMS and Ribble.

From 23rd July 1987 Stagecoach Holdings absorbed CMS, and two years later took over Ribble operations in the South Lakes and Furness.

From 19th May 1990 open top buses were introduced, firstly on the Bowness to Ambleside service operating every 20 minutes (now the 599) and later on the Keswick to Seatoller route (now the 78). The following year the route was extended through to Grasmere.

On 22nd May 1991 bus services in Cumbria and North Lancashire were transferred to Stagecoach (North West) Ltd; by now most of the old coach routes had a modern equivalent, except Honister. Bus services from Keswick to Buttermere went via Whinlatter, and Borrowdale valley services terminated at Seatoller. In 1995 the Traffic Regulation Order for Honister Pass was amended to permit 25 seat vehicles. The Buttermere bus was adapted for this circuitous route, continuing over the pass to Keswick via the west side of Derwentwater.

The following winter the 555 service maintained its hourly summer frequency for the first time.

Bus services in the Lake District are now operated by Stagecoach Cumbria, with a comprehensive network serving the main centres of population and tourist attractions. Mountain Goat still offers a blend of specialty tours, joined by Lake District Tours and Lake District Supertours.

Typical of the modern tour is the Cross-Lakes Experience; Windermere Lake Cruises, Mountain Goat, Stagecoach and Coniston Launch operate a boat-bus-boat service, which carries cycles. From Bowness, passengers take a 15-minute cruise across Windermere to Ferry House, and transfer to a Mountain Goat minibus to Hawkshead, calling at Hill Top. Passengers change to the Stagecoach 505 at Hawkshead for Waterhead (Coniston) via Tarn Hows, then take the Coniston Launch to Brantwood, Coniston pier, and back to the Waterhead Hotel jetty. Once there, steps are retraced back to Ferry House.

Open top Stagecoach bus picking up passengers for Ambleside at Bowness Pier.

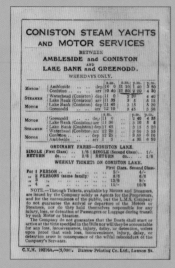

Top: The 1927 LMS steamer timetable for Windermere and Coniston.

Above: The Coniston section, showing sailings that were part of circular tours.

To Elterwater, Ambleside

To Hawkshead

Mines

Yewdale Beck

Low Water

Church Beck

Monk Coniston

The Old Man of Coniston

Waterhead Hotel

MONK CONISTON

Slate Quay

Coniston

Kirkby Quay

Quarries

WATERHEAD

Pier Cottage

Church Beck

Little Arrow Moor

CONISTON

BANK GROUND

Monk Coniston Moor

Slate Quay

Brantwood

Coniston Hall

Park Coppice

BRANTWOOD

TORVER

Torver Common Wood

Torver

Grizedale Forest

CONISTON WATER

To Broughton

SUNNY BANK

PARK A MOOR

Oxenhouses

Oxen House Bay

Peel Island

Bethecar Moor

Beacon Tarn

WATER PARK

LAKE BANK

Nibthwaite Quay

High Nibthwaite

River Crake

Water Yeat

Coniston Water

Blawith

Ironworks

To Lowick

1 kilometre
1 mile

Coniston Water

'Coniston Lake (147 ft) a 'miniature Windermere', is 5½ miles long, about ½ mile broad and 260ft deep at the deepest part. The most picturesque part of it is the N end, with the mountains rising above it, but the beautifully-wooded banks lower down have a charm of their own. The best view of the lake is obtained from Tarn Hows. A small steamer plies up and down the lake (3/4hr each way; fare 1s., return 1s 6d.).'
– Baedecker's Great Britain 1890

Coniston Water – or Thurston Water until the late nineteenth century – is the most south-westerly of the English Lakes, lying on a north-south axis and emptying into Morecambe Bay by the six mile long River Crake. Commercial use predated the advent of steam, as the heavily wooded shore encouraged the development of timber industries. Later, mines and quarries at the head of the lake took advantage of easy water transport southwards, even though transhipment over land was required to reach the sea. Remote from the main tourist destinations of the central Lakes, Coniston was also late in being connected by railway and in developing steamer services.

Documented use of the lake dates back to 1246, when the monks of Furness Abbey – who owned land along the eastern shore – were granted permission by the baron of Kendal to *'place boats on the lake for fishing and carrying'*; the *'carrying'* refers to their use as cargo vessels. They took sheep fleeces farmed on abbey land near the lake to Nibthwaite, and down the River Crake to Greenodd for loading onto coastal vessels for Rampside and Furness Abbey. Timber for building was also shipped by the monks, and the tops of the branches would have been used for charcoal too. The abbey had iron smelters along the Furness coast, and by 1292 was gaining most of its income through this trade.

Other early lakeshore activities included bark peeling and charcoal burning, based on the abundance of local woodland. Bark was used in the tanning industry when turning hides into leather, and charcoal was used for smelting and, later, gunpowder production. The main cargo was therefore timber for construction to service charcoal pits in Low Furness that supplied fuel to the bloomeries (early iron smelters) nearby. Charcoal burning pits appeared along the shore (and on Peel Island) in the thirteenth century, and were well established by the sixteenth century. The woods of Low Furness became depleted, and the ore was brought to the lakeshore where it was then smelted. Large volumes of charcoal were needed for smelting, so bloomeries appeared alongside the charcoal pits as it was easier to move the ore to the charcoal than vice versa.

Gondola at Pier Cottage in post 1903 condition, with seven windows in her saloon.

In the eighteenth century bloomeries were established at Penny Bridge, Newlands and Nibthwaite (where there was also a bobbin mill) and the lakeside sites were left unused. The Coniston Forge, established around 1600, was also extant. The Penny Bridge furnace later came under ownership of the Backbarrow Company, who owned the furnace near the River Leven. Charcoal was transported from the pits by company boats to Nibthwaite Quay for onward shipment to the newer bloomeries, and in the 1770s the *'coal boate'* was repaired. The cost of transporting fuel from Waterhead to Nibthwaite on the 'Short Voyage' was 1s. per twelve sacks, the 'Long Voyage' being the Windermere route from Waterhead to Newby Bridge. Boats could be dragged between the lakes as business demanded.

In 1750 the Penny Bridge Company was in dispute over rights to ferry goods on Coniston Water as they asked the Backbarrow Company to send the following letter;

I am informed that you are timorous about bringing down Coniston Water our Coals, the Partnership have also been acquainted therewith and thereupon ordered me to send a messenger herewith (to prevent the coals being damaged from standing) which is to give you orders to take no stop from any person or persons whatsoever, but to proceed and continue to ferry on the said Water as occasion shall require till such a time as you have contrary orders from the Pennybridge Company, and therein the said Company will against all persons whatsoever protect and indemnify you. Let this be your sailing and fighting orders.

The Backbarrow Company ceased using the lake for moving fuel in 1783.

Water transport was the easiest way of moving copper and slate from the hills above Coniston to the

The goods wharf at Nibthwaite, used latterly for copper and slate. The Copper Houses are situated just out of shot to the left of the image. The site is accessible by a short bridleway.

sea for onward shipping. Copper mining had started in Roman times, and was being worked locally during the Middle Ages. In 1561 the Company of Mines Royal was formed to work mines in the Lake District, beginning initially at Keswick in 1565, where they also built a smelter before taking over the operations at Coniston. The Keswick smelter was fed with copper from Coniston using pack-horses, but plans to establish a smelter at Coniston were thwarted by the Civil War, when the Keswick mines were wrecked and the local operation ceased.

By the late 1700s the copper mines were proving very successful, expanding further after the arrival of John Barrett around 1830. By 1849 he was employing over 400 men, with 250 tons of ore carried monthly to the copper store at Coniston Hall, before being shipped to Nibthwaite, where a wharf had been constructed in 1843. Here three copper stores were established, and houses near the quay became known as the 'Copper Houses'. The company had 4 or 5 vessels for use on Coniston Water that were usually rowed, but were also equipped with an auxiliary sail. From Nibthwaite the ore was carted to Greenodd, shipped to Liverpool and smelted at St Helens. Ulverston replaced Greenodd as the export port after the Ulverston canal was completed in 1795, and in the 1830s over 2,000 tons of copper ore was exported from a yard at the head of the canal.

Green slate was the other major local industry, with the most productive quarries being at Tilberthwaite and Hodge Close. Coniston slate was being shipped from Piel Harbour as early as 1688, and in 1772 around 2,000 tons of slate was sent down the lake. This heavy cargo was carted to the lakeshore at Kirkby Quay, just above the Waterhead Hotel, where it was loaded onto sailing

boats. Crosthwaite's 1809 map shows slate-loading quays at the present day Monk Coniston pier, and near Coniston Hall.

William Green's 1819 guidebook confirmed that the Coniston Hall quay was used to store *'the slate which is dug from the bowels of the mountains of Coniston.'* He noted that David Kirkby, who gave his name to Kirkby Quay, owned land near the head of the lake. Thomas Rigge, owner of many Coniston quarries, employed David and his father to carry slate along the lake. Kirkby had a new boat built for the slate around 1781/2 which was referred to as a rowing boat, although it presumably had an auxiliary sail. Green's book provides a graphic description of the quay;

'The slate quay, already mentioned as being on the road from Coniston Church to Waterhead, is seen from these grounds [Bank Ground]*, and about three quarters of a mile from the house; the unloading from carts, and re-loading the slate to vessels which navigate the lake from head to foot, create a bustle and an animation, which is happily increased by the gliding of those vessels, when with unfurled sails they tack from side to side, presenting thereby every possible variety their forms are capable of'.*

A fleet of sailing boats carried slate along the lake to Nibthwaite Quay where there was *'a fine slate storage barn'*. Some barges may have unloaded at a berth in Allen Tarn – an abundance of slate on the riverbed supports this. Onward transhipment was by horse and cart to Penny Bridge, where the River Crake had been straightened to allow small boats upstream. A small landing quay was built to load boats for Greenodd or Ulverston. From here it was shipped to Bristol, Chepstow and London, and even – during the early nineteenth century – the West Indies. The cost of transporting the slate from quarry to sea was between 6s 10d and 7s 10d. As well as the Kirkbys, other slate carriers in the mid-18th century were Adam Fleming and Robert Kendal. Five carters were employed in moving the slate to the lake from the quarries, and a further six from Nibthwaite to Greenodd. The old slate quays at Kirkby Quay and Nibthwaite are still extant, the latter accessible by a public right of way.

From 1824 saltpetre and sulphur were brought up the lake to Waterhead for the newly opened gunpowder works at Elterwater. It is probable that charcoal – essential in the production of the 'black powder' – was also taken to the works from Coniston Water, although Windermere was also used to supply this site. The finished gunpowder was stored in a large barn near the head of Coniston Water before being shipped down the lake.

Typical of the Coniston barges was *Elizabeth*, built at Ambleside in 1839 by local boat builder William Watson for the Coniston Copper Mines Company. After many years service on the lake she was displaced by the railway and returned to Windermere in the 1880s.

Rowing boats were available for hire on Coniston Water from at least the 1830s and probably for many years before that. 'A Guide to the Lakes and Mountains of Cumberland, published in 1832, mentions;

Gondola at Lake Bank around 1900 with 8 windows.

'CONISTON WATERHEAD INN is beautifully situated on the shore at the head of the lake, of which it commands a fine view. Here boats may be hired, as well as a chaise and horses.'

James Gibson, proprietor of the passage boats on Windermere, published 'A Guide to the Scenery of Windermere' in 1843 which advised readers to take a boat out on Coniston, albeit in an unsurprisingly less than complimentary tone; *'...arrive at Waterhead; here is an excellent Inn kept by Mr Braithwaite, where the party can ... engage a boat for an hour on the water: the latter I should advise, as a row three miles down the lake will repay the trouble, but not further, as the scenery is tame below.'*

There is no reference to any sort of pleasure steamer being available for hire on Coniston until a small snippet appeared in the Westmorland Gazette in October 1846; *'A project is on foot for placing a steamer on Coniston lake by next summer.'* Although this came to naught, it demonstrates that tourism was increasing sufficiently to suggest a steamer could be viable. Pleasure boat operations on Windermere were clearly benefitting from the proximity of a railway, and large villages on its shores. Perhaps the project was abandoned after appreciating the difficulties of getting a steamer to the lake, and the limited accessibility by coach services. Even so, in 1848 J.G. Marshall demolished his hotel at the head of the lake and replaced it with a 'handsome hotel', anticipating the future tourist market and coinciding with the extension of the Furness Railway from Kirkby in Furness to Broughton.

Local entrepreneurs hired out 'wherries' on the lake; wooden slate and copper ore barges converted by the addition of 'thwarts' to seat 3 or 4 tourists, and rowed with 2 or 3 pairs of long sweeps, or oars. A painting of a wherry by Thomas Tolming survives in the Ruskin Museum in Coniston.

The prospect of a steamer on the lake was reported again in the Westmorland Gazette on 16th November 1850; *'A STEAMER ON CONISTON LAKE: – It is now (says our correspondent, who evidently and naturally ranks his statement among the* curious and improbable), a fact, established beyond doubt, that a steamer will ply on Coniston Water next summer'. However no steamer appeared in 1851 and it was another four years before one appeared on Coniston Water.

On 17th July 1855 the Carlisle Courier carried the following report, copied from the Westmorland Gazette;

Steamer on Coniston Lake

A small steamer was launched on Wednesday at High Nibthwaite, upon the glassy surface of Thurston, or Coniston Lake, the twin sister to the Queen of Lakes. The steamer is on the screw principle, and came from Fleetwood. It was transported to Coniston Lake, and is, we understand, the property of the Ulverston Mining (Copper) Company, who intend running it for passengers, and as a tug for the conveyance of ore down the lake.

The following week they noted that the steamer was the property of James Sladen, not the mining company. Little is known about this boat, but local papers mentioned that it had been operating on a body of water near Rochdale. A.R. Bennett's 1927 'The Chronicles of Boulton's Sidings' notes that Isaac W. Boulton built a steam boat for pleasure trips on Rudyard Lake; *'He got an order from the North Staffordshire Railway for a steamboat for pleasure trips on Rudyard Lake near Leek. Boulton built it with a locomotive type boiler and non-condensing engine and it made a successful, if somewhat noisy, debut on the lake at Easter, 1850. After some years Boulton re-purchased the steamer and under the name of Princess Royal ran her on the Irwell between the Albert Hotel, Manchester, and Pomona Gardens. Later still he took her to the Humber and established a passenger*

service between Hull and Grimsby. In 1853 she was once more removed, this time to Hollingworth Lake near Rochdale, where, the lake becoming popular with visitors, he for a time made a profit of £40 per month. Finally the little vessel was sold to a Company formed to exploit the lake as a pleasure resort and ran it there until worn out'.

The dates, locations and name all match, suggesting the Coniston vessel was Boulton's steamer. The Hollingworth Lake Company was established by James Sladen, an engineer at Newall's woollen mill in Littleborough. This was not a success so Sladen took one of the two steamboats to Coniston Water. She probably took the canal from Rochdale to Liverpool and sailed as deck cargo to Greenodd to be dragged to Nibthwaite. A guidebook stated that; *'a beautiful iron steamboat would ply for hire on the* (Rudyard) *lake during the day.'* suggesting she was built from iron. The Kendal Mercury compared her to the boats plying along the Lancaster Canal to Kendal before the railway opened, which hints that she was a long narrow craft.

Sladen intended to use the vessel as a tourist passenger steamer, and a timetable appeared in the Kendal Mercury on the 21st July 1855. Interestingly the *Princess Royal* was scheduled to run on Sundays;

Steam on Coniston Lake

The Princess Royal Steam Boat commenced running between CONISTON WATERHEAD and NIBTHWAITE on Monday last 16th instant, and will continue to run daily, between the above places, for the accommodation of Passengers, calling at different stations, if required.

Down the Lake – 9.30 am; 12.15 pm; and 4 pm.

Lady of the Lake nudges into Lake Bank pier, at the southern end of Coniston Water.

Up the Lake – 10.30 am; 1.15 pm; and 5 pm.
JAMES SLADEN, Proprietor.
Coniston, July 16th 1855.

It seems Sladen had still to confirm the major details. On July 16th, the Ulverston Advertiser carried the following advert for the *Queen of the Lakes;*

Coniston Lake Steamer – On and after Monday, July 16th, the screw steamer Queen of the Lakes will ply from and to the Waterhead Inn, Coniston (weather permitting) taking in passengers from both sides of the lake, viz., Nibthwaite and Lake Bank, as under:
Down the Lake – 9.30 am; 12.15 pm; and 4 pm.
Up the Lake – 10.40 am; 1.30 pm; and 5.30 pm.

Fares for the Round: First Class 1s 6d; Second Class 1s. Parties not returning charged same fare. Children under 12 years go half price. To Tourists: Parties travelling from Ambleside by the coach for Broughton will arrive in time for the boat leaving Waterhead at 12.15 and returning at 4 or 5.30. On Sundays the Queen of the Lakes will ply (weather permitting) as under:
Down the Lake – 9.30 am; 1.30 pm; and 5.30 pm.
Up the Lake – 10.45 am; 3 pm; and 7 pm.

Fares as on Weekdays. The steamer will call at Coniston Hall and Oxenhouses as required.
James Sladen, Proprietor.
Coniston Waterhead. July 1855.

Sladen may have changed the name to make reference to Windermere, then known as the Queen of the Lakes. The vessel called on request at Coniston Hall and Oxenhouses (near Sunny Bank pier where the bay is named Oxen House Bay). There was also potential for a circular tour by taking the steamer from Bowness to Ambleside, boarding the Broughton coach for Waterhead (Coniston) and travelling the length of the lake before returning to Newby Bridge via Ulverston, or reversing the outward trip.

Inconsistent information may well have confused prospective passengers and the venture was not a success. On 11th August the Westmorland Gazette reported; '*The steamer on Coniston Lake, which we announced a week or two ago, has already ceased to ply, the experiment being found to be an unprofitable one.*' Sladen was clearly impatient and the *Princess Royal*'s role as a Coniston steamer quickly ended.

Coniston had yet to become a staple of the tourist trail as it was still remote, coach fares were high and the trade could not sustain the business. It is not recorded what happened next to the *Princess Royal*, but Bennett mentions that she ran on Hollingworth Lake until '*worn out*', suggesting that she returned there after completing her Lakeland service. Another theory suggests that the Coniston Mining Company purchased her to tow ore barges along the lake, but there is no further record of the vessel on the lake. Sladen returned to Lancashire, and on 29th April 1856 put pleasure boats and a steamer on Hollingworth Lake. Perhaps the *Princess Royal* was that vessel. He remained in the Hollingworth area and in 1879 was listed as proprietor of the Beach Hotel.

The outcome of the venture may have been very different four years later, when the railway was extended from Broughton to Coniston. The opening in 1859 heralded the end of two centuries of boating ore along the lake. The demise of this trade was noted in the 'History of the two Conistons'; '*The port of Nibthwaite, with its miniature docks and piers, was formerly a spot of some bustle and liveliness, from being the place of discharge, on their way to Ulverston, for the mineral products of the Coniston hills, which, with quantities of small timber, were brought down the lake in large boats. The trade of Nibthwaite, however, like that of many more important emporia, has been annihilated by the formation of a railway, and the Lake-foot now lies in a state of almost primeval quietude, broken only by an occasional pleasure boat, or the steam gondola on her daily voyages during the months of summer... A visitor, wishing to see too advantage on his approach to it, may hardly do better than take a passage up the lake in this screw-propelled gondola, so styled*'.

The Coniston Railway was to be dependent on freight revenues for the bulk of its income, but the directors were alert to the tourist possibilities. They commissioned naval architect Douglas Hebson to design a passenger steamer for the lake trade, aided by the FR's James Ramsden, a keen sailor who had travelled widely in Italy. His idea was to base the vessel on a Venetian burchiello, but without a traditional funnel; instead her steam exited through ducts on the starboard side at the stern. The railway company did not possess powers to operate this service in their own right, so registered the operation through Ramsden, a typical ploy at the time.

The contract was awarded to Jones, Quiggin & Co. of Liverpool. *Gondola* was built of 1/8 inch steel flush

Lady of the Lake nears completion on the slip at Pier Cottage. (Steam Yacht Gondola Collection)

riveted on to a steel frame at a cost of £1,200. Wrought iron was used in constructing her gunwhale, some of which is still original. Her plates were conveyed by rail and heavy horse to Pier Cottage near Coniston Hall, where she was assembled. She weighed 42 tons with dimensions of 84 feet by just under 14 feet with a draught of 4 feet 6 inches, and she was driven by a 2 cylinder, 16 horsepower engine fed by a coke fired locomotive style boiler, identical to that fitted to Furness Railway loco No.20 of 1863. The engines were supplied by Lawrence and Company of Liverpool. Her fittings were lavish and consisted of two saloons amidships. The first class saloon was based on the interior of Queen Victoria's royal carriage with a mahogany ceiling and wall panels, and blue crushed velvet upholstery. Part of the other saloon was given over to smokers, with open decks at the bow and stern. Hanging over the bow was a golden sea serpent bearing the motto of the Duke of Devonshire *'Cavendo Tutus'* – *'Safety through caution.'*

Miss Boileau of Coniston launched Gondola on Wednesday 30th November 1859 at Coniston Hall – just south of the present day Coniston landings – with the wedges knocked out by James Ramsden. A large crowd gathered to witness the spectacle, which was hampered by water rushing up the exhaust ducts and dampening the boiler fire. After the launch she moved to Pier Cottage, near the Waterhead Hotel, which was to be her new home.

Gondola made a trial trip on Wednesday 21st December. She performed well in a strong northerly breeze heading south, but was forced to seek shelter near Peel Island when facing a headwind on her return. After leaving the shelter of the bay she met more heavy weather, which the Kendal Mercury reported on 24th December 1859 *'swept her boats away, which were cast upon the north shore at Waterpark, one being*

S.Y. "GONDOLA" ON CONISTON LAKE

S.Y. "GONDOLA" & "LADY OF THE LAKE" AT WATERHEAD PIER, CONISTON

Above right: Gondola with long time master Felix Hamill at the wheel.

Right: Gondola and **Lady of the Lake** at Pier Cottage.

almost dashed to pieces and the other considerably damaged.' This suggests that *Gondola* was carrying lifeboats, although no images survive, and it is probable they were not replaced after being lost.

An image in the Illustrated London News on 7th July 1860 depicts rails along the saloon roof allowing passengers to access the top deck, although this is probably artistic license. It was quickly recognised that the small stern exhaust ducts were inefficient, and a funnel was added. Her long saloon had eight windows prior to alteration in 1903 and she was licenced to carry up to 225 passengers.

Gondola was described in detail in the Carlisle Journal in June 1860: *'This vessel is in its outward form and internal fittings a perfected combination of the Venetian gondola and the English steam-yacht – having the elegance, comfort, and speed of the latter, and the graceful lines and quiet gliding motion of the former. It may be said to be the most elegant little steam-vessel yet designed, and is specially suitable for pleasure excursions on lake or river... The centre of the vessel, being thus left for passengers, is fitted up as a saloon, covered with a light roof; the sides, of plate-glass, in large sheets, affording an uninterrupted view of the magnificent scenery surrounding the lake, the summit of the highest mountains being visible to those seated in the saloon. The interior is beautifully furnished in walnut-wood, and is cushioned and decorated after the style of the Royal carriages of our railways. The prow, which is long and graceful, is adorned with a well executed-carving of the arms of the Duke of Devonshire, while the armorial bearings of the Duke of Buccleuch ornament the stern'.*

Her first public season was from June to the end of September 1860, operating one round trip of the lake at 1 pm with additional cruises at 11.30 am and 4 pm if required. The 11.30 am cruise became part of the core schedule from 1861 but when that season finished on 30th September it was reported that: *'The summer has not been favourable for jaunting parties, but those who have availed themselves of the privilege of staying a few hours at the foot of the lake during the return of the boat, have found themselves highly gratified by the rustic strolls and the pleasant scenery to be met with in their rambles.'*

An 1862 Parliamentary Act permitted railway companies to own and operate ships linked to their railheads, coinciding with the FR takeover of the Coniston Railway. The timetable incorporated *Gondola* into the railway schedule from 1863; although advertised as sailing from Waterhead, the steamer ran from Pier Cottage (a short walk through the grounds of the hotel) at 12 noon and 2.45 pm, returning from Lake Bank at 1.30 pm and 3.45 pm. She offered a morning tour if notice was given to the nearby hotel or the master of the vessel. Her tours were well patronised, and the villages of Nibthwaite and Oxen Park were opened to tourists, who responded to the new found accessibility. Adverts for 'Sly's Waterhead Hotel' mention *'A steam Gondola on the lake'* with coaches from all over the lakes.

Train service punctuality suffered amidst the heavy volumes of freight traffic on the Furness network. The railway had been built primarily with the copper mines in mind, leaving Coniston station atop a steep hill above the village. Passengers for lake services transferred at their own pace between the station and pier, which boasted a railway-style name board. Whilst connecting coaches were provided they were not included in the ticket price, so many passengers chose to walk. The stationmaster was instructed to erect a flag at the station to alert the steamer if the train was more than half an hour late. *Gondola*'s scheduled 12 noon departure was often delayed until 12.30 pm to allow passengers to make their way down from the train.

As the railway opened so copper ore output declined; dropping to around 3,000 tons by 1860, and less than 2,000 tons by 1864. By the end of the century the industry was effectively defunct. The FR's answer was to develop the programme of Circular Tours, with Coniston featuring prominently in three of the first four.

The first master of the *Gondola*, Captain Anderson, had travelled with the *Fox* expedition to the Arctic between July 1857 and September 1859, but in 1871 the *Gondola* came under the command of Captain Felix Hamill. He lived in Pier Cottage above the boathouse with his family of nine children.

Gondola's standard timetable in the 1890s left Waterhead four times a day at 11.10 am, 12.45 pm, 2.10 pm, and 4.10 pm, leaving Lake Bank at 11.50 am, 1.25 pm, 2.50 pm, and 4.50 pm.

Minor alterations were made to the *Gondola* from 1900, when the smoking room was removed to create room for a 3rd class lounge at a cost of £35, and in 1903 her superstructure was shortened to build a cockpit at the rear of the saloon. She reappeared with seven windows along her saloon. 2nd class was abolished by the Furness Railway in 1897 due to *'the fact that the through bookings had nearly ceased... it would be better to discontinue the provision of second class accommodation.'*

In 1897 *Gondola* carried 14,264 passengers – a considerable achievement when her capacity was only 200 passengers. Traffic levels grew to 17,572 passengers in 1904, 19,125 in 1905 and 22,445 in 1906, demonstrating the success of the tour programme. The 1907 timetable included Boat Trains connecting with the cross-bay steamers from Fleetwood to Ramsden Dock, bringing Coniston within reach of day excursionists from Blackpool.

The rebuild at Vickers. (Vickers Shipbuilding and Engineering)

The Old Man of Coniston seen
from the lake's eastern shore.

A larger steamer was needed to meet the growing demand and replace the older vessel, which by 1907 was valued at £40. The design was drawn up by W.F. Pettigrew, Chief Mechanical Engineer of the FR, and a £5,600 order was placed with J.L. Thornycroft and Company of Woolston. Transported in sections by rail for assembly at Pier Cottage, she was 97 feet long with a width of 15 feet and drawing 6ft 9in. She slightly resembled the Windermere *Tern* with a canoe shaped bow and a similar funnel, which was probably no coincidence.

Lady of the Lake was launched on 26th May 1908 by Mrs Wadham of Millwood. During the celebratory lunch – probably at the Waterhead Hotel – it was revealed that there had been difficulties in registering the vessel's name with the Board of Trade. The company wanted to revive that of the first steamboat launched on Windermere in 1845 but there were eighteen vessels with her name, including one on Ullswater.

Lady of the Lake pushed the *Gondola* to reserve vessel, as she could carry up to 400 passengers, but she rarely reached this figure. In the Lakes Herald on 29th May her first class cabin was noted to be of panelled oak, her second-class cabin being panelled with teak.

Power was provided by two engines either side of a locomotive style boiler, providing a speed of about 11 knots. Her arrival allowed eight return sailings to be provided between Waterhead and Lake Bank for the 1908 season, two more than in previous years. Captain Hamill skippered the new boat, and Captain Priss assumed the *Gondola's* helm. To celebrate the launch of the new vessel, colourful posters depicting a well-dressed lady symbolically waving a handkerchief at the *Lady of the Lake* at Lake Bank pier were posted across the Furness Railway network. Above the images was written;

CONISTON
NEW STEAM YACHT LADY OF THE LAKE.

Coniston's popularity continued to rise, with a Sunday service between June and September 1909 connecting with excursion trains from Barrow. Mr Brydson objected to Sunday landings on his land at Lake Bank pier, so these became non-landing cruises from Waterhead. Sunday sailings featured up to the First World War with Mr Brydson continuing to deny access to Lake Bank pier. In 1913 these non-landing tours departed Waterhead at 2 pm, 4.15 pm and 5.30 pm costing 1s in First Class or 9d in Second.

In August 1910 the company advertised to increase revenue and find employment for *Gondola*: '*Furness Railway Company give notice that they permit the Towing of Boats, with or without passengers in them, on Coniston Lake by the "Gondola" at the Captains discretion, but not by the Steam Yacht "Lady of the Lake". The charge for towing a boat will be 1/-, whether for the full lake or part thereof. In the case of passengers accompanying Boats, a charge of 6d. per head is to be paid by each passenger, in addition to the towing charge.*'

On 14th May 1913 a breakdown in communication saw *Lady of the Lake* fail to respond to the helm when approaching Lake Bank pier, when the newly appointed engineer McDowell failed to engage the reversing gear. Running ashore she crashed through a smaller boat, and remained hard aground. *Gondola* was called to assist but failed to refloat the grounded vessel, and a gang of men from Barrow were called in to float her off. Damage

Gondola as a Houseboat at the south end of the lake (Steam Yacht Gondola Collection).

Lady of the Lake on Coniston (Reproduced by courtesy of the Museum of Lakeland Life and Industry, Kendal, Cumbria).

was limited to £28 to the vessel and £10 to the pier.

Coniston Water has fewer shallow areas than Windermere or Derwentwater and Captain Hamill once noted 'There are few places on Coniston Lake where I could not put the prow (of the Gondola) into green fields while the stern was in deep water.'

The 'Lady' never proved as popular as Gondola, perhaps due to her similarities to other local vessels, relative to her sister's unique design. With engines at the stern of the vessel, her bow was comparatively high in the water making her difficult to manoeuvre.

The popularity of the circular tours made intensive work for the two steamers. For the 1914 season eight return trips were offered between Waterhead and Lake Bank, with a one-boat service scheduled from September. But the outbreak of the First World War brought services to a temporary stop. Lady of the Lake ceased sailing on 12th August 1914, while Gondola saw out the season before being laid up at Pier Cottage.

Aslett proposed a short operating season for Gondola in 1915, but the FR Board decided against it. In 1916 Gondola was nearly pressed into service after complaints about loss of trade from local residents – including Mr Tyson of the Waterhead Hotel – but she was left tied up. Both vessels returned to service after the war.

Captain Felix Hamill retired in 1921 after commanding Gondola from 1871 and spending many years with Lady of the Lake. He completed over 13,000 sailings and only caused 7s 6d worth of damage. Captain Priss now took command of both vessels.

The LMS incorporated the FR in 1923, and re-boilered the Gondola with a steel boiler and copper firebox, whilst retaining her original engine. The new boiler worked at a pressure of 100lb per square inch, compared to 80lb per square inch of the older copper one.

Gondola retired in 1936 but Lady of the Lake continued until the outbreak of the Second World War when she was laid up alongside Gondola at Pier Cottage. Gondola's engines were removed in 1944 and sold to a sawmill near Ulverston. In 1946 she was sold to Fred McCaddam of Ulverston, converted into a houseboat and moored near Lake Bank. Lady of the Lake was broken up in 1950.

During the late 1950s an attempt was made to revive a service using a small open motor launch named Queen of the Lake. Cruises were operated from the head of the lake, probably from the boat landings, but it proved unsuccessful. Rowing boats could however be hired from the Thwaite family at the boat landings. George Thwaite had commenced hiring in 1894, and his son Godfrey continued the business, including building and repairing boats, until selling up around 1960. Throughout the 1960s Robert Clarke and John Wilson worked from the beach; between them they had about forty rowing boats for hire. Clarke, originally a boat builder at Borwick's in Bowness, brought his fleet across from Waterhead on Windermere.

The severe winter of 1963 took its toll on the Gondola and she sank, ending washed up at Water Park. To make matters worse the River Crake was dredged shortly after and the level of the lake dropped by around two feet, leaving her high and dry. She was purchased by Arthur Hatton for £40, patched up and re-floated by digging a channel back to the water, moved to near Nibthwaite and sunk to preserve the hull plates.

Gondola languished there for over a decade until a group of enthusiasts commissioned a survey in 1975, which showed that the hull plates had deteriorated, in some places only a third as thick as when originally launched. Undaunted, and recognising there might be a chance of saving her, her hull was made watertight with cement, and in January 1977 she was slowly moved to Coniston Hall, where she had been assembled back in 1859.

The National Trust purchased the 119-year-old vessel in 1978 and dismantled her into 3 sections for restoration at Vickers shipyard in Barrow. Vickers constructed an exact rebuild of the Gondola from ¼ inch welded steel plates using the original plans. Slight modifications brought her up to modern safety standards. A new three bladed propeller was fitted, as her original four bladed one had been stolen in 1976. Many original fittings were re-used on the rebuilt hull, including some handrails and railings. Much of her original gunwale was retained, and if seen out of the water it is easy to identify which parts are over 150 years old, and which are not. Locomotive Enterprises of Gateshead supplied a new engine and W Bertram & Sons of South Shields built a high pressure boiler to the same design as the Ffestiniog Railway's 'Prince'; it operates up to a pressure of 150lb per square inch. The engine operates at 40lb per square inch whilst cruising at 8 miles per hour, whilst full power requires a pressure of 80lb per square inch to achieve a speed of 12 miles per hour.

The mild steel hull sections were transported to Pier Cottage in November 1979 and Gondola was launched for a second time on Lady Day, 25th March 1980 by Mrs Sheila Howell, great grand-daughter of Captain Felix Hamill, and wife of the Vickers Shipbuilding Production Director. Her first sailing on 24th June saw the 11th Duke of Devonshire in attendance with passengers dressed in Victorian costume.

For her first season the National Trust operated Gondola with a passenger certificate for 86 passengers for her first public cruises in June 1980. She berthed overnight at Pier Cottage and offered 4 trips daily between the Coniston Boating Centre, Lake Bank and Monk Coniston. These sailings lasted around 90 minutes, and at the peak season an extra sailing was added to the schedule. Gondola was not an immediate success, and in 1982 Sealink – who also operated the Windermere vessels at the time – took over operation of the vessel at the National Trust's request. Sealink operated around 7 circular tours a day from Coniston Boating Centre to Park a Mor on a 55 minute cruise, but carried less than 20,000 passengers throughout the season.

Sealink withdrew from management of the operation, and the National Trust resumed running Gondola in 1983. Under their ownership she ran to Park a Mor, but made fewer trips, which left more time available for maintenance. National Trust property agent Gordon Hall said, *'We will have to accept making only a small profit every year.'* In 1985 she operated four return trips to Park a Mor, with a fifth sailing added during the high season. Calls at Brantwood were added in the late 1980s, with *Gondola* calling there after Park a Mor on her circular cruise.

Gondola has seen several different liveries during her long career on the lake. If early coloured photochrom postcards are accurate, Gondola originally sported a red underside with a black hull and a cream saloon. Later her hull was painted light grey with a white superstructure until settling down to a black hull for the bulk of her service on the lake. When sunk at the southern end of the lake she had a green hull that had probably been painted when she was converted into a houseboat.

Since re-launch, Gondola has mainly sported a brown hull and funnel with a white band and red strip along the top, finished off with a green water line. Her saloon has remained white. For 2012 she had a brown hull and for the 2013 season her hull was painted in an attractive blue. She retained the white band and red stripe along the top, and her funnel was coloured to match the hull whilst her saloon remained white.

In 1992 competition arrived in the form of *Ruskin* operated by Coniston Ferry Services ('Coniston Launch'), a company established by Gordon and Margaret Hall the previous year. *Ruskin* was a diesel launch built from mahogany on oak in 1922 as the *Raglan II* for the Chester Boat Company. Purchased by Coniston Launch in February 1992, she was converted into a traditional Lakeland launch with an open bow and covered stern.

Her cruises started later that year from the shared pier at the Coniston Boating Centre, to Brantwood and

Cygnet arriving at Coniston on 13th June 2013 on a Gilbert Brown & Son boat transporter. (Peter Walker)

Monk Coniston – named Waterhead in timetables. Up to twenty sailings were offered at peak times for her first two seasons in service and she was such a success that attempts were made to construct a pier further down the west shore of the lake at Torver. In 1994, permission was sought for a pier at Park Coppice, just south of the Caravan Park. Leaflets were printed marking the pier in the timetable, but the rent proved prohibitive. Consent was eventually granted to construct a pier just south of Park Coppice at Hoathwaite, although this was never built as the works would interfere with the Raymond Priestley Outdoor Education Centre, which shares the little bay.

The timetable operated for 11 months, from 12th

Campbell and **Cygnet** at the Coniston Boating Centre for the simultaneous 4.40 pm departures on both the Northern and Southern services.

Gondola sunk at the south end of the lake in 1974.

special interest cruises with commentaries were added to the timetable; subjects such as Donald Campbell's speed record attempts, Arthur Ransome's tales of Swallows and Amazons and John Ruskin all featured in these special non-landing trips to the south end of the lake.

Arthur Ransome's 'Swallows and Amazons' stories, draw on his childhood years around Windermere and Coniston. Captain Hamill of the *Gondola* used to let a young Arthur take the wheel of the steamer as she plied the length of the lake. Ransome later said how both the *Gondola* and the *Esperance* (on Windermere) were the inspiration for Captain Flint's houseboat in the books.

Coniston Launch sought access to piers at the southern end of the lake and finally in 1999 secured permission to land at Park a Mor, Lake Bank and Sunny Bank to form the 'Southern Service' (marked in green on the timetables). Initially Sunny Bank pier was not allowed to touch the lakeshore due to access restrictions, but permission was granted to utilise the lakebed. A floating jetty was towed to Sunny Bank, with large anchor rocks placed on top and, once manoeuvred into position, the anchors were dropped into the lake. No part of the pier permanently touched dry land, and a sliding gangway was kept on the pier for embarkation or disembarkation. Nowadays the structure has a permanent connecting ramp to the shore.

The original cruise to Monk Coniston, Torver and Brantwood became known as the 'Northern Service', and was marked in red on the timetables. The following year Waterhead Hotel was added to the timetable, but only for special cruises such as coach groups or the Breakfast Cruise, where passengers took a one-hour cruise at 8 am before breakfast at the hotel. Around this time launches stopped using the *Gondola* pier and moved to share the

Gondola ready to go to Vickers. (Vickers Shipbuilding and Engineering)

February 1994 through to 2nd January 1995, although during the winter *Ruskin* operated at weekends only.

With passenger numbers on the increase it was thought a second launch could be sustained and the *Iris* – renamed *Ransome* – was chartered from Keswick Launch for the 1994 season. Her trial was a success and so another permanent boat was found, allowing the *Iris* to return to Keswick.

The *Empress* was built from pitch pine on oak in 1923 for services around Plymouth. She arrived at Coniston ready for the 1995 season and was renamed *Ransome* to partner *Ruskin* and offer cruises every half hour at peak times.

In 1997 a new pier was built at Torver about half a mile south of Hoathwaite. With two boats in operation

Gondola on her full lake cruise, heading for Nibthwaite, passing Sunny Bank.

pier used by the Coniston Boating Centre.

Ruskin had a brief moment of fame when she carried Donald Campbell's coffin to Coniston on 12th September 2001. The lake was the scene of his tragic death on 4th January 1967 when *Bluebird K7* crashed at a speed of over 300 mph. The Campbell's had a long connection with the lake; Sir Malcolm Campbell set the world water speed record there on 19th August 1939 in *Bluebird K4*. He died in 1948 and his son, Donald followed in his footsteps during the summers of 1949 and 1950 when he trialled a heavily modified *Bluebird K4* on Coniston, and in 1952 achieved 170 mph. Attaining this speed damaged the vessel beyond repair, and the following year an American, Stanley Sayers, raised the record to 178 mph.

Campbell returned with a new boat *Bluebird K7* in the mid-1950s. He had already set several world water speed records in *K7* – on Ullswater in July 1955 and in America on Lake Mead in Nevada. Campbell and *Bluebird K7* became a common sight on the lake, returning annually between trips to Australia and America.

In November 1966 Campbell and *Bluebird K7* returned for a final attempt at the world water speed record, as he was concentrating more on his rocket car *Bluebird Mach 1.1*. The target was 300 mph and after a month of trials, high-speed runs were made in December, reaching 250 mph despite fuel pump problems that starved the engine of fuel. The problems were rectified but bad weather set in, and no runs were made for a few weeks.

4th January 1967 dawned calm, and the lake was

flat, without a ripple. At 8.45 am Campbell set out on his first run and reached an average speed of 297.6 mph, tantalisingly close to the target. He immediately decided to make a second run, rather than refuel and wait for the wash from the previous run to subside; this was not uncommon if conditions permitted. The second run was faster, reaching a peak speed of 328 mph, but the starboard sponson bounced alarmingly, the movement intensified and *Bluebird K7* somersaulted before hitting the water again, and cartwheeling before eventually settling. She sank quickly with much debris floating on the water, having sheared off on impact. Campbell was killed instantly and Navy divers almost immediately tried to find his body. The search was called off without success after two weeks, and his

Marianne, newly arrived at Coniston, undergoes a re-paint prior to launch.

Ransome at the Coniston Boating Centre in 2009.

Marianne at Pier Cottage awaiting sale.

whereabouts remained a mystery. The wreck was discovered on 5th January but it was decided not to raise it without the body. The location of the wreck was not publicly disclosed.

In March 2001 the vessel was raised from its watery grave and Campbell's body was later discovered in May. *Ruskin* played her part loading the body at the crash site and conveying him to his funeral on the 12th September. A small plaque above the entrance to the saloon commemorated the occasion, until the vessel's sale from the lake.

Winter sailings continued to operate, and for the 2001/2 season 35-minute winter cruises were offered between Coniston, Torver and Brantwood. There was no strict timetable, with the launch running on request to all jetties, except Sunny Bank, subject to demand.

The following winter five 25-minute sailings were offered daily except Christmas Day, between Coniston, Waterhead Hotel (included in literature for the first time) and Brantwood only. Torver was added in subsequent winters making it a 40-minute cruise, but sailings were only provided at weekends and holidays.

From 2003, Waterhead Hotel became a permanent timetabled call before Monk Coniston on the Northern Service, but 2005 was the last year that the latter was served. *Ruskin* was converted to electric propulsion when solar panels were fitted to charge banks of batteries stored on board following modification to *Ransome* late the previous year. They both received Solomon Technologies ST74 electric motors powered by a 144dc battery bank, and in case the sun didn't shine they were charged up from the mains overnight at Pier Cottage.

In 2007 Water Park replaced Park a Mor, which was removed from the timetable. Previously one vessel operated the Northern Service, whilst the other sailed to the south two or three times daily. A new sailing was added as the 'Yellow Cruise' which was essentially the Northern Service, extended to Sunny Bank, after Torver and before Brantwood. The Southern Service still operated twice daily, with the new sailing sandwiched in between.

In 2008 the company was sold to Douglas and Gillian Hodgson; operations continued as before but in 2009 slight changes were made to the number of south

lake cruises operated when the Yellow Cruise was dropped, leaving the two Southern Service sailings. Winter sailings on the Northern Service continued as previously, with a limited timetable operated at weekends and holidays.

2010 was *Ransome*'s final season as the 1976 *Exonia* (II), a replacement fibreglass boat arrived in June. She was brought to Hawkshead for a major rebuild, emerging as *Campbell* from Patterson Boatworks looking like a traditional Lakeland launch. She entered service on 18th June 2011 alongside *Ruskin* providing a two-boat schedule for that year.

In 2012 *Ruskin* was withdrawn after twenty years service and *Campbell* operated a single vessel timetable. This restricted the Southern Service although specialist cruises were still offered. 2012 saw a new pier added to the Northern Service at Bank Ground Farm. This was the inspiration for Holly Howe in Arthur Ransome's 'Swallows and Amazons', and offered a tearoom, although the farm only remained in the timetable for one season.

Campbell was joined by a new vessel in 2013, bringing the Coniston Launch fleet back up to two. Arriving at Coniston on 6th February she was painted in the company colours at the car park near the main piers before being launched on 12th March. Named *Marianne*, she was equipped with a bar and upper deck seating, having been built in 1988 as the *Windsor Minstrel* by the Windsor Marina for French Brothers.

Cygnet joined the fleet on 13th June 2013 allowing *Marianne* to be used almost exclusively for private cruises and charters.

Cygnet was painted in the company colours, with much of the work taking place at Sunny Bank pier. She entered service on 1st August still powered by her original Scania DS11 engine. She inaugurated the 'Wild Cat Island Cruise' – similar to the Yellow Cruise of 2007 and the south lake trip, omitting the calls at Water Park and Lake Bank. After calling at Torver, *Cygnet* sails close to Peel Island before returning north to Sunny Bank, Brantwood and the Coniston Boating Centre. She offers four of these sailings daily.

Ransome was sold in 2011 to the Avon for conversion into a holiday houseboat. *Ruskin* had been kept at Pier Cottage, but the arrival of the *Marianne* meant pier space was at a premium, as the service boats berth there overnight. In early 2013 she was laid up alongside Water Park jetty, and in June appeared on eBay for a 'Buy It Now' price of £4,500 without an engine. Her new owners, Pennine Cruisers, have restored her to her former condition and cruise her on the Leeds and Liverpool Canal from Skipton. *Marianne* became surplus to requirements after the arrival of the *Cygnet* in June and was laid up at Torver pier to free up space at Pier Cottage. She was sold back to the Thames in October for use as a crew boat. She left the lake on 9th October 2013. For the 2015 season, Water Park was dropped from the timetable, and at the time of writing it has not been determined wether the call will reappear in the future.

Gondola's call at Park a Mor ceased in 1999 and

she sailed a 45-minute cruise between Brantwood and Coniston. Monk Coniston was added on Saturdays only from 2006 and then daily from 2009. Leaving Coniston Boating Centre she took a circular route to Brantwood, returning to Coniston via Monk Coniston. This route is still the mainstay of her timetable although full-length sailings were included in the timetable in 2010; non-stop on Mondays and Thursdays, continuing to Brantwood and Monk Coniston on Sundays. The following year Park a Mor was re-introduced, with a short time ashore for 'non-landing' passengers for photography, providing time to oil the engine.

From 1859 *Gondola* burnt coal, but from March 2008 it was decided to use Blazer Logs. These are made from compressed sawdust and burn more efficiently with little smoke. They are also more environmentally friendly as they are carbon neutral.

2010 was *Gondola's* 150th anniversary and to celebrate, the National Trust had her totally refitted prior to the commencement of the season. A special cruise took place at 4 pm on 8th June; amongst the guests were the 12th Duke of Devonshire, Lord Cavendish and Sheila Howell, the great granddaughter of Captain Felix Hamill. On Saturday 19th June a replica 'Middle Circle' tour was operated; guests started with a trip on the Lakeside and Haverthwaite railway and continued along Windermere to Ambleside. Vintage transport conveyed

them to Coniston where they boarded *Gondola* for a return cruise to Lake Bank.

2012 saw full lake sailings call at Brantwood and Monk Coniston. Until 2013 Lake Bank pier had only seen occasional use since the re-launch, but this southern-most pier was added to full lake sailings, on Saturdays only, from Easter 2013 – too late for inclusion in the season's literature. For the first time in decades it was possible to sail between the two original piers *Gondola* had been built to serve. In 2014 Lake Bank was once again a pier reserved for special occasions. In 2015 the timetable was changed again, this time including one full lake trip and three 45 minute sailings every day, and once again, Lake Bank was a scheduled call on weekend mornings. Her full lake cruise commentaries give a detailed and varied history of the lake and the surrounding area, as well as covering the literary connections of Arthur Ransome and John Ruskin, and Donald Campbell's record attempts.

With two operators on the lake supplying contrasting cruises, Coniston has plenty to offer. *Gondola* provides a link with the grandiose age of Victorian luxury, whilst *Campbell* is more reminiscent of a traditional Lakeland launch, and *Cygnet* provides all weather accommodation. From the Coniston Boating Centre rowing boats, kayaks, canoes, sailing boats, and small self-drive motorboats are still available for hire. There is something for everyone.

Ruskin in Skipton after restoration by Pennine Cruisers. (Colin Greatorex)

Ruskin departs Brantwood for the Coniston Boating Centre.

A Keswick on Derwentwater Launch Company ticket from the 1960s.

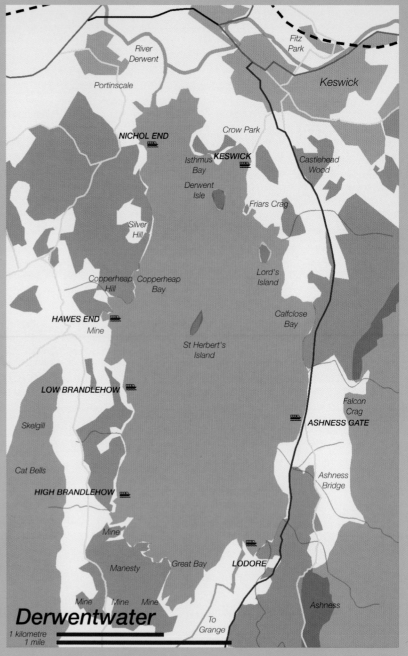

A handbill for sailings on Derwentwater from 1947.

Derwentwater

Derwentwater (244 ft above sea-level), 2¾ m long and 1¼ m wide, with a maximum depth of 72 ft, is perhaps the loveliest of the English Lakes. Its compact form enables it to be taken in at one view. The wooded crags and green hills rising from its banks are picturesquely varied, and the grouping of its islets is very beautiful.

– Baedecker's Great Britain 1937

The story of the Keswick area dates back to Neolithic times; there is evidence of a Roman and Norse presence around Bassenthwaite, and Derwentwater has three islands with a long history of habitation. Derwent Isle has been occupied since around 1569, and Lord's Island was inhabited by the Earls of Derwentwater after they left their stronghold on Castle Rigg. When in residence, legend dictates that the approach to the island was via a drawbridge.

St Herbert's Island was home to the saintly hermit of that name. A friend of St Cuthbert, he constructed a small chapel and cell on the island. Herbert lived alone and prayed that he and Cuthbert would go to Heaven together. His wish was granted as they died within the same hour in 687. This tale inspired Wordsworth to write a poem about St Herbert, further encouraging pilgrims to visit the island. The ancient pilgrim's route brought them to the lake near Portinscale where there was a small shrine to St Nicholas, the patron of sailing men, and they were ferried over to the island. The pilgrims offered a prayer before crossing to the island and it is thought that is how Nichol End got its name.

Friar's Crag, described by Ruskin as one of the three most beautiful scenes in Europe, can be traced back to ancient times, when it was an embarkation point for Lindisfarne monks and other pilgrims visiting St Herbert's Island – a short distance to the south west – and the landing place for monks who lived at Grange in Borrowdale. Crossing the lake was an easier proposition than tackling the hilly packhorse route, which ran from Grange to Rosthwaite, then over via Watendlath to Ashness and Keswick. The Grange monks were an outpost of Furness Abbey – just 25 miles away as the crow flies, but considerably further away on foot.

The development of the lake for transport purposes was linked with the mining industry. From the 1560's there were workings at Brandlehow and in Newlands Valley, and German miners were present at the time of Elizabeth I. In 1567 there was enough lead and copper mined to keep six ore smelters in operation at Brigham, then the largest operation of its kind in Europe. Copperplate Mine alone, at the head of the lake, shipped 174 cwt (9.7 tons) of copper to Brigham in October 1567. The copper had many uses, including cladding sea-going ships to prevent encrustation. Many German miners were housed on Derwent Isle (then known as Vicar's Isle) and tensions sometimes ran high between the local population and the miners, who were accused of 'taking the bread out of their mouths'. In 1561 the Company of Mines Royal was formed and their most profitable copper mine was at Goldscope in the Derwent Fells. The miners from Goldscope ferried from a pier at Copperheap Bay (near Fawe Park) to Keswick, where the landing area was then known as Middingstett. Ore was then taken on to the Greta valley to be smelted at Brigham. There were 4 boats in use by the company which were also used for the transport of timber, stone, and other goods from the southern end of the lake. The company had a building at Copperheap Bay which was used as a shelter for the boatmen, which may also have been a store room. The name 'Copperheap' was given to the bay after a boat laden with copper ore sank there. They were probably the first to use the Foreshore as a commercial embarkation point for goods and passengers, the latter mostly headed for the island on which they resided.

Mining spoil was dumped around the Brandlehow area and is still visible when disembarking from the launch at High Brandlehow. These mines were first worked in 1567, but became properly established in the 1840s. This was the site of the first steam engine in the Vale of Derwentwater in 1851. By then half a dozen tons of copper and lead ore were brought up from the mine each week which was boated to Middingstett, carted to Cockermouth, and boated to Workington for transfer to larger ships for Wales. Here the ore was smelted to create pure lead. The Brandlehow mine employed around 100 men, but struggled with flooding and required a steam engine to pump water from the levels. This impacted on profits and the mine eventually succumbed to the water in 1891. The operations at Goldscope ceased in 1923, but the method of shipment across the lake had long since finished.

Early launches at the Foreshore, including **Lorna Doone** and **May Queen**.

107 BOAT LANDINGS DERWENTWATER.

Timber was also transported across the lake, and in 1749 a contract to harvest woodland was given by the Greenwich Hospital to a man named Matthews, who owned the wood on Lord's Island and at Crow Park. He was allowed ten years to remove the timber and eventually sold his contract to merchants from Whitehaven.

On Crosthwaite's map of 1783 there were also lead and copper mines at the head of the lake, with ores from these locations loaded onto boats at Great Bay. The easiest transport to Keswick was by barges, propelled by oars and often fitted with an auxiliary sail.

The remains of a thirty-foot long boat were discovered when the slipway was built at Nichol End, near Portinscale. Inside were pieces of ore and coal, suggesting that the north west corner of the lake was used as a landing point. It is known that coal was brought from Whitehaven to Nichol End and shipped across to the Keswick Foreshore for residential use. Portinscale also had a resident boat builder as far back as 1764.

From August 1781 a series of annual regattas were held on Derwentwater when yacht races and mock naval battles were played out. These celebrations attracted huge crowds, with the lake covered in pleasure barges and beaches thronged with spectators. They were organised by Peter Crosthwaite and Joseph Pocklington; the latter lived on Pocklington's Island – now Derwent Isle – where he built a grand mansion with manicured grounds, inspired by Thomas English's development of Belle Isle on Windermere. The regattas continued until 1790 and were accompanied by shore-side activities in marquees on the Foreshore and at Crow Park.

These regattas were the first recorded use of Derwentwater as a pleasure venue, and from this point on the Foreshore became a popular venue for tourists seeking a boat. Early pleasure barges were rowing boats available for sole hire or with a guide. Local gentry conveyed notable tourists along the length of the lake, and there were undoubtedly men employed as guides and boatmen in the later 18th century, supplementing their income with other trades, such as fishing.

John Walker, *'the far-famed guide and boatman'* guided the King of Saxony around the fells near Keswick in July 1844. Walker impressed the King when offered wine with lunch, by taking the bottle straight to his lips and finishing it on his own – His Majesty later admitted to enjoying a hearty laugh at Walker's naiveté.

Henry Marshall purchased Derwent Isle in 1844 and the island remained in his family until 1951 when David Marshall gifted it to the National Trust. The family established a private ferry between the island and the Foreshore. A bell was placed in the grand boathouse to summon ferryman William Glover if there were passengers or goods to be ferried across. Nowadays the island is open to the public several times each year with a small ferry operating from the Foreshore.

The first scheduled passenger service on Derwentwater was introduced in 1848, when on the 3rd June the Westmorland Gazette reported; *'There is at present a number of tourists in the capital of the Lake District, and for their accommodation an enterprising individual has commenced plying a passage boat four times a day, from the foot of the lake, to the Lowdore Hotel, at the other extremity, capable of carrying twenty passengers, which will be found very convenient to parties visiting the Waterfalls, Bowderstone, Black-lead mine, and the*

Stunning reflections in Derwentwater with snow-capped Skiddaw behind.

much admired vale of Borrowdale.'

The Cumberland Pacquet gave more information on 6th June, and divulged the name of the boat, the *Spec*. Unfortunately this foresighted individual withdrew his boat after one week in service, as on the 10th the Westmorland Gazette reported; *'The passage boat which was announced last week as plying between the foot of Keswick Lake and the Lowdore Hotel, through the interference of Mr Hudson, of the Royal Oak Hotel, (who foresaw that some unpleasantness was likely to accrue), has been discontinued.'*

Part of the reason for the withdrawal of the *Spec* was revealed in the Cumberland Pacquet on 13th June; *'As we more than hinted would be the case this day week, another passage boat has been placed upon Derwent Lake, Keswick, by a party of guides, and as cheapness in all things is the order of the day, it is not a matter for wonder that this principle should have been laid hold of by the new passage boat company. They ply their boat from the beach near the town to the head of the Lake at half the fare of their opponents, so that a backward movement or bankruptcy we apprehend awaits the original projectors of the scheme. 'Cheap trips up the Lake' for Whitsuntide visitors have been announced at 'half fare there and back,' being just one-fourth of the charge demanded by the originators of the Spec.'*

Both the Cumberland Pacquet and the Westmorland Gazette were weekly papers, hence the overlap of the dates. The new boat was larger than its predecessor, being capable of carrying between thirty and forty passengers. It is not clear how long the new passage boat company remained operational, but on 19th July 1850 the Carlisle Journal reported that a new service had started four days earlier; *'PASSAGE BOAT ON DERWENTWATER. – On Monday last a splendid*

new passage-boat commenced plying on Derwent Lake, Keswick. This handsome craft was launched on Saturday last. The boat is calculated to accommodate from thirty to forty passengers, and is supplied with an excellent awning, which will be used when the weather may render such an agreeable shade from the warmth of the mid-day sun necessary. The present arrangement, we understand, is to ply thrice daily between the boat landings at Keswick, and the Lowdore inn, at the head of the lake.'*

The Cumberland Pacquet gave an update on the 23rd. The vessel was named *The Steamer* and would ply four times daily between Lodore and the Foreshore. There is nothing to suggest this was a new undertaking; the passage boat company had been operational throughout, and the new boat was an addition, not a replacement, as their article started *'Another passage-boat, named The Steamer, now plies regularly...'*

A visitor to the area in 1852 took a *'small pair-oared boat, at the usual boat-landing, at the foot of the lake.'* He noted there were around *'a score or more of boats'* moored there near piers made of either wood or stone. Mr Marshall, the resident of Derwent Island received an annual rent for each boat for hire on the lake, collecting rent of a guinea per boat on the 2nd August each year. It was believed that there were around 40 boats available for hire in 1852.

In 1860 Richard Mitchell re-commenced the ferry to St Herbert's Island, trading between Portinscale and the Keswick Foreshore. The island was a request call after leaving the beach between Fawe Park and Derwent Bank, and passengers were rowed between the landings. After Mitchell's death in 1893 his son carried on the service, in turn handing it to his son. The Mitchell family also hired out rowing boats from Portinscale and

Annie Mellor (1935) on Windermere as a steam launch before her move to Derwentwater in the 1950s.

Right: The Tea Gardens by the Foreshore, with two launches at the piers.

Below: **May Queen** approaching the Foreshore with Cat Bells behind.

Bottom left: The Foreshore with (L-R) **Waterlily**, **Lady Derwentwater** and **Princess Margaret Rose**.

Middle right: The landing stages with **Waterlily**, **Doris** and another launch.

Lower right: **May Queen** as an electric launch.

Bottom right: **Iris** at Lodore, before her modifications.

would row passengers anywhere they wanted to go, for a price. From 1920 the service was upgraded to a motor boat and in the mid-twentieth century Mr Newby of Keswick took over the ferry.

In 1865 Herman Ludolph Prior wrote that; *'In its normal condition, the usual 'excursions' on the lake, as distinguished from its general navigation, are to Portinscale; Lodore; and the lead mines. The landing place for Portinscale is a short distance down the (River) Derwent, just before its junction with the (River) Greta. The approach to it, which it is difficult to hit otherwise, is marked by a pole with a flag flying upon it… There is also a very pretty landing-place for the Catbells, in a little bay just beyond Sir John Woodford's residence… Boats are also kept at the Derwentwater Hotel; Poole's; and elsewhere.'*

The proximity of Keswick to the lake helped to secure the popularity of the 'Queen of the Lakes', and in 1865, Derwentwater became much more accessible as the town found itself on the Cockermouth, Keswick & Penrith Railway linking the main line at Penrith with Cockermouth and Workington. The station at Keswick lay on the north side of the town, some distance from Derwentwater, and the line skirted the western shore of Bassenthwaite as it headed to Cockermouth.

The Ordnance Survey map of 1867 shows 17 jetties along the Foreshore offering pleasure cruisers and rowing boats for hire. Severe competition broke out between boatmen as they undercut prices and touted for customers, and it was not uncommon for them to employ a lad to meet travellers at the station to secure a customer.

In 1880 a branch from the Cockermouth, Keswick and Penrith Railway was proposed from Braithwaite station to Honister Crag Quarries at the head of Borrowdale. The surveyed route crossed the Newlands Valley and climbed steadily along the western shore of Derwentwater to reach the quarries. Widely opposed at the time, it was never realised. The proposed railway would have opened up the upper reaches of the valley but with a detrimental effect on the tranquil nature of the valley.

On 16th March 1898 it was deemed newsworthy to record the arrival of a steam boat on Derwentwater; the Edinburgh Evening News noted;

A STEAMER FOR LAKE DERWENTWATER.
During the coming season a screw-steamer is to ply on Lake Derwentwater, Keswick, having been procured by Mr Ceasari, the manager of the Lodore Hotel. The steamer which will accommodate about 50 passengers, was formerly the property of the earl of Lonsdale, and was used by him on Lake Ullswater.

The West Cumberland Post told how the steamer had been dragged by *'seven fine chestnut dray horses'* from

Lady Derwentwater approaching High Brandlehow.

Ullswater the previous Thursday, and was intended to ply between the Lodore Hotel and the Foreshore.

Hotel adverts after this date major on the availability of a steam launch service. The size of the vessel suggests it could be the *Lorna Doone,* capable of carrying 53 passengers and known to be on the lake in the early 20th century. A 1901 advert confirms the availability of a steam yacht and rowing boats.

Hire boats were also available from Portinscale. Here in the 1890s one of the boatmen was Edward Reed with five boats of his own, and Mr Mitchell was still rowing passengers to Lodore at the advanced age of 84. At the Foreshore, amongst others, were Mr Joseph Sparx and Mr Broatch. Many of the rowing boats they used were built locally, and one builder was John Milburn.

The 27 jetties at the Foreshore marked on a map from 1900 suggest the scale of a business that could support many different operators. Each rented their small patch of land from R. D. Marshall, but in late 1908 he sold the land to the Keswick Urban District Council, and thereafter rent was paid to the council. Old postcards show signs on the end of each jetty displaying the name of the owner and his boat, or guesthouse.

A committee was formed to put an end to the era of intense rivalry and competition with agreement reached on 30th July 1904. Rules were created to govern the hire of rowing boats, banning fishing in certain parts of the lake, and insisting that no sails were installed in boats that weren't designed for them. And if a boat had an 'injury' it had to be attended to as soon as possible, but above all, '*No touting will be allowed*'. The committee also set prices to eliminate undercutting. Rowing boats could also be hired with a boatman; in

1904 the charge for a trip to Lodore was 3s 6d, but the fare could also be negotiated for hire by the hour.

Steam was well established on Derwentwater by the early twentieth century. Early steam launches *Lorna Doone* and *Derwent* – amongst others – were vying for custom on the Foreshore. *Lorna Doone* was a converted 'herring boat' a coal fired steamer latterly owned by Joseph Hodgson (presumably after Mr Ceasari had sold her). She was sold to interests from Whitehaven and beached on the Isthmus prior to handover, but when re-floated she sank as her sea-cocks hadn't been closed. Re-floated with the help of barrels she was hauled ashore by tractor but not all the water had been drained from her hull and part of it fell through. She was deemed irreparable and broken up on the spot, although her windows were salvaged by Mr Hodgson. *Derwent* could carry just 23 passengers and was later fitted with a petrol engine before being broken up for scrap.

Waterlily was a launch built by Shepherds of Bowness in 1903, closely resembling their other products, *Osprey* and *Swallow*, now both at the Windermere Steamboat Museum. Originally a steam vessel, *Waterlily* had a diesel engine later in her career, but may have had a petrol paraffin engine in between.

The Keswick Electric Launch Company ran the electric boats *May Queen* and *Iris* from the Lodore Hotel to Portinscale, where the company also owned the Derwent Hotel. *May Queen* was built in 1904 by Tom Hayton in Bowness on Windermere and later nicknamed 'The Great Thief' as she stole business from other boatmen. *Iris* followed shortly after from the same builder; both were transported to the lake using teams of horses. The vessels were based at the Lodore Hotel

Douglas Hodgson clears Hawes End pier of snow ready for passengers on the winter service whilst Lakeland Mist waits alongside.

and charged up overnight by a turbine installed in the Lodore waterfalls. The charge was stored in banks of accumulator batteries kept under seats in the bow. On the way to Portinscale they called at Brandlehow and the Keswick Landings, where their stone jetty and boathouse still stand at the south end of the Foreshore. They remained part of the lake scene for the next 80 years.

It was reported in August that; *'Two electric launches driven by current obtained from the famous falls of Lodore have been placed on Lake Derwentwater. There being no noise or smell and but little wash, and the boats being small and low, there*

Above: **Lady Derwentwater** heading north from Hawes End.

Left: **Annie Mellor**, **May Queen**, **Princess Margaret Rose**, **Waterlily** and **Lady Derwentwater** sit at the Foreshore in the 1960s.

Lakeland Star and **Princess Margaret Rose** on the Isthmus.

Annie Mellor and **Lakeland Mist** at the Foreshore during the winter timetable.

is little to object to them from an aesthetic point of view, but naturally the boatmen of Keswick do not look on the innovation favourably, more especially as it coincides with a rise of 25 per cent in the boat rents they render to the lord of the manor. Indeed, so sorely do they feel it that they have clubbed together and bought a little steam launch as opposition to the Lodore and Portinscale craft. Fortunately it burns smokeless coal and its crew is not very aggressive, but it is difficult to see in what way its owners' rowing-boats profit by its presence.'

The 'small steam launch' may refer to the *Derwent*. Early petrol paraffin boats also emerged prior to the First World War and by 1910 there were 8 separate operators at the Foreshore; the Lodore and Derwentwater Hotels, the Blacks, the Fishers, the Hodgsons, the Millburns, the Scotts, and Sparks, Smith & Telford. The hotels operated together, advertising as the Keswick Electric Launch Company.

Around the same time, the National Trust – an increasingly large landowner of the Foreshore -became actively involved in resolving the question of whether the public had rights to boat on Derwentwater at all. Arguments raged over whether these rights had been in place since 'time immemorial', with the dispute eventually settled by buying the right for 'all subjects of his Majesty' to navigate the portion of the lake owned by Lord Leconfield.

In 1916, the Derwentwater Launch and Motor Company was formed, operating between Lodore and Portinscale, although this was probably just a renaming of the Keswick Electric Launch Company. Quite when *May Queen* and *Iris* ceased as electric vessels is unclear,

but an advert from the early 1920s for the Lodore Hotel stated that *'Two Electric Launches run to Keswick and Portinscale, landing several times daily.'*

After the First World War there were numerous small electric, steam and petrol paraffin launches operating from the Foreshore. The *Iris*, *May Queen*, *Waterlily*, *Lorna Doone*, *Derwent*, *Water Nymph*, *Dolly*, *Mayflower*, *Swan*, *Ino*, *Trojan* and *Doris* are known but few other names have been recorded, although there were undoubtedly other public pleasure boats on the lake.

In 1924 Keswick Urban District Council, unhappy that the appearance of the Foreshore was cluttered with empty petrol cans and tourists' rubbish warned boatmen regarding their continuing touting. Later in 1927 they threatened to take licenses away from the more notorious boatmen who boisterously touted and used bad language.

In 1928 the Keswick Tea Gardens opened near the piers for the convenience of the tourists. They were run by Anthony Spedding of Penrith who also sold guide books; an extract from one of these noted; *'Boats on Derwentwater 1/- per hr., 5/- per day. Motor boats ply on the lake calling at Lodore, Brandlehow and Portinscale (single journey 1/-, tour of the lake 1/6).'* The Tea Gardens were demolished in 2013 to make way for redevelopment.

Despite the 1904 agreement it appears touting was still widely practiced, as in May 1932 the following appeared in the newspaper;

DERWENTWATER BOATMEN TO SACK TOUTS
No More Pestering Of The Public

The boatmen on Derwentwater have decided this season to employ no tout to attract the custom of visitors. In the past visitors have been much annoyed by these men, who sometimes have gone the length of following people to Friar's Crag in an effort to persuade them to take a trip. Many complaints were made by those who were pestered this way, and the boatmen, who paid out a total of £40 a week to these touts, lost much custom. This year the takings from 60 odd boats and launches are to be pooled. Each boat and launch owner is to take custom in turn instead of fighting through touts for passengers. It is expected under this new arrangement that during a busy week £250 will go into the pool.

The creation of the Keswick On Derwentwater Launch Company Ltd in 1933 formalised the arrangements of the previous year, the main founders being Victor Hodgson and Walter Walker. The first large boats incorporated into the company were the *Waterlily*, *Iris* and *May Queen* as well as the fleet of rowing boats. It is likely that a few smaller launches were used in the early years as well, before being joined by a larger vessel in 1935.

In 1935 the company acquired a new steam launch. A decade previously, Sir George Mellor had commissioned a private day boat from Borwicks for his personal use on Windermere, named *Annie Mellor* (I) after his sister. Regarded as one of the finest boats on the lake, she conveyed the entourage of H.R.H. the

Lakeland Mist. Built as a waterbus, she now sports a wooden deckhouse, with an open stern.

Lady Derwentwater and **Princess Margaret Rose** at Keswick.

Prince of Wales, when in 1927 he sailed from Waterhead to the Royal Windermere Motorboat Club at Bowness in the *Badger*. Arriving at Waterhead the Prince made to board the larger *Annie Mellor* (I) before being directed to the smaller *Badger*! Although the larger and finer of the two boats, *Annie Mellor* (I) was slower, capable of 12 knots compared to the *Badger's* 15 knots. *Annie Mellor* (I) was replaced by a larger steam launch – *Annie Mellor* (II) – in 1935, and sold for use on Derwentwater. The Keswick on Derwentwater Launch Company brought her over Dunmail Raise and through Keswick to the lake before renaming her *Lady Derwentwater*.

The only vessel built specifically for the company was *Princess Margaret Rose*, constructed by Shepherds of Bowness in 1938 and transported to Keswick by traction engine, where her arrival boosted the pre-war fleet to 5. In the same year floods hit the lakes and on the August Bank Holiday the level of Derwentwater rose 6ft 8in in a 24 hour period.

Austerity measures limited Derwentwater services during the war but they resumed in 1946 when the route of today's cruise circuit was created. The boats left the Foreshore operating alternately clockwise – calling at Ashness Gate, Lodore, High Brandlehow and Low Brandlehow before returning to Keswick – or anti-clockwise around the lake. Notably there was no call at Portinscale, as bus services had superseded the ferry, and cruises were for tourists, not locals. By the mid-1950s calls were being made after Low Brandlehow (in a clockwise direction) at a new jetty at Hawes End. The *Annie Mellor* (II) was purchased from Sir George Mellor and retained her name on Derwentwater. She still

operates alongside her older sister *Lady Derwentwater*. Both of Sir George's former boats are twin screw vessels and now incorporate diesel engines

Dates are hard to ascertain regarding the *Iris's* history. At some point after the Second World War, she operated on Windermere for the Ambleside Motor Launch Company. Her cabin was moved from the centre to the stern giving her a more traditional look, but it is unclear whether this was done before or after her transfer to Windermere. After the amalgamation with the Bowness Bay Boating Company in 1968 *Iris* remained in operation with the new company but by the late 1970s she had re-commenced operations on Derwentwater.

The winter of 1963 was one of the hardest in memory and 14 inches of ice covered Derwentwater. Cars were driven onto the lake and four landing stages were destroyed by the power of the ice. A new landing stage was added to the timetable at Nichol End in the 1980s, between Hawes End and Keswick Landings in a clockwise direction and the current total of seven landing stages was reached. By then the ferry operated by Mr Newby between Nichol End and the Foreshore had ceased operations.

Lady Derwentwater underwent a major overhaul in the 1980s. Built originally with four windows and an open stern, her cabin was extended aft and she operated with six windows. From 2010 she had five windows and her canoe stern was replaced with a square transom. *Princess Margaret Rose* has also been modified, changing her aft roof with open sides to a full cabin. *Waterlily* was withdrawn from service in 1988 for a total rebuild, but when the relevant authority was

Annie Mellor. Built in 1935 as a steam vessel, she now has twin diesel engines.

Left: **Princess Margaret Rose** approaching High Brandlehow on the anti-clockwise circuit of Derwentwater.

Below: **Lakeland Mist**'s arrival in 1998. (Carol and Andrew Wray)

approached for the plans, it was discovered they had been sold. She lay at the Isthmus until the mid-1990s but was too far gone to be rebuilt and was burned, as was *May Queen* nearer the end of the decade, after laying up around 1993.

Iris was chartered to Gordon Hall of Coniston Launch in 1994 and after her return continued in service before being laid up in the early 2000s. She still lies under cover on the Isthmus and it is hoped to return her to service after a rebuild.

The next new vessel on the lake was a small waterbus named *Lakeland Mist*, built in 1954 as *Prinses Juliana*, and arriving at Derwentwater on 19th June 1998. Lakeland Mist is a similar vessel to Windermere's Miss Cumbria class. She served her first couple of seasons with a fully enclosed saloon, but was tastefully modified by the removal of her original saloon and the installation of a wooden deckhouse. At first glance she looks just like a traditional launch.

In 2004 the 1978 built *Twin Star II* was purchased from the Thames to accommodate larger groups. The 162 passenger vessel made a coastal trip from London to Workington with a four-man crew, before continuing to the lake by lorry. Renamed *Lakeland Star* she operated her first season in her original blue, red and white livery before being painted black and brown for subsequent years. However her draught proved too deep and she spent time laid up on the Isthmus. She was sold in 2011 to the Dartmouth Steam Railway and Riverboat Company, and renamed *Kingswear Princess*.

Towards the end of the 2000s the three larger wooden launches were stripped back and rebuilt to target another eighty years service, and today the Launch Company operates *Lady Derwentwater*, *Annie Mellor* (II), *Princess Margaret Rose*, and *Lakeland Mist* whilst the *Iris* is laid up. Their service runs daily from Easter to mid-November with boats leaving every half-hour, alternately in each direction. Extra services run at weekends and holidays and a single-boat weekend

winter service is offered, with extras used when demand dictates. Boats are overhauled on the Isthmus on the promontory visible from the Foreshore, where rails with cradles allows for two boats to be pulled up simultaneously; one is pulled into a tent and the other is left outside on its cradle. The rowing boats and self-drive motor boats are also overhauled on the Isthmus. *Lady Derwentwater*, *Annie Mellor* (II), and *Princess Margaret Rose* are all on the National Historic Ships Register, as was the *May Queen*.

A leaflet from the 1960s with the newly added Hawes End pier marked.

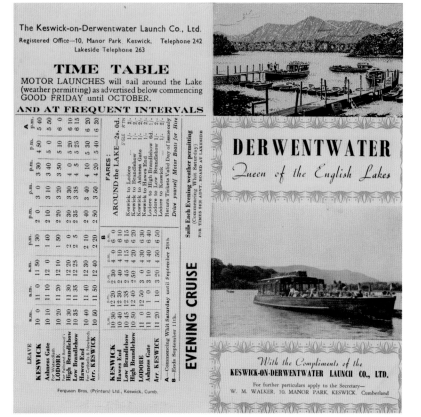

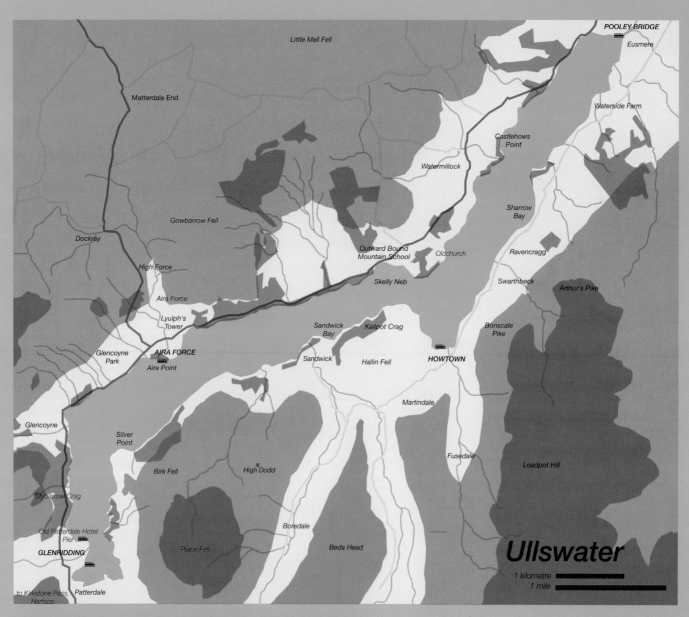

Ullswater

1 kilometre
1 mile

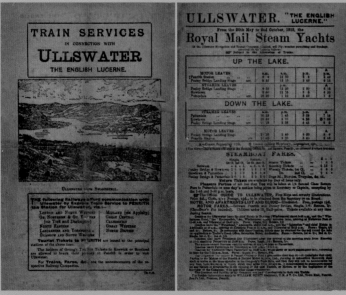

The timetable from 1915 showing 4 sailings along the lake. At busy periods, the boats would run in tandem.

Ullswater

Ullswater (476ft; 'Ulf's water') is the second in size of the English Lakes, measuring 7 ½ M in length and ¼ – ¾ M in breadth. Its greatest depth is 205 ft. The N. bank belongs to Cumberland, the S bank to Westmorland. The scenery of the lake, which some prefer to Derwentwater and Windermere, increases in grandeur as we approach the head. No general view of the lake is obtainable, as its bends divide it into three reaches, each of which from some points seems a complete lake in itself. There is a good road along the whole of the W side of the lake, but on the more precipitous E bank the roads stop at Sandwick. Boats may be hired at the hotels, and there is free fishing in the lake.

The steam yachts which ply on the lake in summer (mid May to end of Sept. ; three or four times daily, except Sun. in either direction; fares 3s,. 2s., return 4s., 3s.,) taking 45-50 min to reach the upper end, start from a small pier, ¼ M from Pooley Bridge
– Baedeker's Great Britain 1937

Ullswater flows from west to east and empties through the River Eamont to the River Eden and the Solway Firth. Some of the Lake District's most productive lead mines lay close to the head of the lake, but water transport did not play a significant role in carrying the ore. Opening up of the lake by steamers made the very remote dales near Howtown accessible, helping Patterdale and Glenridding to become thriving tourist destinations. Ullswater never had a railway connection, the nearest station being Penrith, 6 miles from Pooley Bridge, making it more challenging for tourists to reach. The story of the Ullswater steamers is an interesting one, with recent fleet expansion to a size that would have been unimaginable in 1859. The combined age of Ullswater's present fleet adds up to nearly 450 years, and the two oldest vessels have nearly three centuries of service between them.

Commercial use of the lake in mediaeval times was linked with sporadic workings of lead veins above Glenridding, but the lake was later split into different fisheries and used for the transport of heavy materials by those residing along the shore. Joseph Budworth recorded a fortnight's ramble to the Lakes in 1792, noting that John Mounsey, the 'King of Patterdale' … *was reckoned the best boatman between Patterdale and Dunmallart Head, and he used to convey his own slate and wood, or when other people wanted him, for a trifling sum per load:- he was once deeply laden with the latter, and was drove by a violent gale of wind upon the largest island; in this situation he remained with his assistant two days; the poor fellow, expecting a short passage, had made no provision, his majesty always carried bread and cheese …'*

During the canal revolution William Chapman proposed a branch from the Tyne-Solway canal to Ullswater via Penrith to ease the transport of heavy goods and allow mines at the head of the lake to expand. However the only stretch to come to fruition was between the Solway and Carlisle.

In 1833 John Robinson noted; *'The fish in Ullswater are trout, perch, eels, char, skellies, and a fish which is peculiar to this lake and to that of Buttermere, and is called the grey trout'.* Land owners rented fisheries and adjacent land to local men to fish the lake for a living; these fisheries and associated lands would later pose a problem to the Ullswater Navigation Company in 'The Great Ullswater Case'.

Early visitors were intrepid explorers, often men of wealth who could afford to spend time and money for costly excursions into the heartland of the lakes. In the eighteenth century Clarke's Survey of the Lakes described a popular excursion from Pooley Bridge on-board the Earl of Surrey's barge, an 8-oared vessel mounted with 12 brass swivel guns which were fired where the echo could be heard best – the record was 13 times. Gilpin tells us that The Duke of Portland also had a vessel on the lake, with brass guns for the purpose of *'exciting echoes'* for his guests. Tourism was evidently on the increase and Otley's 1834 edition of 'A Description of the English Lakes' advised that hotels at both Pooley Bridge and Patterdale had boats for hire.

Long before tourists started to arrive there were plans to introduce a steam boat to Ullswater to serve the mining industry. The Helvellyn field had been mined from around 1690, with operations gaining momentum when the Greenside Mining Company exploited the extensive lead deposits from 1822. The Carlisle Journal reported on the 13th August 1836 that; *'The spirited mining company, who are now working the mines in Patterdale, have resolved to put a steam boat on Ullswater Lake, for the purpose of conveying pig lead down to Pooley Bridge, a distance of nine miles, instead of conveying it by the slow operation of carts, a distance of not less than ten miles. The steamer on conveying down the lead, will return laden with the most useful of all articles to a mining establishment, viz. coal. – We think the day cannot be far distant when pleasure boats, for the accommodation of tourists, will be propelled by steam, on all the larger lakes, such as Windermere, which is 13 miles in length, and Ullswater, which is nine miles in length.'*

The paper correctly predicted the arrival of pleasure boats to Ullswater, although the Greenside Mining Company did not introduce a steamer and it was nine years before a regular steam service was inaugurated on Windermere. The idea was raised again in the Carlisle Journal on 2nd February 1843; *'The Greenside mines, in Pattersdale, are at present very rich in ore, the low level having exceeded the expectations of the*

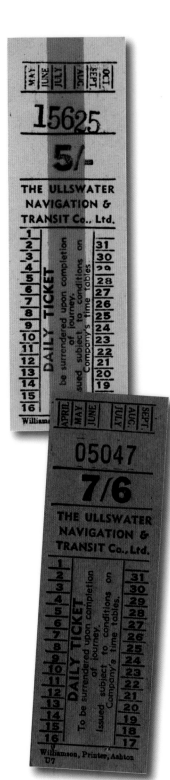

A couple of tickets from The Ullswater Navigation and Transit Company.

Enterprise's first timetable.

shareholders. Should the projected railway between Penrith and Carlisle go forward, the company contemplate running a steamer on Ullswater Lake in order to expediate and economise the carriage of the lead; they having recently purchased pieces of ground at each extremity of the lake for that purpose.'

The proposals had moved forward with the purchase of land at Patterdale and Pooley Bridge. The company had progressed from using carts to carry lead across mountain roads, to utilising barges, in line with contemporary practice on other lakes. Flat bottomed boats with a capacity of 8 tons of lead ore also carried slate from Hartsop Quarry.

In September 1846 a letter to the Kendal Mercury noted that steamers on Windermere were thriving and proposed placing one on Ullswater with a connecting coach service between the two lakes. The writer pointed out that Ullswater was suited to a steam service, with an inn at each end and the new railway just 6 miles away at Penrith. He even proposed to enrol himself as a large shareholder.

There were plenty of boats available for hire on the lake in the 1840s; William Ford mentioned in his 1843 'Description of Scenery in the Lake District' 'In advancing up Ulles Water, we should recommend the south or Westmorland side of the shore to be taken as far as How Town, where a boat should be in readiness to carry you across to Old Church, Watermillock, in as much as the views are incomparably finer, both with regard to the foregrounds and the combinations of the distance.'

There is no mention of safety, but the January 1847 Kendal Mercury reported, 'There are some boats on Ullswater which are a disgrace to the Lake District. We often hear of men who narrowly escape drowning by venturing over the water in these schooners.'

The report tells of a man crossing from Howtown to Newchurch (now known as Oldchurch), whose boat started to fill with water. He rowed back to Howtown 'as if the fate of Europe depended on his exertions' and made it ashore.

Royal visits placed Ullswater firmly on the map. In 1840 the Dowager Queen Adelaide stayed at Patterdale with her sister Ida, the Duchess of Saxe Weimar. Both the King of Saxony and Prince William of Prussia followed on separate visits in 1844 and more Royal visits were to follow. 1857 saw the Prince of Wales attend a church service in Patterdale, whilst the Kaiser came in 1895.

The absence of a steamer service and a direct rail link to Ullswater did not deter trippers and excursions were offered via Penrith by the Lancaster and Carlisle Railway in June 1851. Passengers were carried thence 'by coach from Penrith Station to the Crown Inn, Pooley, and back, 1s. each way', and a tour of the lake was offered 'by boat … to the Head of the Lake and back, allowing sufficient time for viewing all objects of interest, 1s. 6d. each.'

Coaches met the trains on Sundays, Mondays and Tuesdays, and this continued in later years. It is probable that large barge-type vessels propelled by oars with auxiliary sails and an awning over the stern, were

utilised, similar to those used by Gibson and White on Windermere. Personal rowing boats became more common on the lake; some came with a guide, and many tourists must have wished for a scheduled service.

The Pooley Bridge to Glenridding coach road was perilous, with a steep and rocky ascent and descent at Stybarrow Crag, which limited traffic on the road. In July 1855 a minor accident on the coach 'Helvellyn' – running between Patterdale and Penrith – highlighted the case for a lake steamer. They had now been plying successfully for ten years on Windermere, supporting three steamers. Steam would reduce the time taken to travel between the railway and Patterdale, and increase comfort levels, as the coach would only be needed between Penrith and Pooley Bridge.

The Ullswater Steam Navigation Company was formed in 1855 to place a steamer on the lake to serve both the Glenridding mines and intrepid tourists. Adverts were placed in December 1858, 'for a WOOD-PADDLE STEAMBOAT of 20 Horse-power, and Fittings complete, constructed to carry 250 Passengers, and not to draw more than Three Feet of Water, to be Launched upon Lake Ullswater ready for the use of the Company.' By 21st January the specification for the new-build had been amended, as a new advert required 'An IRON PADDLE STEAM BOAT of 18 Horsepower, with Fittings complete, 70 feet length over all, and 14 feet beam, and not to draw more than 2 feet 6 inches of water.'

Liverpool shipbuilders Jones, Quiggin & Co. successfully tendered to build the iron steamer, whilst R. M. Lawrence and Co. provided the engines. As with most lake steamers, they set about constructing the vessel at the lake, while the company went in search of staff. In March they placed an advert signed by company secretary J. W. Brunskill, for; 'A CAPTAIN, ENGINE DRIVER and GENERAL ASSISTANT, to manage a PASSENGER STEAM BOAT (Condensing Engines), upon LAKE ULLSWATER, for the ensuing season; their duties to commence about the middle of June next.'

Launch of the Enterprise

On a very hot Saturday 16th July 1859, the stage was set for the launch near Pooley Bridge, close to where the River Eamont leaves the lake. The Carlisle Journal carried the story; 'Several hundreds of spectators assembled to witness an operation novel to the inhabitants of these dales-the inland navigation of Ullswater having hitherto been restricted to skiffs and oar boats, and a light yacht or two. A party with a band of music were present from Penrith, and boat after boat came down the lake with its load of passengers, until the lower reach assumed almost the appearance of a regatta … The boat, which is of iron, had been constructed at Liverpool, by Messrs. R.M. Lawrence and Co., bought in pieces to Ullswater, and put together on the shore close to the boathouse. The launch took place without the engine, which has not yet arrived, being put in. The boat is otherwise still in a state of incompleteness, but it is calculated that she will be ready for a trial trip by the end of the month-

the 28th instant, having indeed been fixed upon for that event … By some exertion the arrangements for the launch were completed in due time, and she was decorated by a full set of signal pennants, as well as by floral garlands, wreaths and devices. At two o'clock therefore, when the expectations of the spectators had reached their full height, the supports and impediments were removed, and Mrs Slee of Tyrrel was conducted to the platform at the bow to perform the ceremony of baptising the new addition to the Ullswater fleet. The proper signal was then given, the last wedge that kept her on the slips was knocked out, and, as the boat began to move, the fair sponsor dashed the customary bottle of wine against the bow, and named her "THE ENTERPRISE". Thus christened, the boat glided gracefully into the blue waters of the lake, amidst the cheers of the onlookers. The impetus carried her half-way across, and as she righted with her head to the wind and began to drift downwards, she was taken in tow by several boats and brought to the place where she is to be completed.'

The newspaper erroneously credited R. M. Lawrence and Co. as builders. The *Enterprise* was 80 feet long, 14 feet broad and had a draught of 30 inches when fully loaded. After the launch a celebratory meal was held at the Sun Inn to toast the success of the new venture.

A further trial for shareholders took place from Pooley Bridge at 12 noon on Thursday 28th July, with the Yeomanry Cavalry Band on board. *Enterprise* completed a tour of the lake and returned for a *'Grand Public Banquet'* at the Sun Inn at 4 pm. Special trains were laid on from Kendal and Carlisle.

The Carlisle Patriot updated their story after the trial run; *'A commodious vessel with accommodation of*

BOWNASS' ULLSWATER HOTEL. PATTERDALE.

superior character. She sails swiftly and steadily, and although the arrangements for landing passengers and the discipline of the crew are not yet completed, yet, in the course of a lifetime, and with a little experience of two or three more trips, there can be no doubt she will prove another great source of attraction to this beautiful location.'

The Jones, Quiggin & Co. builders' book details her internal fittings. The after cabin was lined with yellow pine, with panels painted to imitate oak *'or any other wood that may be decided upon.'* It had a mahogany table, carpets and a stove in the corner, complete with a copper funnel. The ladies cabin had a water closet and

Enterprise in front of the Ullswater Hotel in the 1860s.

One of only two known photographs of the **Enterprise**. Seen here at Patterdale.

Lady of the Lake as built, with ten windows.

'a neat looking glass'. The fore cabin boasted a teak table, plenty of deck lights and an oilcloth floor. Seats were provided on the upper deck, constructed from yellow pine and made to be let down on hinges. Enterprise had iron rudders at each end steered from wheels at each extremity.

On 6th August *Enterprise* was officially transferred to the directors. Mr Lawrence, contractor for the engines, took charge of the engine room for the trip which commenced at 2 pm from Pooley Bridge, and set out for Patterdale. Arrival at Patterdale was enlivened by the following incident. *'When the vessel reached the pier, the steward, an active fellow, threw the rope to a man to make it fast to the post; but instead of doing this, he took the opportunity of converting himself into a post, and, assuming a definite attitude, he attempted*

Lady of the Lake at Silver Point, with twelve windows.

to stop the vessel and pull it up to the landing place. Whilst the little steward was in the act of remonstrating him on his folly, he was suddenly caught by the ankle and drawn up by the rope, his head being where a minute before his feet were firmly placed. A young man who was standing near the paddle-wheel was for a moment fixed to the spot by the rope passing across his face, which, as he afterwards explained, was anything but a comfortable position.'

Public service commenced the following Monday. *Enterprise*'s first timetable from the 15th August consisted of three round trips daily, except Sundays, leaving Pooley Bridge for Patterdale at 8.30 am, 11.10 am and 4.15 pm, calling at Howtown en route, ending her day at 6.35 pm. Pooley Bridge pier had not yet been completed and embarkation was made by bringing the vessel close to the shore and lowering a gangway.

A first class circuit of the lake cost 3s – in second class it was 2s 3d. Coaches left Pooley Bridge to connect with trains at Penrith, the 11 am steamer arrival connection leaving at 12.30 pm, but for those arriving at 1.30 pm, their connection was at 7 pm! Clearly the coaches took time to adjust their schedules to match the *Enterprise*. In September the *Enterprise*'s times were altered to leave Pooley Bridge at 8.15 am, 11 am and 4 pm, but this was probably for operational reasons and didn't improve coach connections.

Captain Cornett, one of the first masters of the *Enterprise,* retired in the mid-1870s, handing over the vessel to Thomas Metcalfe Thompson, former master of the *Swan* (I) on Windermere. He eventually took command of the *Lady of the Lake* and the *Raven.* Other skippers included Robert Lowe of Silloth and William Garnett (Garnett and Cornett were perhaps the same, inconsistently spelt in local newspapers). These early skippers played a sly trick on tourists; as the steamer passed Kailpot Crag, they would say that to throw a coin into the hole in the rock on the crag was good luck. Coins would pile up, only to be collected later by the crews!

The remote townships of Martindale and Boredale near Howtown benefitted greatly from the new service as Penrith and places further afield became more accessible, making what was formerly an arduous proposition a leisure activity. Patterdale Pier was originally sited outside the Ullswater Hotel, built by Richard Bownass. As well as the daily steamer departures rowing boats were available from the hotel grounds.

Enterprise also carried the post along the lake, the steamers later justifying the title 'Royal Mail Steam Yachts' until they ceased carrying mails around 1910. But the vessels were built with the Patterdale mines in mind and heavier loads of lead could now be moved faster and quicker to Pooley Bridge for onward transportation.

By 1861 *Enterprise*'s timetable had changed again with three round trips connecting properly with the coaches from Penrith station. *Enterprise* left Pooley Bridge at 10.15 am, 3 pm and 6 pm, returning from Patterdale at 12.30 pm, 5 pm and 7 pm. In 1862 the later sailing was dropped, with minor alterations being made to the earlier trips. Coaches connected at the Ullswater Hotel, one for Bowness and Windermere, another for Troutbeck (North) and Keswick.

The Company was summoned to the Westmorland assizes in 1862 over a land claim dispute. The assizes found in favour of the plaintiff, so the Company appealed and the case went to Westminster in November 1862. Lord Chief Justice Cockburn, Mr Justice Wightman, Mr Justice Blackburn and Mr Justice Mellor heard the 'The Great Ullswater Case' concerning issues about ownership of the lake-bed.

The Company had purchased land on the shore from Henry Askew to build a pier and hotel for the convenience of their passengers. The plaintiff, Mr Marshall, owned land adjacent to the steamer pier, and a hotel at Glenridding. He claimed that as owner of the manor of Glenridding he owned the lakebed there, and that the building of a pier 20 to 30 feet out from the shore was an infringement on his lands. He further claimed that steamers disturbed a fishery in the same area and sought to sue the Company for these claims.

The hearing reviewed the history of lakebed ownership with the defendants claiming that it was owned by different manors around the lake. Mr Pickering QC argued in favour of the Company, pointing out that fishery ownership does not include ownership of the soil, and being assumed, does not mean it is given. The Lord Chief Justice stated that lands surrounding the lake were originally all part of the same barony, and if they had not been split up, he may have claim to the ownership of the lakebed. As it had been divided, no party could claim

Top: **Lady of the Lake** at Glenridding in July 1989. (George Woods)

Above: **Lady of the Lake**. (George Woods)

Lady of the Lake with 8 windows, prior to her 2013/14 refurbishment.

ownership. The Lord Chief Justice found in favour of the plaintiff; as owner of the fishery he had sufficient interest in the soil to enable him to maintain an action of trespass, but the public had a right to navigate and travel over the lake in steamers and other boats. The pier became the property of Mr Marshall.

On May 13th 1865 the Ullswater Company was again at the Exchequer Chamber in regard to the *'placing the piles of a pier in Ullswater Lake for the purpose of steamers calling.'* The plaintiff was again Mr Marshall, raising the question of lakebed ownership, and whether the Steam Navigation Company had the relevant permission to build their pier. Again, the courts found in his favour, but reminded Mr Marshall about the right of navigation over Ullswater.

The issue returned to the Courts in November 1871 in regard to trespassing on the jetty at Glenridding, owned by Mr Marshall. His barrister, Mr Manisty QC argued that; *'the public only had the right to navigate Ullswater from one particular terminus to another, and that boats must only land passengers at places where the water was deep enough without using jetties or gangways.'* He claimed the Company was trespassing by continuing to call there and wanted control over the pier to regulate the alleged abuses of sailings taking place on Sundays.

This time the Judges found in favour of the defendants, as Mr Marshall had allowed the jetty to remain, and the steamers had a right to use it. Whilst Mr Marshall had the right to remove the pier, he couldn't close it or interfere with the right of way. Finally the Judges remarked that; *'the public has a right of navigating over Ullswater without any restriction as to the nature and size of vessels, and can use all reasonable means for getting to or from the shore.'*

'The Saturday Review of Politics, Literature, Science and Art' carried a rather rude description of the *Enterprise* in 1866 – in an article which patronised residents and traditions of the area; *'Steamers, yachts, 'gondolas', and a miscellaneous flotilla of row-boats are common to most of the larger lakes, though some of the craft especially on Ulleswater, are decidedly Charon-looking, and do not tempt the cautious tourist.'*

The *Enterprise* was becoming dated by the mid-1870s and the Ullswater Steam Navigation Company sought to replace her with a screw steamer. They looked at second hand tonnage on Windermere and in 1875 purchased the steam launch *Wyvern*, an 1872 product of T.B Seath & Co. But plans to transport her over Kirkstone Pass proved optimistic and the scheme stalled. Winter 1875 was a very hard one, and on 24th February 1876 the *Wyvern* sank in Mitchell Wyke on Windermere. The cost of raising and restoring her proved prohibitive and the steamer was sold to a Barrow contractor.

Shareholders met in Penrith and confirmed an order with Thomas B. Seath and Co of Rutherglen for a steamer to be named *Penrith Castle*. Ullswater residents protested at the proposed name, and by the launch the vessel had become *Lady of the Lake*. Designed by Douglas Hebson, she was constructed of Low Moor puddled iron, and transported by rail in three sections to Penrith whence she was taken to Eusmere by horses and

Opposite: **Lady of the Lake** en route from Howtown to Glenridding, with Dunmallard Hill in the background.

Below: **Lady of the Lake** on the slip at Waterside Farm.

carts. Rebuilt on the newly constructed slip, she was launched on the 26th June by Miss Eliza Williamson of Fernilee, Barton. The vessel *'took to the water in a most handsome manner, and was admired by all present for the faultless symmetrical proportions of her lines, and the graceful ease with which she floated on the water.'*

Weighing in at 43 tons *Lady of the Lake* was 97 feet long, nearly 15 feet wide with a draught of just 2 ½ feet, and capacity for 260 passengers. A twin screw vessel, she was originally fitted with non-compound engines delivering 34 horsepower on an 8 inch bore with a stroke of 9 inches. Built by Rankin and Blackmore, they pushed her along at a respectable 12 knots.

The fate of the *Enterprise* remains uncertain, although speeches at the launch of *Raven* in 1889 referenced her coming to grief; no detail was mentioned, nor can reference be found in local papers. *Lady of the Lake* definitely assisted *Enterprise* in the late 1870s, after her paddle wheels became clogged with hay. One local theory is that *Enterprise* was hauled ashore at Howtown during the First World War and broken up, with some parts recycled as munitions. But images of Howtown Bay in this period don't depict a wrecked vessel. Parts of the steamer survived, as Elizabeth Thompson – daughter of Thomas Metcalfe Thompson – had a table built from *Enterprise*'s timbers and a window made from a porthole.

In 1881 the *'Lady'* sank at her moorings and could not be raised for several weeks due to bad weather. Once the weather abated, her owners gathered a team of divers from Liverpool to assist in raising her.

Trade improved, building throughout the 1880s, but in 1888 another high season breakdown took *Lady of the Lake* out of service for some weeks. One

shareholder –Thomas Cook – persuaded the directors that a new vessel must be commissioned. This would permit a more comprehensive service during the high season, and allow for charters and breakdowns. Cook had been organising tours to the area including lake cruises for many years.

Raven was launched at Eusmere on the 11th July 1889 by 6 year old Winifred Parkin of Kent, a relative of Mr Parkin of Raven Crag, Ullswater, after which she was named. The boat slid down the slip at 3 pm with directors, builders and friends on board. She had been constructed from iron and steel by T. B. Seath & Co at a cost of £2,865. Like *Lady of the Lake*, she was assembled in Rutherglen using pegs instead of rivets, then transported in sections by rail to Penrith, thence to Eusmere by horse and cart, where assembly commenced in April.

She was launched with engines in and steamed to Pooley Bridge under her own power. Once landed she was boarded by many more people *'which completely filled her'*, for a short return trip to Howtown. This trial apparently took 22 minutes prompting the Cumberland and Westmorland Herald to declare; *'It is questionable if there be any boat to beat or even equal this little craft on any lake in the country.'* *Raven* could carry 420 people at a speed of between 12 and 14 miles an hour. She was 112 feet long, 15 feet wide with a draught of 2.9 feet. She had twin steam, non-condensing, engines providing around 100 horsepower.

The obligatory launch meal was followed by speeches, and Mr Seath said the *Raven* was the 270th vessel his yard had built, and expressed his hopes that the railway would reach the shores of Ullswater so they would need a larger steamer! This had been proposed a year earlier

Opposite: Ullswater and Place Fell from near Glenridding.

Below: **Lady of the Lake** after her 2013/14 refurbishment, with 9 windows.

Raven approaching
Patterdale.

by the LNWR, leaving the main line at Yanwath and following the Eamont valley to Pooley Bridge.

On 25th July 1889 *Lady of the Lake* and *Raven* raced from Sandwich Bay to Patterdale; the *Lady of the Lake* arrived first, much to the disdain of the crew of the newer boat.

Douglas Hebson, contemporary designer of Windermere steamers, who lived on the shores of Ullswater, designed the *Raven*. A highly regarded ship designer, his work could be seen on Ullswater, Coniston and Windermere, and elsewhere. Born in Penrith in 1818, he studied engineering and ship design at Fawcett, Preston & Co on Lydia Ann Street, Liverpool and went on to design many Mersey-built ships. He helped fund several churches around Liverpool before retiring in 1889 to Swarthbeck Cottage near Ullswater. He continued to help build churches, including Martindale, and died in February 1906 aged 87; three vessels of his design perpetuate his legacy in the Lake District today.

Soon after the *Raven's* launch the company slip moved from Eusmere to Waterside Farm where more

Raven approaching Pooley
Bridge. (Reproduced by
courtesy of the Museum of
Lakeland Life and Industry,
Kendal, Cumbria)

space enabled both vessels to occupy adjacent shore slipways simultaneously.

Both *Lady of the Lake* and *Raven* were built as two class vessels. Their first class forward saloons were fitted with carpets and cushioned seats, whereas the second class lounges had wooden seats. Each originally had a raised steering position, with Raven's aft of the funnel and '*Lady's*' forward. By the 1920s the wheelhouses were fully enclosed for the comfort of the crew, and replaced the waist-high 'dodgers' which offered little protection from the elements.

Kaiser Wilhelm II, Emperor of Germany, visited Lowther Castle as the guest of the Earl of Lonsdale on Wednesday 15th August 1895. His first planned visit to Ullswater was postponed due to heavy rain, but he took a train to Penrith and cruised along Ullswater on the *Raven*. The piers were adorned with crimson bunting and a '*really artistic arch was erected. It was in the castellated style. Purple heather formed the outer border, contrasted with a wreath of evergreens, the whole being surmounted with the inscription "Welcome to Ullswater"'*. Major Parkin and Mr Winn, directors of the Ullswater Company, greeted the Kaiser. He sat forward on the Raven, contemplating the view to Patterdale in silence, before travelling over Kirkstone Pass to Bowness for a sail on board the steam launch *Maru*.

The Kaiser returned in 1902 and 1912, both times enjoying a cruise along the lake. For the 1912 visit *Raven* had a yellow line painted around her after deck to mark the occasion. The Earl of Lonsdale was known as the 'Yellow Earl' after his sandy hair and love of the colour; his carriages and cars were painted yellow, and as a founder of the Automobile Association, he ensured they adopted the distinctive livery that they retain today. He

remained friends with the Kaiser during the War, refusing to remove a bust of the German from his hallway.

For the summer 1901 season a one-boat service offered 4 daily return sailings from Pooley Bridge. These offered a tight coach connection to and from Penrith, allowing just 5 minutes at the foot of the lake. Most full length sailings took 45 minutes, with the coach adding an extra hour to the journey. At the turn of the century the company produced guidebooks, which are now much sought after. Both hardback (with red covers) and softback (with black covers) editions were produced, and they proved very popular. They gave a commentary and history of what could be seen around the lake, information on the steamers and contained many adverts. The 1903 edition noted:

The steam yachts 'Raven' and 'Lady of the Lake' are both twin screw boats. The 'Raven' was built in 1889 by Messers. T. B. Seath & Co., or Rutherglen, Glasgow, and the same firm in 1877 also built her sister ship, the 'Lady of the Lake.' Both vessels are handsomely furnished with every convenience, and care is taken to ensure the comfort of the passengers. The carrying capacity of the 'Raven' is 420, and the 'Lady of the Lake' 366, as certified by the Board of Trade.

A full lake return cost 2s in first class, and 1s 6d in second class.

In January 1904 the shareholders increased the powers of the company, changing the name to the Ullswater Navigation and Transit Company Limited. By 1907 the new company was looking to obtain a third vessel, named *Osprey*, but chose instead to re-boiler *Lady of the Lake.*

Coke or coal for the steamers was delivered by rail from the northeast to Penrith and carried to Pooley

Bridge by Mr Lancaster in his horse and cart. Coke blocks were broken up each morning by the steamer crews, and taken to the pier using a four-wheeled hopper before being thrown down a chute to bunkers on the lower decks. The laborious daily exercise of washing down had to be completed before passengers could board. The invention of the internal combustion engine must have proved a blessing for the crews.

The pier at Patterdale was moved west to the present site at Glenridding in the 1920s, and calls at the hotel pier ceased. The new site had been home to a boathouse owned by the combative Mr Marshall of Patterdale Hall, with Mr Robinson's rowing boats

A bow shot of **Raven** at Patterdale.

Raven approaching Howtown in 2014.

Below: **Raven** seen from above Kailpot Crag. She has just left Howtown Bay for Glenridding.

available for hire from the adjacent beach. The new pier became the 'home' of the boats from the mid-1940s with the steamers berthing overnight at the head of the lake rather than at Pooley Bridge.

New motorbuses began to reduce the travelling time between Pooley Bridge and Penrith, and longer day trips could be offered. During busy periods it was commonplace to catch the steamer one way along the lake and return by motorbus. 1929 saw the introduction of Ribble bus services over Kirkstone Pass to connect with the Windermere steamers.

Pooley Bridge pier was washed away during a terrible storm in November 1931 and rebuilt in time for the 1932 season – not the last time the pier would be severely damaged by storms.

In the winter of 1932/33 *Raven* had a new foredeck fitted, then both vessels were converted to motor ships. *Lady of the Lake* was first in 1934 receiving a Crossley two-stroke oil engine. *Raven* followed in 1935 with a four-cylinder oil engine from the National Gas and Oil Engine Company Limited. These were similar to contemporary bus engines and the conversions saw their old funnels replaced with squat motor funnels, creating

controversy amongst aficionados at the time. The wheelhouses were moved just ahead of the new funnels.

Lady of the Lake hit the limelight in July 1935, rescuing three army officers who had capsized their sailing dinghy in rough weather. Both vessels were in use that day and were making their final journey in tandem to Pooley Bridge from Patterdale. Captain Baird of *Raven* failed to notice the distressed dinghy, but Captain Jackson of the '*Lady*' thankfully did; '*He hove to, and got almost alongside the overturned dinghy. Three buoys were thrown to the officers, but they failed to reach them, and drifted away. The men were then near Swarthfield, nearly a mile from where their boat overturned. Captain Jackson and his staff then threw ropes, and after considerable difficulty due to the rough state of the water, the officers were hauled on board…*'. Two of the officers clambered aboard, but the third was rescued using one of the ship's lifeboats.

The 1937 season ran from 1st May until 30th September with the single boat service still based at Pooley Bridge. Four return sailings along the length of the lake were provided, between 10 am and 6.40 pm, with a limited Sunday service. A full lake return cost 2s.

During the Second World War *Lady of the Lake* was laid up on the slipway, while *Raven* operated a limited service, sometimes carrying soldiers to Glenridding for training at the Ullswater Hotel. Servicemen practiced using mini-submarines on the lake during the War.

Raven was slipped next to the '*Lady*' in late 1946, as both slipways were still serviceable. *Lady of the Lake* re-entered service in summer 1947, but ice had moved *Raven*'s slipway below the waterline and she could not accompany the '*Lady*' until repairs had been carried out, so she operated alone. *Raven* was not launched again until May 1955, after having new hull plates fitted and internal floors re-laid.

Liveries and windows

The Ullswater fleet had no standard livery until the mid-1930s. The boats were initially painted brown, and then cream as successive managers altered their colour scheme. During the late 1940s the fleet gained the standard colours of green hull, white superstructure and red funnel, copied from the Cunard White Star Line (of *Titanic* fame) steamer *Caronia*, which had been launched in 1948 and served until 1974.

For a period in the 1960s the boats sported a grey hull, and a red and black funnel, with a white awning over the stern. This did not last long and the fleet reverted to the *Caronia* livery. A surviving part of the earliest livery is the stag's head emblem, which is easily visible today on the ships funnels.

Both *Lady of the Lake* and *Raven* were similar in their original condition but distinguishable by their window arrangements. *Lady of the Lake* had ten windows, extended to twelve when she received a wheelhouse just forward of the funnel. By 1934, she had eight windows, probably after her new engines were installed. She now has nine after her 2013/14 refit. *Raven* retained eleven windows until 1935, when she received an additional window during the motor ship conversion.

More trouble

1950 saw *Lady of the Lake* sink again. On Saturday 16th September Captain Band took the last trip for Pooley Bridge. The lake had a slight swell due to a stiff breeze and it proved difficult to tie up at the pier, so she was left stern-to the wind, instead of the more protected bow. It was thought she was taking in water as the crew left for the night, and Captain Band undertook to check the boat later. He returned at 11.30 pm, with some help and pumped the '*Lady*' out before returning home. The weather worsened throughout the night and by morning the *Lady of the Lake* had sunk in six feet of water. The paper reported; '*In a 90 m.p.h. gale the Lady of the Lake, a 98ft. long pleasure steamer on Ullswater Lake, sank at her moorings at Pooley Bridge, Westmorland, early yesterday.*'

She remained on the bottom for nearly eight weeks before she was salvaged. Raising her was a tricky operation involving engineers G and J Thomson and local joiner Tom Craig, as well as company staff.

It took over two weeks to seal the boat using clay and steel plates and fire hoses brought from Workington, Penrith and Brampton to help her float, despite concerns over whether the decks could handle the strain. Hard work by the crews ensured the engines were running in two weeks, but it was the 1951 season before she sailed again.

Hard times hit in the early 1950s and there was talk of suspending lake services, until Sir Wavell Wakefield (later Lord Wakefield of Kendal) purchased a majority share in the company in 1953. He later purchased the Ravenglass and Eskdale Railway. Lord Wakefield was also a Director of the Preston company who built the jet powered Bluebird K7 for Donald Campbell's speed record attempts. He provided a temporary boat-house and launching facilities at Glenridding, where the original slipway stands adjacent to the Pier House. Campbell broke the world speed record on Ullswater on 23rd July 1955 with measured mile runs of 215.08 mph and 189.57 mph setting a new world record of an average 202.32 mph.

Meanwhile on Windermere the *Cygnet* of 1879 had been withdrawn and was awaiting sale. In 1955 she was purchased by Lord Wakefield, gained a new funnel

Lady Wakefield (left) heads for Pooley Bridge, as **Raven** nears the pier at Howtown.

Right: **Lady Dorothy**. Small and sturdy, she offers all weather sailings and is ideal for the winter service.

Below: **Lady Wakefield** underneath Hallin Fell.

and was painted in the Ullswater colours. However she never left Windermere, as plans to transport her by road through Kendal and Shap to Pooley Bridge proved abortive, and was converted into a houseboat.

A popular excursion by steamer was to be dropped off at Howtown and walk to Glenridding. In the 1950s ponies were carried on board the boats to be dropped off at Howtown – the first livestock to be carried since the turn of the twentieth century. Bicycles have since been substituted for ponies, and nowadays the only livestock regularly carried on board is of the canine variety.

A local tale recalls huntsman Joe Bowman arriving at Howtown pier with his hounds to catch the steamer back to Glenridding. On hearing he would have to pay 6d per dog, he paid for himself and sent his dogs running along the shoreline to the head of the lake. Continuously blowing his horn to encourage them, they kept up with the boat all the way back – one hopes there is a hint of truth to the story!

During the early 1960s a two-ship service was operated during the high season, one from each end of the lake, reducing to a single vessel during the shoulder seasons. The ships had been operating at an annual deficit of around £1,000 since the late 1950s, which had been recovered from the director's reserves. The company planned a pier near Lyulph's Tower at Aira Force to boost revenue. The Lake District Planning Board refused permission, but with the help of two MPs, the outcome was overturned and a temporary floating pier was built in 1964. The new pier allowed visitors to access the waterfall, just a short walk from the berth.

For the 1964 season the Sunday service operated during the high season and omitted the call at Aira Force. Access problems forced removal of the pier before the 1965 season, despite the success of the previous year when over 56,000 passengers were carried between May and September.

The 1930s engines were now in need of replacement, so in 1964 Raven received a pair of Thornycroft engines at a cost of about £5,000, each providing 150 horsepower and allowing her to cruise comfortably at 11 knots using relatively little fuel; on a two hour round trip she used just five gallons of diesel. At the same time her wheelhouse was moved to the bow of the vessel.

Lady of the Lake was due to receive her new engines in 1965, but disaster struck before they could be installed. Whilst on the Waterside slip, one of the nearby sheds caught fire when a gas cylinder exploded, and the 'Lady' was close enough to be considerably damaged. Initially it was thought she could be repaired for Easter 1966, but her condition proved far worse and she remained out of service until 1979, leaving Raven to operate alone. Raven offered three daily return cruises from Glenridding at Easter, then from June to October. She was slipped next to Lady of the Lake for her own overhauls. The hull of the damaged 'Lady' was surveyed in 1977 and a £70,000 rebuild commissioned. Lifted by two cranes from where she had lain for over a decade, she was placed on the slip at Waterside Farm.

Lady of the Lake finally got her new Kelvin engines

in 1978. She was re-launched on 31st October, but after floating in her cradle became stuck when reversing into the lake. It transpired that one of the 'Lady's' engines was going ahead instead of astern as it had been connected the wrong way and she remained motionless on the cradle. Raven towed the refurbished vessel into open water and the problem was quickly rectified. Her official re-launch ceremony took place on 19th May 1979 by the Deputy Prime Minister, MP William Whitelaw and she soon entered service alongside Raven.

The 1979 timetable showed Raven still operating three cruises from Glenridding, with Lady of the Lake available for charter. Usually Raven would operate during peak season with the 'Lady' covering the shoulder season. In the height of the summer, Lady of the Lake offered unscheduled extra sailings, usually of an hour's duration from Glenridding. This continued throughout the 1980s, and in 1989 the Raven celebrated her centenary year, by having much of her hull re-plated. The 'Lady' was now in operation too, offering five cruises from Glenridding to Howtown and back. Confusingly both vessels departed Glenridding at

Birkhouse Moor seen behind the Ullswater Hotel as Glenridding is approached.

Western Belle nears Pooley Bridge on an autumn day.

4.30 pm, one for Howtown and back and one for Howtown, Pooley Bridge and back.

A 10 mph speed limit was introduced in July 1983, dramatically reducing the number of private speedboats on the lake. Many moved over to Windermere, where speeding was allowed until 2005, and the water-ski jump had to be removed from Howtown Bay making the pier approach safer.

The timetable remained similar until 2001 with both boats based at Glenridding, operating full and half-lake cruises. The 2001 timetable offered an earlier full lake sailing from Glenridding at 9 am to cater for walkers. Glenridding Pier was renovated to house a tearoom and shop overlooking the arriving and departing vessels.

2001 also saw the first addition to the Ullswater fleet in over 110 years.

Lady Dorothy was built in 1967 for Herm Seaways (part of the Trident Charter Company). After purchase in March 2001 she sailed from St Peter Port to Poole, where she was loaded onto a lorry. Her arrival was followed by restoration by local boat builder Frank Howard, before an official re-launch on 5th November. Her arrival allowed sailings to be introduced during winter 2001-02, with two sailings daily between Glenridding and Howtown. She left the head of the lake at 10.30 am and 1.30 pm returning an hour and a half later. For this first winter Pooley Bridge was not served, except by prior arrangement for private groups.

The following winter sailings were extended to Pooley Bridge, offering two full lake sailings leaving Glenridding at 9 am and 1.30 pm, as well as a shorter return trip to Howtown at midday.

Western Belle at Calstock on the River Tamar during her early career.

Designed for the sea, *Lady Dorothy* does not have the fine lines of the older vessels, but handles weather well. Still the mainstay of the winter weekday service, *Lady Dorothy* can be seen at a floating mooring in St Patrick's Bay when not in use.

The three-vessel fleet enabled radical change to the 2003 summer timetable. *Raven* operated her traditional three round trips from Glenridding, *Lady of the Lake* made one circuit to Pooley Bridge then four trips to Howtown, while *Lady Dorothy* made one return trip to Glenridding from Pooley Bridge, before making six return trips between Pooley Bridge and Howtown. During the shoulder season before the winter timetable commenced, *Lady Dorothy* received her overhaul while *Raven* and the '*Lady*' ran a two-boat service.

A further vessel was added in 2005 when *Lady Wakefield* brought the fleet up to four.

She sailed from Plymouth to Whitehaven for lorry-transfer, and was craned into the lake in early May to begin a two year restoration. Her Gardner engines were refurbished in 2006 and she entered service in April 2007 to be officially renamed by HRH Princess Alexandra. She displaced *Lady Dorothy* in the timetable, so a three-boat service was still offered. The two original vessels were re-engined for a third time in the mid-2000s, *Raven* receiving a pair of Cummins engines in 2004, with *Lady of the Lake* following in 2005.

Slight changes to the 2008 timetable still saw full lake services and short cruises offered from each end, but from 2009 services changed to their present form.

Ullswater was hit by extensive flooding in late 2009. The pier at Glenridding survived intact with *Raven*, *Lady Wakefield*, and *Lady Dorothy* tied alongside and *Lady of the Lake* weathering the storm on the slipway at Waterside Farm. Luckily no boats were berthed at Pooley Bridge as it was wrecked, and anything tied to it would have been damaged as well. The pier was unusable and emergency repairs were undertaken in December to allow a winter timetable to operate. By the following year, and with a new vessel on the cards, permission was being sought to build a new improved pier.

Work began in September 2010, with vessels operating to an amended timetable between Glenridding and Howtown. There were plans to undertake the work during the winter, but the annual salmon migration forced work to be brought forward to reduce the environmental impact.

Continuing their tradition of restoring classic pleasure boats, instead of building new ones, the Ullswater Navigation and Transit Company launched *Western Belle* in 2010. A 1935 Great Yarmouth build, she was taken to McTay's, Bromborough yard for a total refurbishment. On 12th July 2010 she arrived at Ullswater from the Wirral by lorry, being craned into the lake from the A592 between Glenridding and Aira Force. She was towed to the Waterside farm slip by *Lady Dorothy* to have final modifications made and engines fitted. Entering service late in 2010, she was officially launched on 30th June 2011 by Jane Hasell McCosh, owner of Dalemain House near Pooley Bridge.

Western Belle displaced *Lady Wakefield* on the three

boat roster, accompanying *Lady of the Lake* and *Raven*. One vessel, usually *Western Belle*, is now based at Pooley Bridge with two at Glenridding, each operating three full-lake cruises. A two-boat service operates during the shoulder seasons and as required, with the two spare vessels *Lady Wakefield* and *Lady Dorothy* covering the timetable during overhaul periods, charters and breakdowns. A one-boat winter timetable is offered with *Lady Dorothy* providing the weekday service, and a larger vessel covering the busier weekend sailings.

A new development for 2013 was a proposal to build a new pier at Aira Force, where the boats had called for a short while in 1964. This pier is a joint venture between Ullswater 'Steamers' and the National Trust, and is to be built on the National Trust land at Aira Green near the junction of the A592 and the A5091. The pier will allow access to the famous waterfalls and Lyulphs Tower. The structure will be 46 metres long and built from timber. Services will commence on the 23rd May 2015 with seven direct sailings from Glenridding daily at peak periods. Initially it will be served at the main periods only, but it is hoped to receive a regular service eventually. It will not be a call on the round the lake services, but will instead be served by *Lady Dorothy* or *Lady Wakefield* on a direct service from Glenridding, returning to Glenridding.

Over the winter of 2013-14 *Lady of the Lake* had a major overhaul and refit. Her main deck was extended forward, resulting in an enlargement of the passenger saloon downstairs with an extra window being added. The toilet facilities were moved too, into space previously used as part of the engine room, which was made smaller by the creation of a new bulkhead. Previously the saloon could accommodate 15 people, now 50 can be seated comfortably. The wheelhouse and funnel were moved 4 feet aft creating a large open deck space in front of the helm position. The bow area was inevitably made slightly shorter, but it is a small price to pay for the vast improvements made to the near 140 year old vessel. In total she spent over 7 months out of service and was welcomed back into passenger sailings on the 24th May 2014 with a passenger capacity for 200. The latest construction work undertaken by the company was the raising of Howtown pier by 2 feet in early 2015 to enable landings even when the lake is at high levels.

With five boats at their disposal the Ullswater Navigation and Transit Company now operate 363 days of the year using their fleet of historic vessels. From near closure in the 1950s a thriving service has been established. As well as the standard timetable, special events are advertised, many of which are repeated year on year. Events include the 'Marmalade Madness' day, various RSPB cruises, photography workshops, cruises with commentary given by a park ranger, excursions to see the red deer rut in October, Cumbrian Fish Supper evening trips, a charter to view the Birkett Cup yacht race, and Yuletide afternoon tea cruises. More special days are aimed at children. Santa specials depart each December; a pirate themed trip operates a couple of times a year, and in October a 'Ghostly Galleon' sails on Halloween.

The boats are overhauled on the slip at Waterside Farm, a short walk along the lake shore from Pooley Bridge. The boats pulled out on the slip are available to view at close quarters as a public footpath passes within metres of the bow of the boat on the cradle! The whole fleet, with the exception of *Lady Dorothy* is on the National Historic Ships Register, making Ullswater the home of one of the largest heritage fleets in the UK.

Western Belle on the slip at Waterside Farm, taken from the public footpath.

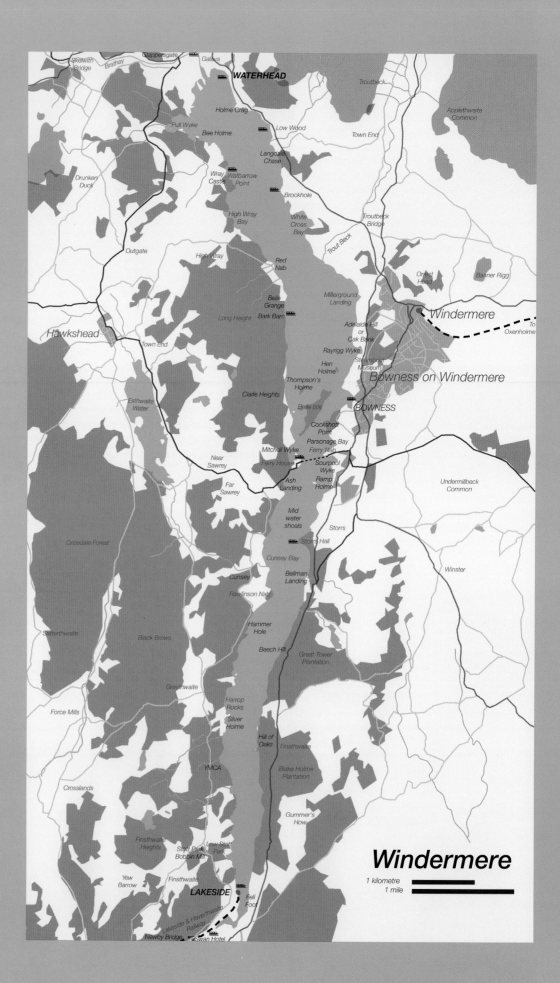

58885

AMBLESIDE
TO BOWNESS
Issued subject to weather
DAY RETURN

DAY	MONTH	YEAR

BOWNESS TO
AMBLESIDE
BOWNESS BAY
BOATING CO., LTD.

58885

AUTOMATICKET LTD.

A Bowness Bay Boating
Company ticket for the trip
from Ambleside to Bowness.

Windermere

1 kilometre

1 mile

Windermere

Windermere, or Winandermere (the 'winding lake', or, perhaps, Windar's lake'), is the largest lake in England, being 10 ½ m. in length and 1/3 – 1 m. broad. It lies 134 ft above the sea level, and its greatest depth is 240 ft. Its banks are beautifully wooded and enlivened with numerous villas. The N. end of Windermere is enclosed by an amphitheatre of lofty mountains. At the S, end of the lake, 6 M. from Bowness (reached by crossing the Ferry, ¾ M. below Bowness, and following the shady road on the W. bank), lies Lakeside (Lakeside Hotel; Railway Refreshment Rooms), the terminus of the railway from Carnforth.

– Baedeker's Guide 1890

Windermere's north-south alignment has long formed a natural highway, and has been instrumental in helping industry and tourism flourish. Ferry services date back to at least the fifteenth century, but the arrival of the railway provided the catalyst to the development of steamer services. Windermere is the busiest of the lakes with the largest pleasure fleet and over 6,500 registered boats, 1,000 moorings and 600 jetties, slipways and boathouses around its shores. To many visitors it is the first lake they come across, with some never getting further than Bowness. Over the years many different companies have operated on the lake but they now come under the aegis of Windermere Lake Cruises, apart from the vehicle ferry crossing at the narrowest part of Windermere. A comprehensive timetable of services is offered 364 days a year, with a fleet of historic 'steamers' and launches running alongside more modern waterbuses.

Early use of the lake as a highway

Man first visited the Windermere area as early as 8,000 B.C. when nomadic people came to the heavily wooded area in search of valuable flint. Later Neolithic settlers established communities in clearings hewn from the forest, quarrying stone and sending rough lumps to the coast to be finished and polished into axe heads. The lake was a natural export route with dugout canoes possibly carrying the stone from Waterhead to Newby Bridge for shipment down the River Leven and across Morecambe Bay. Demand grew, and axes from Great Langdale have been found in Furness, Morecambe, the Isle of Man, and in southern England. These pioneer settlers also used the lake for fishing and getting from one shore side community to another.

In the last decade of the 1st Century A. D. a Roman expedition established a fort at Galava near Waterhead and used the lake for transporting goods, especially grain. Materials were probably taken by road from Dalton in Furness to Conishead, up the River Leven to the tidal limit, thence by packhorses to Windermere and barge to the head of the lake. This first wooden fort was replaced by a larger stone fort by 125 AD and the Romans dredged a channel up the River Rothay to a quay next to the fort, where stone piers accommodated a handful of vessels, but they remained primarily reliant on the road network, and Galava was finally abandoned in the fourth century. The locals reverted back to their old ways, sustainably fishing the lake and farming the pastures.

Six hundred years later a peaceful influx of new blood, with a similar language and shared religion, arrived from Scandinavia via Ireland to lay claim to the area. Locally constructed boats allowed these Norsemen to fish and trade around the lake; present place names reflect their influence, especially in the use of 'Holme' – Old Norse for island. The lake also gained its name at this period.

Fishing rights

After the Norman Conquest, ferrying rights on Windermere were directly linked with fishing rights on the lake. Fishing is the most obvious industry associated with the lake, dating to the time the shores were first settled. The lake has a wide variety of fish, especially the char, a relative of the arctic variety, trapped in the lake after the last ice age. Others include perch, pike, trout, eel, and salmon at different times of year. The first references to fishing date to around 1157 – 1163 when Henry II accepted an agreement between the monks of the Furness Abbey and William Fitz Gilbert, defining the boundaries of lands surrounding the lake. In 1223, the Abbot of Furness Abbey summoned Baron William de Lancaster III to Westminster, accusing him of seizing his fishery of Windermere. In court the Abbot

An engraving of Newby Bridge showing a steamer about to enter the River Leven at Lakeside.

NEWBY BRIDGE

pleaded that William had forcibly seized their fishery on the lake and destroyed their boats. William stated that the Abbot had not been granted any claim to the fishery, so when the Abbot sent his boats they had been impounded. The outcome was in favour of William, and Windermere was deemed the boundary of the Abbots lands, not part of them.

Feelings improved, and in 1240 William de Lancaster III granted the Abbot the rights to have *'two small boats, one in Winendremer, and another in Thurstinewater* (the original name of Coniston Water)*, for carrying their wood and building material and other things which may be necessary'*. De Lancaster also allowed *'two smaller boats, one namely in Winendremer, with twenty nets for fishing constantly without interference from myself or my heirs'*. But William did not fully trust the monks, noting *'if any servants of the said monks, who shall have been navigating their boats in the said waters, shall have given offence in my forest, he shall be sufficiently punished. If, indeed, any of them shall refuse to submit to a fair trial, he shall be discharged from the service of the monks, and shall forfeit his wages'*.

It is unclear whether the Abbot took advantage of his Windermere fisheries, as records list fisheries at Blelham Tarn, Haverthwaite, Finsthwaite and Esthwaite, of which the River Leven at Haverthwaite was the most valuable. Whilst the Monks of Furness Abbey owned the rights to fish the lake the actual fisheries were included in the Barony of Kendal. In 1246 this barony was split, half becoming the Richmond Fee, the rest split between the Marquis and Lumley Fees. Windermere lay in the Richmond

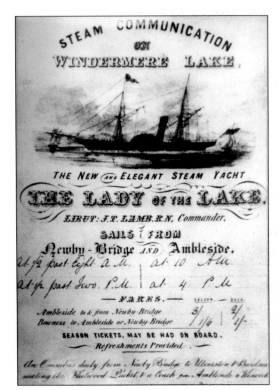

Fee, except Rogerholme (now Ramp Holme) and its fishery – a part of the Lumley Fee. The Richmond Fee passed to Walter de Lindsay who built a home on Wynandremere Holme (now Belle Isle). The De Lindsays held the Richmond Fee until the 15th Century but suffered from a lack of heirs. The Fee, including the fishing rights, reverted to the crown and in 1513 was granted to Sir Thomas Parr, father of Catherine Parr, who leased it to residents along the lake shore.

Although owned by the Lord of the Manor, the rights were split between landowners or farmers*,* who paid an annual rent. Before 1570 the lake was separated into three Cubbles. The Upper Cubble stretched from Rothay Bridge to Ecclerigg Crag, the Middle Cubble from here to Ash Landing, and the Lower Cubble – by far the largest – from Ash Landing to Newby Bridge. Each Cubble owner had rights to boating, fishing and ferrying in that area, but landowners with shore frontage had no claim to fishing. Twelve fisheries made up the lake; one in the Upper, five in the Middle, and six in the Lower Cubble. The Cubble owners paid annual rent of £6 to the lakebed owner which also gave the right to ferry. The proprietors sold licenses to ferry to make up their fee; only residents of Belle Isle were exempt from paying.

Boats sold locally usually came parcelled with rights to fish or ferry in one of the Cubbles, often being handed across the generations. In 1693 Roger Parke sold, *'a moiety or half fishing in the highest and middle cubbles'* to the highest bidder, John Philipson of Rayrigg. These rights were frequently flouted and a few became repeat offenders, ferrying people around the lake through all the Cubbles. One man referred to as J.B., plagued the Lower Cubble without paying ferrying or fishing rents; he *'built a new boat and ferrys at pleasure not only within that cobble but thro' other two cobbles and often times takes and kills fish, sinks timber in the draughts of the fishers whereby the fishers are hindered to draw with their nets to their great prejudice and often rows his boat thro the nets of the fishers when set out in common draughts and disappoints 'em of catching fish. The Impunity of J.B. has encouraged several other People to erect boats to carry and fish on the said Water without ay Lycence contrary to Usage or Right and thereby do great Damage to the said Fishers and Fishery and Ferrying'*.

By the 19th Century the fisheries were in the hands of local gentry who sub-let the fishing or employed men to fish. The Lowther family held the Manor of Windermere, and received rents until 1939, although commercial fishing of the lake ceased in 1921, when the fisheries were bought by the Board of Conservators (set up to restore fish stocks), who refused to lease rights to fishermen. In 1939 Henry Leigh Groves donated £9,000 to Windermere Urban Council to support purchase of the lakebed from the Earl of Lonsdale and today it remains in the hands of the local authority. Fishing resumed in 1941 during rationing – when Perchines (tinned perch in a tomato sauce) were sent as far as London – and continued until 1947. Today leisure fishing requires a rod permit.

Ferry services

Over time a number of ferries crossed the lake in an east-west direction. Furthest north was Millers Crossing linking Millerground with a point just south of Belle Grange and connecting bridleways between Kendal and Hawkshead, joined in the east with the bridleway to Keswick. The service was irregular, as the inhabitants of Applethwaite and Millerground rowed prospective passengers across in fishing boats on demand.

Tradition holds that monks from Kendal and Windermere used this route to Hawkshead, and perhaps Furness Abbey. It was ancient and operational at the same time as a ferry further south at Nab End; known as 'Gurt Boat' (Nab) and 'La'l Boat' (Millers) – Great Boat and Little Boat – to distinguish the two. This crossing was still in use by the 15th Century but may have been less regular than the Nab crossing, as there are few mentions in early literature; however local tradition recalls a ferry here.

Millerground was the usual landing place for Applethwaite, and the route across the widest part of the lake is the shortest to Hawkshead. The Wynlass Beck bridge near Millerground shows the track's antiquity; on the opposite shore the cobbled pony track known as the Bogey Road from Belle Grange to Hawkshead shows signs of engineering, indicating its historical importance. Bark Barn is situated on the western shore, so it is probable that bark, charcoal and other goods were brought across by ferry to be taken into Westmorland by pack-horses. It was likely used by the corn mill at Millerground for moving products to and from the mill with ease. The landing site on the west shore is not known; a man-made promontory 300 yards south of Belle Grange could have provided a sheltered berth in both northerly and southerly winds. Near Bark Barn and Bass Rock were the remains of an old landing stage – until recently a few stakes could be seen driven into the shore.

The ferry seems to have ceased by 1535 when the miller, John Dicson (Dixon) had to allow 'one able and leaffull hie waie wynter and somer for hors and man through the Oake banke and so down to the under Syde off the Scottyshe bushe'. The document makes no reference to crossing the lake. Oakbank was the name for Millerground and Queen Adelaide's Hill, and the bridle path leading to the shore from St Mary's church and Bowness is still a popular footpath today.

No further reference can be found until the late nineteenth century so it is unlikely that a service was being operated. The crossing lay within the Middle Cubble, and from at least 1570 the holders of the ferry rights were lessees of the Nab Ferry, the only party allowed to ferry for profit here. The accounts of rents payable from 1675 for ferrying and fishing rights within the Richmond Fee does not distinguish between ferrymen and fishermen. An unrelated document from 1693 shows that Roger Parke of Millerground sold 'a moiety or half fishing in the highest and middle cubbles'. No reference to ferrying was made.

In 1740 John Robinson of Millerground paid 6s 8d 'for his fishing', but again no reference is made to ferrying; George Braithwaite of the Nab Ferry in the Middle Cubble paid the same rent.

The building with a belfry to the west of Millerground built in 1612, is known locally as the ferryman's cottage. The oldest surviving lakeshore building, it probably marks the site of an older dwelling used by the ferryman. In the seventeenth century the Dixon family lived at Millerground and Crosthwaite's map of 1783 marks the ferry at Nab End, but not Millerground; Clarke's map of 1787 does the same. As the most accurate pre-Ordnance Survey maps it is unlikely they would omit one ferry, but include another.

James Gibson's mid-1830s ferry service picked up and dropped off passengers at Millerground, and probably Belle Grange, and so a cross-lake service may have operated a couple of times each day. Cargo boats

The 1870 Nab ferry at Ferry Nab. (Reproduced by courtesy of the Museum of Lakeland Life and Industry, Kendal, Cumbria)

Below: The 1870 Ferry and the Ferry Hotel steamer pier c1881.

Below middle: The 1870 Ferry loaded with Bruce Logan's coach, and private steam launches at the Ferry Hotel.

Below right: The 1870 Ferry at Ferry Nab with a coach and four aboard.

Bottom left: The 1915 Ferry unloading at the Ferry Hotel.

Bottom right: The 1915 Ferry nears the Ferry Hotel on a busy summers day.

may have called here too when summoned by the cottage's bell. After 1793 ferrying was allowed anywhere on the lake although it is likely a ferry service was operational until the early twentieth century. Herman Ludolph Prior – writing in 1881 – warned passengers crossing at Millerground that 'If it is wished to return the same way, an arrangement must be made with a Millerground boatman to meet you at Belle Grange at an appointed hour'.

In 1885 Harriet Martineau told passengers walking to Langdale from Bowness to 'cross the lake at Millerground'. By then the steam ferry at Ferry Nab had been in operation for 15 years, so Belle Grange ran for tourists, probably operated on request by the Baines family who hired out the rowing boats there until 1947.

In the Middle Cubble, the busiest crossing was the Nab Ferry linking Ferry Nab and Ferry House. Early writings describe it as the Horse Ferry, perhaps the only ferry capable of conveying a horse; other ferries used rowing boats and only carried passengers. By the late nineteenth century a steam ferry was operational here and this is covered later in the book.

South of Storrs Hall it is probable that a small ferry linked Bellman Landing on the east shore with a stone jetty on the west shore near Ling Holme, in the Lower

Cubble. References are scant but in 1713 Myles Sandys of Graythwaite left to his grandson Myles Sandys 'all that his right and title to ferry and fish upon Windermere water....without stopp, lett, suite, trouble, disturbance, molestation, interruption or incumberance..' This suggests the right to ferry was maintained within the Lower Cubble. In 1740 Mr Sandys paid 4s. 0d for the right to ferry within the Lower Cubble, but the limited settlements would not have generated much demand.

On 13th January 1912, Beatrix Potter wrote in 'Country Life' that 'the ferries at Miller Ground and Rawlinson Nab are cobble boats yet, and little used'. This suggests a service was operating, which probably landed at Bellman Landing on the east shore – a public landing site.

A toll was levied on the ford between Fell Foot and what is now Lakeside. The route from Kendal to Furness went by way of Crosthwaite, Gummers How, Newby Bridge (a ford until the 1620s), Ealinghearth, Bouth, Penny Bridge and Ulverston prior to the A590, and the ford at Fell Foot provided a short cut to the Lancashire side of the lake. This land was owned by Furness Abbey, the eastern shore by Cartmel Priory (after 1290). Toll clerks, known as St. Nicholas clerks (after the patron

The Ferry, Lake Windermere. S320

S 3614   FERRY BOAT, WINDERMERE

6691.   THE FERRY CROSSING. LAKE WINDERMERE.

saint of travellers) were employed by each order, but tolls were abolished in the late 1530s after the dissolution of the monasteries. The western landing was known as 'St Nicholas Landing' or 'Nichol Ending', later just 'The Landing' and this name was given to a calling point for steamers from 1845 to 1869, when the River Leven was too low to be safely navigated.

Five large one-ton boulders were laid over the bottom of the shallow to aid crossing of the fifty-five yard ford; it was considered safe to cross when the centre stone (known as the 'cheese press' due to its shape) appeared above the water level. The cheese press also marked the 'Bass Hole' – a deep hole just above the crossing. These boulders later posed a navigational risk to cargo boats, but boatmen dropped pieces of limestone to identify a safe channel.

Tinkler's Ford lay just above the River Leven bend known as the Dog Hole or Dog Tarn (a 30ft pothole in the river bed), near Landing How, was eighty yards across and about two feet deep with the lake at normal levels. According to legend a tinker (in dialect a tinkler) drowned here; he was found standing with his feet stuck in mud, having veered off into the deep Dog Tarn.

A mile further downstream, at the southernmost navigable point, was Newby Bridge ford where the flag stoned river bed allowed carts to cross. A wooden bridge was built around 1622 and replaced by a stone structure in 1652; this precipitated decline for the ancient fords. In 1763 the turnpike from Kendal to Dalton across Cartmel Fell was completed, followed in 1819 by the road from Milnthorpe to Ulverston. These improvements transferred traffic from the fords as carriages took the new road instead of the rocky riverbed. Until the 1850s the original flagstones were visible from the bridge, but these became hidden when the lake level was raised.

The steamers finally put the fords out of use. When *Lady of the* Lake was constructed in 1845 the river was dredged to five feet, and the fords – originally around two feet deep – became unsustainable. The boulders at Fell Foot were removed using horses and chains, being left on the shore near Landing How. Still visible in 1872, the fourth stone from the north was reckoned to be the cheese press. Although hard to spot today, one of the boulders is visible south of the Fell Foot piers on the eastern shore. Until 1869 steamers passed dead slow over the shallow fords.

Industrial uses

The shoreline's deciduous woodland supported many local industries, illustrating the role played by the lake as a swift convenient way of getting goods to market. In the 17th and 18th centuries Windermere was busy with fishing boats, cargo boats and the Nab Ferry. Even before the steamers and pleasure boats, the lake was a thriving highway between settlements, enabling businesses to expand and industries to grow along its shores.

These woodland industries were ancient; one of the earliest detailed references is in the King's Commissioners' Report of 1537; *'there is moche wood growing in Furneysfells in the mounteynes there, Byrk, Holey, Asshe, Ellers, Lyng, lytell short Okes, and other underwood ... profytte commying and growing of the said Woods, called Greenehewe, Bastying, Blecking, byndying, making of Sadeltrees, Cartwheles, Cupes, Disshes, and many other thynges wrought by Cowpers and Turners, with making of Coles and panage of Hoggs'.*

Large tracts of deciduous woodland covered the Furness Fells and shores of Windermere. These were a valuable commodity containing birch, ash, elder and oak and supporting cottage industries of keeping pigs, making cups, dishes, mats (bastying), barrels (bynding), packhorse pannier frames (sadeltrees), and drying bark for soap (blecking). The main woodland industries of charcoal burning, bark peeling, spelk basket and bobbin making, and using timber for building lasted until the nineteenth and early twentieth centuries. Charcoal continued to be used for gunpowder production and iron smelting.

500 years ago, charcoal was the only effective way of smelting iron, copper, lead and silver, and the local history of charcoal burning is closely linked with the iron smelters. The earliest charcoal burning pits were in Low Furness, where plentiful iron ore was available, but

Below: The third chain ferry, Drake, as a steam vessel.

756 *The Ferry Boat on Windermere*

The many rowing boats available for hire at Bowness. Note the 'Cushion Huts' to the right with the oars stacked up outside. The Old England Hotel dominates the view, and was built in 1869. (Reproduced by courtesy of the Museum of Lakeland Life and Industry, Kendal, Cumbria)

woodland was soon depleted. Charcoal burning pits became a familiar sight with their pale blue smoke in the woods surrounding Windermere. In 1798 Joseph Palmer's poem 'Windermere' depicted; *'columns of smoke bursting out, from the process of charcoal-making, hanging on tops of trees, by the fields of hills, has an enchanting effect'*.

Ore production required plenty of charcoal which needed plentiful supplies of wood; one ton of charcoal used five tons of wood, and one ton of iron consumed nearly four tons of charcoal. Consequently it was sensible to have multiple pit steads and move the coals after production. There were at least nine charcoal pits along the west side of Windermere between Canny Hill and Blelham Tarn, the largest being at Graythwaite. To the east there were only two; at Rayrigg Woods near Millerground, and Holbeck Ghyll. Early iron smelters, known as bloomeries, relocated from Furness to Millerground, Blelham Tarn, Matson Ground, Fell Foot and near Rawlinson Nab to be nearer to charcoal pits. The men working the coals lived in crude round huts.

Some pits were owned by the monks of Furness Abbey who brought in ore, rather than move charcoal to the Low Furness bloomeries. Whilst the ore was probably carried on packhorses, the shoreside sites were served by boat, with the Monks making use of their rights from the grant of 1240 by William de Lancaster. In 1537 the King's Commissioners' Report mentions *'the Abbots of the same late Monastery have been accustomed to have a Smythey, and sometime two or three, kepte for making Yron to those of their Monastery'*. The *'late'* Monastery was dissolved by Henry VIII. An order dating from 1570 refers to coals being delivered out of Furness Fells on *'the water of Wendermyre'*.

Keeping charcoal pits supplied required good forest management and by the time of the King's Commissioners' Report of 1537 the ancient woodland

was being used faster than natural regeneration could replace it. In 1564 the inhabitants of Hawkshead and Colton complained to the Queen that her woods were *'sore decayed'* due to the operation of iron smithies.

In the 18th century two large smelting furnaces were built, making the smaller lake-side sites redundant. The Cunsey Company opened in 1712, although a forge operated there in 1675 and references go back to 1623. Ore from Low Furness was brought along the lake to the mouth of Cunsey Beck or the landing at Hammer Hole below Rawlinson Nab, whilst charcoal was brought south from woods surrounding the northern end of the lake. Construction of the furnace commenced in 1711 and the Cunsey Company, officially known as Edward Hall & Company, remained operational until 1750 when the premises and nearby forge were sold to the Backbarrow Company, *'together with the Liberty and free passing and re-passing of boats for the carriage of any material whatsoever to and from the said premises in and upon the water or meer commonly called Windermere'*. The site was never worked again, being partially demolished in 1760, and losing its remaining machinery in 1800.

The Backbarrow works, built by William Rawlinson, John Machell and others, also opened in 1812. They employed Windermere boatmen *'to row the Company's Coals upon Windermere to our landing nigh Newby Bridge at 16d per dozen from above the Nabb, and 11d from below it'*. This was 'The Long Voyage' ('The Short Voyage' being from Waterhead to Nibthwaite on Coniston Water), with an annual payment of 4s being made to the Earl of Lonsdale for the *'privilege of rowing'* charcoal along the lake. The charcoal was collected from pitsteads at Ambleside, Skelwith, Troutbeck, High Borrans and Winster and shipped to Backbarrow along the lake. In 1726 the Braithwaite family – who owned the ferry rights on the

Bowness Pier.

One of the sisters, either **Teal** (I) or **Cygnet** at Bowness in the late nineteenth century. Note the white ensign flying at the stern of the vessel.

lake – were employed as boatmen but the company complained about the handling of charcoal; (The man) *'crowds such quantities of Coals into the Boat as not to be able to get her up to the stage without discharging many upon the meadow tho' we expect he should deliver every sack upon the stage.......I now tell you we shall suffer ourselves to be imposed upon no longer. You will therefore hear from us in a very different manner in a few days if the matter is not remedied immediately. I am really ashamed to have forborn so long'.*

At least one boat was kept on each lake but the company dragged them between Coniston and Windermere as required. After leaving Clappersgate loaded with coals, the charcoal barges called at Bowness to load coal and charcoal brought from Westmorland by packhorse. The coal trade operated in both directions here; William Gilpin in 1772 noted that charcoal was regularly brought to Bowness for onward carriage *into* Westmorland by packhorse. The boats would call as required at the Ferry, Cunsey Beck, and Hammer Hole to offload coals. The boats unloaded cargo at a specially constructed landing stage at Newby Bridge whence the finished product was conveyed to the iron works by horse and cart.

Town Head – on the eastern shore opposite Lakeside – was used if the River Leven was too low to allow passage. The company contemplated the need to '... *dam, lade and dress out ye pool at Newby bridge'* to overcome this. The Town Head landing is still visible above the water level as a grassy shelf about 100 yards long, 10 yards wide and 3 feet deep.

Charcoal burning continued until the mid-1930s, but the Backbarrow Company stopped boating their fuels along the lake in 1783, and although the Company's

Drake as a diesel ferry, post 1960.

boats were sold, private carriers continued to trade well into the nineteenth century. The Backbarrow Iron Company finally closed in 1967. Prior to the railways reaching the area, product from the Company was shipped out by sea, and in the eighteenth century they had a fleet of sloops named after local ports and rivers such as *Backbarrow*, *Milnthorpe*, *Leven*, *Kent*, *Bardsea*, and *Pennybridge*.

Coppicing was practiced to maintain the flow of wood. Trees were cut just above the ground, and ten to twenty shoots allowed to sprout for harvesting every fifteen or sixteen years. Thicker shoots were sent to bobbin mills while much of the rest was used for charcoal. The same team would frequently manage both coppice and charcoal pit.

Bark peeling also took place along the shore. Near the Bike-Boat pier at Belle Grange stands Bark Barn used for storing bark peeled from the oak trees. Peeling was easiest when sap ran up the trees between May and

Waterhead pre development. (Reproduced by courtesy of the Museum of Lakeland Life and Industry, Kendal, Cumbria)

early July, and the bark was transported from a crude stone jetty to tanneries at Rusland and Ulverston. These ceased operations towards the end of the nineteenth century when bark was sent to Cheshire and Lancashire. Bark was also used for making mats and soap.

Demand for gunpowder was high in the eighteenth century and the Lake District was perfect for a powder works. The process required charcoal, sulphur and saltpetre, and the finished product could be used in local quarries and mines, or exported – much of it to Africa. The expanding railway networks also made use of the powder when constructing earthworks. Two gunpowder works were established near Windermere; one at Lowwood (also known as Low Wood) near Haverthwaite in 1798, and another at Elterwater in 1824. The latter was producing 4-6,000 pounds of powder a week by 1826. The main ingredients including timber were brought through Greenodd and along Windermere, where a pier was built at the head of Pull Wyke.

The finished product was shipped to Newby Bridge, onward to Haverthwaite by cart, then by barge to Greenodd. This was a dangerous occupation; in 1845 one of the barges carrying saltpetre on Windermere blew up leading the company to stop using the lake. From 1847 horses and carts from Elterwater went overland to the railhead at Windermere. Saltpetre (also known as brimstone and brought from as far as Sicily), and sulphur were dangerous in combination, so horses pulling carts from the pier to the works had copper shoes to avoid sparks. The works at Lowwood had an internal tramway linking to the FR at Haverthwaite, using non-ferrous metals for the same reason. From the early twentieth century motorised vehicles were used, but demand fell after the First World War and the powder works at Elterwater closed in 1928, with Lowwood following in 1934. Life in these factories was hard work; Jim Clark of Backbarrow worked at Lowwood from 1912, twelve hours a day from 6 am until 6 pm, for just 5s a week.

Timber was also sent to the powder works as the mills had a cooperage where storage barrels were made. In October 1866 some seasoned cherry wood had been sent down the lake for the Lowwood works from the

wood merchant Robert Fell. The boat was so overloaded that the landing was problematic, and the cargo was tipped into the water and had to be collected over several days!

Wood for building was gathered from Claife Heights – a log chute lay just south of Belle Grange, near the 'old ferry landing'. Photographic evidence from August 1902 shows logs being towed by rowing boat from near Fell Foot to Lakeside. Fuel for heating was also carried on the lake, including peat which was widely used for domestic fuel in the eighteenth and nineteenth centuries. A letter of 1716 written by Lady Otway to Benjamin Browne of Troutbeck mentions a peat house in Pull Wyke where it was *convenient to come to ffor a boat to carie the peats over the water'*.

The Fell family of Troutbeck Bridge owned local bobbin mills, and Christopher Fell would help his father take coppiced wood from around the lake to the mills. The introduction of the spinning wheel increased demand for bobbins, making coppiced woodland even more valuable. The first local bobbin mill was opened at Skelwith Bridge in 1789, and in 1829 the old mill at Troutbeck was converted. Horrax's bobbin mill on Stock Ghyll in Ambleside opened in 1839 following Stott Park that opened four years earlier. This last named is still operational, restored by English Heritage. The old bloomery at Cunsey was converted into a bobbin mill before being used as a charging station for electric launches.

Spelk baskets, also known as swill baskets, were made from woven oak shavings. In 1476 the Customs of the Manor of Windermere ordered; *'whoso felleth any wands of spelks in the dales of his neighbours without leave or any green wood forfeits 6s 8d'*. Spelk basket making remained important in Bowness but when tourism took over the industry was confined to the Leven, Crake and Duddon valleys. Lowick, Spark Bridge, Torver, Haverthwaite, Backbarrow and Broughton all produced these baskets; it was said that the best of them could even hold water. With many potential uses they were shipped as far as Liverpool, being used for cockling in Morecambe Bay, carrying coal, rubbish collection, farming, and even as baby cradles!

Coppiced wood was used for burning lime to create fertiliser and mortar for building. Lime forms the base for the whitewash which covers many local buildings. A narrow limestone belt across the head of Windermere supported several lime kilns during the seventeenth century – Dove Nest lime kiln is still visible adjacent to the road from Low Wood to Ambleside near the Samling Hotel. Other kilns were at Borwick Ground and Wray – both near Blelham Tarn – and at Pull Beck. The quality of this stone was poor, but it was worked for local use. Wood and charcoal was delivered to the shoreside kilns and Stockdale mentions in his 'Annals of Cartmel' (1872) that barges conveying Langdale slate down the lake also brought Cartmel limestone back up for the kilns. This stone was of a better quality and came from quarries at Fayrigge, Field Broughton and Headhouse. It was taken from the quarries to Newby Bridge for shipment, or used as building stone in its raw state.

Mary Anne, of 1870, at the Windermere Steamboat Museum. She was the last of the row ferries built for the Nab Crossing.

Sir Daniel Fleming's account book of c1690 mentions a boat used for carrying lime along the lake, largely for his estate at Rydal. There is another reference to this trade in the Hawkshead Parish Register on 16th September 1697; '*James Braithwait late of Crofthead did goe to the waterfoote for a boate load of lyme stones for William Braithwait of briers, and as he was comenge backe Againe was drownd in Windermere water and three men that was with him by Gods great mercy gott all out of the water and sav'd there lives; the boate which they were in beinge loaden with lyme stones was lost & did sinke into the bottom of the sayd water; and hee was buried the day of the moneth first mentioned'.*

On the eastern bank of the River Leven close to Nickerhole is an old stone wharf that may have been where lime from Staveley in Cartmel was loaded onto barges.

Slate quarries in Lakeland lay primarily around Coniston and Derwentwater, but William Birkett's Troutbeck Park Quarry produced the best quality 'London Slate'. It was transported by road to Windermere to be shipped to Newby Bridge, then by horse and cart to the tidal River Leven at Haverthwaite whence lighters carried it to Greenodd and Ulverston. In 1727 slate flags for the repairs of St Anthony's Chapel on Cartmel Fell were carried to Bowness by boat from Clappersgate and onward by road.

The Rigge family ran quarries around the Tilberthwaite area and shipped their slate along both Coniston Water and Windermere. Rigge's product was carted to Pull Wyke from where it was boated to Bowness, for onward carting to Kendal and the sea port of Milnthorpe. The cost of moving the slate this way was between 6s 7d and 7s 10d per ton, and in 1786 it was selling in Kendal for between £1 3s 4d and £1 15s 0d.

Quarries at the head of the lake near Chapel Stile, Elterwater and Skelwith Bridge used Clappersgate wharf at the confluence of the Rivers Brathay and Rothay. The artist John Harden depicted the slate wharf in a painting entitled 'Head of Windermere'. Ramsey Richard Reinagle also painted the Brathay slate wharf and William Green stated that Clappersgate was still being used for loading slate in 1819;

'*The slate trade of Langdale is aided by the lake – the slate is brought in carts from the quarries to the landing at the junction of the rivers Brathay and Rothay, and from that place navigated to Newby Bridge, where it is again put into carts, and sent by the side of the Leven to the sea below the Low Wood powder mills'.*

Parson and White's 'History, Directory and Gazetteer of Cumberland and Westmorland' in 1829 referred to Bowness as a slate port, but the arrival of the railway put an end to the lake trade. Other quarried stone was also moved along Windermere. During construction of Wray Castle between 1840 and 1847, stone was moved from Ecclerigg Quarry at White Cross Bay to the shoreline near Wray. This quarry now forms the dock area for the Cragwood Hotel. In 1756 Henry Williamson was paid £1. 10s 0d. per ton for moving six boat loads of slate from Ecclerigg to the foot of the lake.

When the Round House was being constructed on Belle Isle in the 1770s, 828 tons of building stone was shipped to the island by three boatmen including Henry Williamson. They used barges with a capacity of between only six and ten tons.

Windermere cargo boats were large flat-bottomed, heavily built sailing barges with auxiliary oars for navigating rivers, and when there was no wind. They travelled from Newby Bridge to Clappersgate, calling at landing sites at Nickerhole, Lakeside, Town Head, Graythwaite, Ghyll Head, Hammer Hole, Rawlinson Nab, Bellman Landing, Storrs, Cunsey, Ash Landing, the Ferry, Harrowslack, Bowness, Rayrigg, Millerground, Belle Grange, Ecclerigg, Low Wood, Wray, Pull Wyke and Waterhead.

In 1899 Cowper noted '*Clappersgate, near Ambleside, was the charcoal and slate port at the north-end of Windermere as late as 1819'.* The wharf on the River Rothay at the confluence with the River Brathay, was known as 'Three Foot Brandreth' – a possible reference to the depth of vessel able to use the berth. The port was a natural location for serving the Brathay valley and the townships of Langdale, Chapel Stile and Elterwater, being also closer to Rydal and Grasmere than Waterhead. Clappersgate wharf was incorporated into the boathouse and harbour of Croft Lodge around 1830.

A later barge was the *Elizabeth*, built in 1839 by William Watson of Ambleside. She worked on Coniston for the Copper Mines Company, returning to Windermere in the 1880s as a sand barge. Steam launches were by then common, so it is probable she was towed behind a powered vessel. Barges continued on the lake until the late nineteenth century, being phased out when the 1871 FR cargo vessel *Raven* took most of the trade. More efficient and quicker, she was only superseded by road transport.

The build up to steam

The first person thought to keep a pleasure boat was parish priest William de Biggynges. Sometime before 1411 he was granted the chantry of Lady Holme and associated fisheries and land, by the Duke of Bedford, entitling him to a tenth part of all the fish taken in the lake. He built the rectory – an oak panel marked '1416' still remains in the kitchen – and kept a boat at Parsonage Bay, close to the rectory, at a jetty now in a poor state of repair. In 1777 Nicholson and Burn reported that '*the rector hath for time immemorial had a pleasure-boat upon it'* (the lake).

It is not known when people started ferrying the length of the lake; early ferries were linked to fisheries, so until the mid-seventeenth century it was hard to ferry legally as rights were restricted to the various Cubbles. By 1670 Thomas Braithwaite, lessee of the Nab Ferry, had '*the due right, to ferry and carry all and every the said cubles both horse and man and all sorts of goods and commodities whatsoever to his best advantage'.* The Braithwaite family carried limestone up the lake and slate back down, and in 1683 took stones for the corn mill at Rydal Hall. In July 1701 George Braithwaite, presumably the son of Thomas, granted Dame Elizabeth Otway of Ambleside the privilege of fishing on Windermere, allowing her to move goods by boat along the length of the lake for 5s a year.

On 12th January 1711 George Braithwaite, who had sole rights to ferrying, complained that Thomas and John Elleray of Storrs, and George Robinson of Under Millbeck, also kept a boat for ferrying purposes in contradiction of his right, whereby he *'from time immemorial lawfully possessed a common ferry-boat upon Windermere Water, to carry and recarry passengers across from K. Kendall and other places in co. Westmorland to Hawkshead and other places in co. Lancashire…'*

He observed that James Kendall of Bowness also ferried passengers and goods; Kendall was fined 1d. Braithwaite took the law into his own hands throwing one of Kendall's oars into the lake, where it was lost. He was fined 2s 6d. George Braithwaite and friends then used their boat to block Kendall in at Bowness, and again he was fined 2s 6d. Kendall continued to break the law; in 1712 he was fined 6d for carrying slate along the lake through the *'High Cubble and the Middle Cubble belonging to George Braithwaite, who has the sole right to carry goods in the said places'*.

The Kendall family were involved in more mischievous ferrying and an agreement was drawn up in October 1731; *'Mr Thos Philipson and Jon Robinson for his father agree that the fishermen have no right of ferrying (saving their own goods) neither have they any right to allow the liberty of ferrying to any other person. Robert Kendall promises to pay the Ferry Rent provided the fishermen neither Ferry themselves (saving their own goods) nor encourage other people in ferrying. Robert Kendall does agree that he has no right of fishing upon acct of his ferry rent. It is agreed that if any of the fishermen pay part of the ferry rent such fishermen shall have the right of ferrying in proportion to the rent he payd'*. The agreement gave the fishermen no rights of ferriage, although anyone paying part of the ferry rent, would have a share of the ferry rights.

Until the nineteenth century there were no scheduled boats running from Ambleside to Newby Bridge. Locals rarely travelled far beyond the nearest market town, and early visitors spent weeks getting to the area, struggling to get around on the poor roads. Fishermen took paying passengers for pleasure trips. By the 1770s (but possibly as early as the late 1740s) Lord Lonsdale no longer collected rents from ferrying, just gathering his fishery rents. On 18th July 1793, the proprietors of the Windermere fisheries met in Bowness to organise charges for navigating the lake; a surviving document from that meeting is worth noting; *'Resolved that no Carriage Boat navigating on the lake of Windermere with the Goods and Commodities of the Public, shall be suffered to pass on the said Lake, but upon the following conditions – (Viz) Every Boat so navigating shall pay to the owners of the said Fisheries*

the sum of 15— annually for the Priviledge of such Passage, and also be subject to the following Rate and Regulation……. ……Carriage, for carrying the Goods of the Public – (Viz) from Newby Bridge to Bowess 9d per ton – From Newby Bridge to the Head of the Water or any intermediate place North of Bowness, 1-7 per ton –

	d
For every Bushel of Lime to Bowness	*1-½*
Ditto to Waterhead	*2*

and so in proportion for every other Article according to the above prices –
Resolved that every Boat not the Property of any owner of a Fishery, navigating the Lake of Windermere, usually denominated a Pleasure Boat, not carrying Goods and Merchandise, shall annually pay the Sum of five shillings to the owners of the Fisheries –
Resolved that in case any Person refuse to comply with the aforementioned several payments and Regulations, the Proprietors of the said Fisheries hereby agree to enforce the same at their Joint Expence, by such Methods as the Law directs –
Resolved that the Sums so collected shall be appropriated to the payment of the Lords Rent and the surplus if any equally divided amongst the Owners of the said Fisheries…..
Signed by Jer. Dixon
John Fleming
G. Braithwaite
J-C-Curwen
James Wilson
John Stuartson'

The above charges became lucrative for the proprietors of the fisheries, as pleasure boats serviced the growing tourist trade just as the traditional local economy slumped. As wool sales dropped sharply, tourism and pleasure boating provided extra income. How long these charges were enforced is unclear, as in 1876 it was noted that *'the public have been allowed to Boat upon and angle in the Lake without license or payment of any kind'*.

Tourists needed accommodation. In the eighteenth century the only inns along the shore were the White Swan at Newby Bridge (later the Swan Hotel), the Ferry Inn, the White Lion in Bowness and the Low Wood. The Crown – the first tourist hotel in Bowness – opened in the 1820s. The White Lion, owned by John Ullock in 1819 and sometimes referred to as 'Ullock's Hotel', became The Royal in 1840 after the visit of the dowager Queen Adelaide. These hostelries provided accommodation and most had a bowling green outside. The Gentleman's Magazine published a widely read account in 1748 that mentioned that boats were available for hire from Bowness.

Custom increasingly came from tourists coming to take a trip on a lake. Pleasure boat facilities in Bowness Bay couldn't cope with demand, and proprietors hired out boats, acquiring maybe half a dozen boats and employing boatmen to take trippers for a fee; hired by the hour, day, or even week. Boatmen charged as much as 1s per mile. In 1770 Arthur Young recorded that the landlord of the White Lion kept a boat, and could provide rowers for visitors. Some of these early boatmen have survived history; Robin Partridge of Bowness was mentioned in 1792; others included Billy Balmer, William Garnett, Tom Stevenson, and Jack Stevenson. *'Let us descend to the White Lion, and enquire about Billy Balmer. Honest Billy has arrived from Waterhead – seems tolerably steady – Mr Ullock's boats may be trusted – so let us take a voyage of discovery on the lake. Let those who have reason to think they have been born to die a different death from drowning, hoist a sail. We to-day shall feather an oar. Billy takes the stroke – Mr William Garnett's at the helm – and Row, vassals, row, for the pride of the Lowlands, is the choral song that accompanies the Naiad out of the bay…* It appears Balmer worked for the proprietor of the White Lion, although Professor Wilson of Elleray also hired him.

'Blackwood's Edinburgh Magazine' mentioned the early boatmen, and who was best to employ for a tour of the lake; *'After Christopher North, the best guide on Windermere, unquestionably, is Billy Balmer. But Billy can not, any more than a bird, be at above half-a-dozen places at one time; and should he happen to be at Lowood, Waterhead, the Ferry, and Newby bridge, you will be in good hands should you for the day engage Tom or Jack Stevenson. There is no such thing as a bad boat on Windermere'.*

It is unsurprising that Christopher North was rated above other boatmen as this was the pen-name of Professor John Wilson of Elleray, a founder of the magazine. Born in Paisley in 1785 Wilson went to Oxford after discovering the poetry of Wordsworth. Resident at Elleray near Windermere from 1807 until 1815, he moved to Edinburgh after losing a substantial part of his fortune. Two years later he founded Blackwood's Magazine, making enough money to return regularly to Windermere. An admirer – and later friend – of Wordsworth and De Quincey, he loved life in the lakes and took part in wrestling, fishing, walking and cock-fighting. His main interest was the lake and he commissioned Whitehaven boat-builders to build a fleet of boats for him as the self-styled 'Admiral of the Lakes'. Wilson died in Edinburgh in 1854.

The article describes how many hire boats resembled Thames wherries, with the first on the lake being named *Swift*. A later paragraph reads *'If you are so fortunate as to yet be a bachelor, take a wherry or a skiff – if a Benedick, then embark with Betsy and the brats in that bumboat, and Billy, with a grave face, will pull you all*

The Langdale Valley and Waterhead Bay viewed from Waterhead.

away round by the back of the Great Island…'.

Mrs Gordon, John Wilson's daughter and biographer described Balmer; *'Billy was the neatest and best rower on Windermere, and knew that beauteous water from head to foot, in all her humours, from sunrise to night-fall, and even later. There was not a more skilful boatman, or a steadier steersman on the lake, and he was about the best judge of a pretty craft and good sailing to be found. He could sing a sailor's song, had an undeniable love of fun, understood humour, and felt the difference of wit. No one knew how to tell a story better, and with a due unction of excusable exaggeration combined with reality; and in every tale of Billy his master was invariably the hero. He was a little man, weather-beaten in complexion, and much marked from small-pox. His hair was of a light sandy colour; his eyes blue and kindly in expression, as was also his smile; his gait, rather doglike, not quite straight ahead, but, like that honest animal, he was sure-footed, and quick in getting over the ground. That pleasant broad Westmoreland dialect of his, too, gave peculiarity to his voice; and there is a grateful remembrance of the hearty grasp of his little, hard, horny hand when it greeted welcome, or bade adieu, while the whole picture of the man, in his blue dress, sailor fashion, stands distinctly before me, either as he steered the "Endeavour" or mowed the grass on the lawn at Elleray'.*

In 1822 tourists could be conveyed by *'careful boatmen'* from Bowness. William Green's 1819 guide tells how, in 1815, he set out walking from Ambleside to Coniston with his fourteen year old daughter. After bumping into Windermere boatman 'Honest Jonathan' of the Salutation Inn, they were taken to a pier in Pull Wyke from the Brathay slate wharves; a regular destination for the boatmen, not exclusively for cargo boats. Waterhead, where rowing boats are available today, only become prominent with the introduction of paddle steamers. Green notes that boats were available from Ambleside (Clappersgate Wharf), provided by the Salutation, Commercial, and White Lion hotels, Low Wood, Bowness, the Ferry Inn, and Newby Bridge.

Leigh's guide of 1832 noted some of the rates; *'Boats for Windermere may be hired at the Inns. The charge for a boat to visit the Island and the Station House, and return to Bowness, is 2s.; to go to the head or to the foot of the lake and return, 5s.; or if the boat is hired by time, 1s. per hour. The boatman will also expect something for himself, as he depends entirely on such donations, the boats belonging to the proprietors of the inns'.*

Gentlemen living by the lake moored their fleets at quiet anchorages; at Belle Isle John Christian Curwen had 17 at his disposal. A major draw for early tourists was the prospect of watching these sailing vessels race. One of the earliest documented races was noted in a 1775 letter to George Browne of Troutbeck from the Rev. Otley. A famous regatta of 1796 sparked widespread interest, with the yacht *Peggy* sailing from the Isle of Man to Greenodd before being dragged to Windermere. Once on the lake the owner Mr Quayle took part in a race against Curwen.

Regular regattas were organised from the start of the nineteenth century, the first being advertised in 1802.

Windermere and the Coniston Fells viewed from Orrest Head.

These were initially sporadic affairs based at the Low Wood Inn, but in 1824 over 60 boats turned out. A regatta was proposed for the Low Wood every two years from 1825, with a sailing festival planned in intermediate years at the Ferry Inn. These yacht races became a focal point for the local community, supplemented by tourists who brought good business to Bowness boatmen carrying passengers to the Ferry Inn, and to the ferry between the Nab and the Inn.

Wrestling and fox hunting took place, along with some more specialist events such as the 'Pig Race' (which involved catching a soaped pig), and 'Donkey Race' (riding your neighbours donkey – the slowest animal was the winner). As well as the yachting, there were different categories of rowing racing on the water; fishermen's boats, innkeeper's boats, and gentlemen's boats. Mr Wilson was a regular winner of the latter category.

The plan for annual events proved easier in theory than in practice, as the next event was at the Low Wood in 1830. The 1831 festival at the Ferry Inn was lost due to bad weather and in 1832 a cholera outbreak in Kendal led to cancellation. Interest declined and in 1847 it was reported that attendance was lower than in previous years. A revival in the 1850s saw annual regattas or festivals between 1853 and 1860, usually at the Ferry Inn, with spectator numbers increasing. The introduction of a passenger steamer in 1845 allowed easy access to the regatta sites and after the introduction of a second steamer in 1846 also provided a floating spectator grandstand. The arrival of the railway in 1847 allowed Lancastrians to take a day trip to Windermere for the festivals, but the regattas didn't remain a regular feature of Windermere's calendar. A victim of their own success, they outgrew the Ferry Inn's ability to accommodate spectators, and 1861 the sports moved to Grasmere, where they remain a famous attraction.

The tourist trade was now significant enough to be worthy of a mention in Parson and White's History, Directory, and Gazetteer of Cumberland and Westmorland', published in 1829; 'Bowness is the chief port on the lake, and has a few fishing vessels, a number of pleasure boats, and a trade in charcoal and slate....From its admirable situation it is much frequented by tourists, and has excellent accommodation for them in two good inns, the White Lion and the Crown...'.

Boats operated independently of the hotels became available and Bowness in the 1830s and 40s was a busy place. Rowing boats, fishing boats, barges and yachts filled the bay, floating at moorings or pulled up the beach. A popular excursion by rowing boat headed to Slape Scar and on to Waterhead; another went around the islands, stopping on Belle Isle before visiting the Ferry Inn and the Station. This was one of Thomas West's original viewing platforms just south of the Ferry Inn. By the 1780s, Mr Braithwaite of Harrowslack had built a two-storey building with coloured stained glass in large windows; this represented seasonal colours, moonlight, and thunderstorms, allowing tourists to envisage the views through the year. The building fell into ruin, but in late 2013 the National Trust started a restoration project.

William Wordsworth mentioned a boat running the length of the lake to his friend Henry Crabb Robinson in a letter of 11th July 1836;

My dear Friend,
............from Liverpool there is a steamer to Ulverston, from which, if convenient, see Furness Abbey, and come to us by Windermere, up which lake there is at present a boat in connection with the Liverpool steamers to Ulverston.

No other reference to scheduled passenger services for 1836 has come to light; local boatmen probably met coaches to convey passengers wherever they wished to go, akin to a modern taxi. The first definite scheduled passenger boats commenced in 1837, operated by James Gibson of Ambleside. A grocer, he hired rowing boats from Waterhead, sometimes providing a guide – Wordsworth's service may have been operated by Gibson. His unadvertised service between Ambleside and Bowness was recorded on 1st July 1837 in the Kendal Mercury; *We have been informed that Mr James Gibson, of Ambleside, intends to commence plying a boat between Waterhead and Bowness twice a-day during the summer months. This is quite a new undertaking, and as it will be a great convenience to Lakers, we wish the projector every success.*

Steamboats were soon proposed for the lake following the success of Gibson and the continuing rise in tourism. As early as 2nd February 1838 plans were announced when the Westmorland Gazette reported; *'PROPOSED STEAMER ON WINDERMERE – It is reported that a steamer will ply between Waterhead, Ambleside and Newby Bridge, during the ensuing summer months, for the convenience of parties visiting the lakes via Ulverston. We have no doubt but it will be found very convenient, not only to parties coming that way, but to those who reside on and near the banks of Windermere, – not only to strangers but to the inhabitants of Ambleside and neighbourhood, and we heartily wish the projectors of the scheme success'.*

A similar prediction appeared in the Blackburn Standard which stated; *'The report has again been revived that a small steam-boat will be launched upon Windermere...'* alluding to an even earlier attempt at introducing steam. This never materialised and it was another seven years before Windermere's waters were disturbed by the paddle wheel.

In 1840 James Gibson extended his services to connect with coaches at Newby Bridge. The boats were large and heavy, propelled by four long sweeps and fitted with an auxiliary sail for use in favourable winds. Adverts were published for the first time, appearing in the Kendal Mercury and Westmorland Gazette on the 15th August;

DAILY CONVEYANCE ON THE LAKE OF WINDERMERE

THE Public are respectfully informed that a DAILY CONVEYANCE by BOAT on the LAKE of WINDERMERE, between AMBLESIDE, BOWNESS, and NEWBY BRIDGE, for Passengers and Goods is established, being the shortest, cheapest, and best conveyance Southward, as it is in connection with the Lancaster and Ulverston Coaches, the Steam Packet to Liverpool, and the Packet to Fleetwood, which leave Ulverston daily.

Times of departure from Ambleside every Morning at Eight o' Clock; Bowness at Ten; Newby Bridge at One P.M.; and from Bowness to Ambleside at Three.

Terms for passengers;
To Bowness . . . . .1s. 3d.
To Newby Bridge . . . . .2s. 6d.
To Ulverston . . . . .5s. 0d.

Other particulars may be obtained on application to MR JAMES GIBSON, of Ambleside, the Owner; MR T. HOLT, Stag's Head Inn, Bowness; and of MR JOSEPH BELL, Harrison's Landing, Newby Bridge, which is half a mile from the Bridge, on the West Side of the Lake,- the Road to which is round the West End of the Swan Inn.

– Ambleside, August 12th, 1840

Gibson operated a single boat timetable, based in Ambleside. Passengers could be conveyed to Low Wood, Millerground, Storrs, the Landing (near the present Lakeside pier) or any suitable intermediate landing. Gibson took on a partner, Thomas White, of the Swan Hotel at Newby Bridge and introduced a second boat, connecting at Newby Bridge with coaches to Ulverston or Lancaster. Gibson's boat left Ambleside in the morning calling at Bowness, whilst White's left Newby Bridge. Meeting halfway at the Ferry Inn, they transferred passengers and goods before heading back to their starting point. The fare was 3s for the full trip or 1s 6d to the Nab Ferry. A trip from Ambleside to Newby Bridge with Gibson and White would have taken 3½ hours, weather depending of course. Today the same journey takes 1¼ hours.

Shortly before departure, a boy – for many years James Gibson junior – blew a horn in the Market Place in Ambleside to warn intending travellers to head for the piers.

James Gibson was also a writer and his 'Handbook to the Lakes' lasted many editions. In 1843 he published 'A Guide to the Scenery on Windermere' recommending arriving by coach from Lancaster or steamer from Fleetwood via Newby Bridge. Gibson gives a full description of the pre-steamer lake and advertises his sailings; *'At Newby-bridge is an excellent Inn, with first-rate accommodations for Lake Visitors; gigs, cars, carriages, and boats, are kept there; there are likewise two public Boats, daily to Bowness and Ambleside, up the Lake a distance of 14 miles; the first Boat leaves Newby Bridge at 8 o'clock in the Morning, meeting the one at the Ferry Inn which leaves Ambleside at the same hour; the second Boat leaves each place again at 1 o'clock in the Afternoon, and meets as before at the Ferry. This is a very great accommodation for*

visitors, as it affords an opportunity for seeing the whole Lake at a light expense, the fare being only three shillings; a private boat to the Ferry Inn, is charged five shillings, besides the Boatman, and five shillings to Bowness, the Boatman in such cases expects three shillings or three shillings and sixpence, as he has no other pay but what visitors give him'.

He describes Bowness and the boatmen, and recommends his cheaper conveyance; *'Visitors will find pleasure boats in abundance, and watermen always at hand to attend them to any part of the lake, the charge for a boat and man, one shilling per hour, to the island and station, two shillings is generally expected, and the fare for a private boat to Ambleside is five shillings, and the boatman two shillings and sixpence, or three shillings; by the public boat the fare is only one shilling, including luggage and all charges; parties will learn about this boat at the Bazaar in the Market-house, which is always open, during the summer months, by Mr. T. Belshar…'.*

On Friday 3rd May 1844, Ambleside boat builder William Watson, launched two new rowing boats for Gibson and White, at a grand occasion for the inhabitants of Ambleside. Named *Victoria* and *Prince of Wales*, they were built to be the most comfortable vessels upon the lake; *'They are fit up in a very superior manner with cushions, carpets, and waterproof awning which reach nearly the whole length. In short they are the most complete boats of the kind we have ever seen, and do great credit to the owners, who have spared no expense in fitting them up; and to the builder, who has shown himself to be a workman that needeth not to be ashamed of having his work examined'.*

The boats took guests to Bowness – where more joined – then to the Ferry Inn to be met by Mr White and the Ulverston Brass Band. A procession of boats dressed with flags and banners joined the celebration that continued to Fell Foot, where flags were hoisted and guns fired. At Newby Bridge, a dinner was laid on for *'upwards of 90 persons'*.

During 1844 boats left Ambleside and Newby Bridge at 8 am and 2 pm; the former arrived at Bowness at 9.15 am (to connect with coaches for Ulverston and Lancaster) and 3.15 pm. The boats met at the Ferry Inn at 9.30 am and 3.30 pm, returning after passengers and goods were exchanged, to Bowness (to connect with coaches to Keswick from Bowness at 10 am and 4 pm) and Ambleside. Arrival back at Ambleside and Newby Bridge was at 11.15 am and 5.15 pm.

On 21st May the wind was so strong that the Newby Bridge boat remained berthed. The Ambleside boat dared to venture out *'and after a boisterous and dangerous sail arrived in safety at Newby Bridge. The boat, in returning, only got as far as the Ferry Inn, Mr. Gibson and his man being completely exhausted with striving against the waves'.* Passengers would have enjoyed a swift if bumpy journey! Despite these problems, the year was a success; it was reported in September that the new boats had carried between fifty and sixty people daily, *'all of whom appeared highly satisfied with the comfort and safe accommodation of the boats, and the civility and attention of the owners and boatmen'.*

The King of Saxony visited Bowness in July 1844 staying at Ullock's Royal Hotel near the lake. He enjoyed a trip around Bowness Bay before supper, and the next day continued to Ambleside by boat. Whether utilising the hotel's rowing boats or the plush boats of James Gibson is unclear.

The boats operated for the 1845 season, even after the introduction of the paddle steamer *Lady of the Lake*. Their advert appeared in the Kendal Mercury in October under one for the steamboat timetable. Passage boats were timed from the opposite end of the lake to the steamer, but the higher speed of the *Lady of the Lake* meant she soon caught them, and a simultaneous departure was timetabled from Newby Bridge at 2.30 pm.

Gibson tried underhand tactics to win passengers, writing a letter about the unreliable steam service, first to the Kendal Mercury who refused to publish it, and then, after changing his name to 'A Resident' to the Westmorland Gazette;

TO THE EDITOR OF THE WESTMORLAND GAZETTE
Sir, – No doubt you will have a long account this week respecting the introduction of the first steamboat on Windermere. Be careful not to allow your correspondents to give it a colouring above what it deserves, as I wish to put you in possession of a few facts connected with the event. In the first place she is not able to navigate the River Leven, and hence she has taken up her abode at Harrison's Landing (A. Bell's beer-shop), a mile from Newby Bridge. Tuesday was the day set apart for the proprietors and their friends, but the attendance was very small; Wednesday was a public invitation to the gentlemen of the Lake District, but they almost to a man absented themselves, not only from the steam boat and dinner, but also from the Lake and neighbourhood for that day, as not one was to be seen at Bowness or Ambleside; and so great is the dislike to such a projection, that they have entered into a subscription and are about to commence an action of law against them. Bell's Life three weeks ago gave an account of her first trip (of course wholly incorrect), and put Professor Wilson in the chair; but so far has that prophecy failed of its fulfilment that on Tuesday that gentleman honoured the passage boat with his presence, and steered the Prince of Wales, the property of Mr J. Gibson, of Ambleside, going at a speed superior to that of the steamer, so wishful was Professor Wilson to prove his patronage and support to labour and industry. The passage boats are supported more than ever, being full every day, and this arising, we believe, wholly from a determination in the minds of the inhabitants and visitors to prove to the Windermere Steam Company that their boat was not wanted, nor will be supported.

I only wish to put you in possession of the above facts, and hope you will select two or three here and there and insert them.

The Kendal Mercury, wise to Gibson's tactics, published the following condemnation on the 9th August;

TO CORRESPONDANTS
Our attention has been directed to a letter in the columns of our local contemporary, signed James Gibson, Ambleside. The aforesaid James Gibson favoured us the previous week, with an epistle, but it was conceived in so ill-natured a spirit, and expressed in so illiterate a manner, that we consigned it to our Balnam Box. Mr James Gibson has, it would appear, got some kind friend, or, it may be, the good natured editor, to touch up his address, and so obtained access to the public as a writer of ridiculous prose, being previously well known as the inditer of very absurd verses. Mr James Gibson must not flatter himself that we are going to engage in a controversy with him; but we will remark by the way, that he might as well have stated what are the assertions he accuses us of making without foundation, and which, he says, are calculated to bring into contempt and disrepute all other boats on the Lake. Mr James Gibson is evidently a very conceited man, and, instead of advertising his boat, has most effectually advertised himself to the public as also a discontented and disappointed personage. One might be tempted to fancy, from the tone of his effusion, that he has been anxious for a birth on board the Lady of the Lake, and had not succeeded in extorting from the proprietors what he deemed an adequate remuneration for his valuable services. But, however that may be, the proprietors had as much right to put their steam yacht on the lake, as he had to commence his passage boat, which no doubt injured the old watermen, who, before that time, had as much as a shilling a mile. We will only add, that, if the statements of Mr James Gibson, in his published letter, are on a par with those contained in the epistle addressed to us, as for instance in regard to Professor Wilson and his hospitality to the steamer, his facts are more imaginative than his poetry.

In 1846 the *'Original Passage Boats on Windermere (Not Steam Boats)'* were advertised with an eight-oared passage boat – presumably the 1844 boat. Twenty passengers would *'go at a speed surpassing that of former years; and fit up in a style which cannot fail to give general satisfaction'*. The boats would be *'manned by civil, intelligent, and experienced boatmen'*. This was their last year in operation and they withdrew from the lake transport scene.

James Gibson Jr, and John Braithwaite of Bowness also rowed passengers for Gibson and White, and Christopher North sometimes steered the packet boats. He owned the *Endeavour*, *Eliza*, *Palafox*, *Roscoe*, *Clyde*, *Jane* (after his wife), *Billy* (after Billy Balmer his boatman) and *Nil Timeo*; the latter was a ten oared Oxford Barge. After his death in 1854, Harriet Martineau described North at the helm of Gibson's boat in an unforgettable tribute;

Not less striking was it to see him in a mood of repose, as he was seen when steering the packet-

boat that used to pass between Bowness and Ambleside, before the steamers were put upon the lake. Sitting motionless, with his hand upon the tiller, in the presence of journey-men and market-women, his eye apparently looking beyond everything into nothing, and his mouth closed above his beard, as if he meant never to speak again; he was quite as impressive and immortal an image as he could have been to the students of his moral philosophy class, or the comrades of his jovial hours, He was known, and with reverence and affection, beside the trout stream and the mountain tarn, and amidst the deep gloom of Elleray, where he could not bring himself to let a sprig be lopped that his wife had loved. Every old boatman and young angler, every hoary shepherd and primitive dame among the hills of the district, knew him and enjoyed his presence. He made others happy by being so intensely happy himself, when his brighter moods were on him; and, when he was mournful, no one desired to be gay. He has gone with his joy and his grief; and the region is so much the darker in a thousand eyes.

The Windermere Steam Yacht Company

The Windermere Steam Yacht Company was formed in 1844 to build a screw steamer to sail between Newby Bridge, Bowness and Ambleside. Shareholders subscribed from the surrounding area, with Kendal and Ulverston being well represented. From the lakeshore came two from Ambleside, one from Troutbeck, and Mr Ullock from Bowness.

There was outcry from conservationists – led by Wordsworth – when these proposals became public. Already opposing plans for a railway from Oxenholme to Ambleside they saw this as a further intrusion. Wordsworth was invited to the launch of the steamer but declined with a short but curt letter. 'Punch' magazine got wind of the opposition and satirically poked fun, creating a protest poem in the style of Wordsworth which was published in Autumn 1844;

BY THE LAUREATE
What Incubus, my goodness! Have we here,
Cumbering the bosom of our lovely Lake?
A steam boat, as I live! – Without mistake! -
Puffing and splashing over Windermere!
What inharmonious shouts assail mine ear?
Shocking poor Echo, that perforce replies -
'Ease Her!' and 'Stop Her!' – frightful and horrid cries,
Mingling with frequent pop of ginger beer.
Hence, ye profane! – To Greenwich or Blackwall,
From London Bridge – go! steam it if ye will,
Ye Cockneys! and of whitebait eat your fill;
But this is not the place for you at all!
I almost think that, if I had my will,
I'd sink your vessel with a cannon ball!

The Company, chaired by Thomas Roper of Newlands,

commissioned a wooden boat from Greenodd boat builder Richard Ashburner. Built on a specially constructed slipway near the Swan Hotel, it was originally planned as a screw steamer but as the vessel would navigate the shallow waters of Bowness Bay and the River Leven, she was built instead as a paddle steamer.

Launch was set for Saturday 31st May 1845 at Newby Bridge; a grand occasion attended by local reporters as well as The Illustrated London News. Mr Fell attended with guests, and took a trip to Blakeholme in two boats before the launch. Crowds gathered from 11 am to witness the historic launch of the first inland public steamer in England and Wales. The Ulverston Brass Band, dressed in scarlet uniforms, kept spectators jovial and when Miss Fell broke a bottle of champagne on the bow, *Lady of the Lake* slid into the water without engines. A rope pulled taught at the right moment to point her upstream, before she was hauled in to the small jetty. Her pennant was placed on board, and then the public inspected the vessel. Invited guests enjoyed a meal at the Swan Hotel, and over fifty carpenters ate in an adjacent room. The day was finally rounded off at around 8 pm.

The Kendal News and Northern Advertiser on Saturday June 14th announced; '*Steam communication on Windermere Lake. The new and elegant steam boat the Lady of the Lake. Lieut. J.T. Lambe, R.M.S. Commander. Intended to sail regularly (Sundays excepted)'*. This was premature as the steamer required both internal fit out and engine fitment, and remained at Newby Bridge. Whilst lying there many people went to view the steamer. One had an accident whilst boarding across a narrow plank; *Mr Pickthall, who is a man of remarkable bulk and stature, fancying that it was giving way beneath him, jumped to the bottom. The water was very shallow, and the effect of the fall, which was half jump, half tumble, was to break one of his legs very badly, a little above the ankle joint. The bone protruded through the skin, and the blood flowed copiously…..*

Mr White, proprietor of the old passage boats, organised a boat to convey Mr Pickthall to Bowness, where the bone was re-set.

The mishap didn't delay fitting-out, and once engines were fitted, *Lady of the Lake* commenced some special excursions in July; the first on Tuesday 22nd was recorded by the Westmorland Gazette in detail.

The proprietors of the new and elegant little steamer, the Lady of the Lake, together with a large party of their friends, spent a delightful day on Lake Windermere on Tuesday last, in celebration of the opening of the enterprise. About eleven o'clock the company proceeded on board the vessel, which was anchored in the beautiful bay of Bowness, the miniature metropolitan harbour of the Queen of Lakes.

The average speed of the trip on Tuesday, was, we believe, not much more than seven miles an hour, but this is by no means the ultimate power of the vessel. A finely proportioned figure head of the Lady of the Lake forms an appropriate emblem of the name of the vessel, and the snowy whiteness of this tutelary image, and the elegant gilded moulding which decorates the vessel, contrast very effectively with the dark hue of the hull, which is painted black. Her engines of twenty horsepower with their oscillating cylinders, worked admirably, and it was the general opinion of the company on board that no steamer could voyage with greater ease and freedom from unpleasant vibration. Her interior fittings up correspond with the beauty of her form; the saloon is especially commodious and tasteful, the prevailing colours being pink and white, to which handsome carpets, mirrors and cushions of crimson velvet harmonise most effectively. The saloon is lighted by a skylight projected from the deck, contrived to admit air as well as light at pleasure, and at each side of the framework are seats for the deck. This arrangement, although convenient enough on larger steamers, narrows the passage too much between the sides of the vessel, and as it appears that the saloon may be sufficiently lighted from the port windows, it is intended to remove the projected frame of the skylight, and so afford a complete and commodious promenade upon the deck. This alteration will perfect the exterior accommodations of the vessel.

At the appointed signal the vessel started from the bay with the union jack and her own streamer, mottoed, Lady of the Lake, floating from her masts, to make the circuit of the northern portion of the lake, and proceeding to Ambleside, soon came alongside the noble woods of Rayrigg, with its wide reach of prospect and deeply indented bay. It is useless to try and particularise the beauties of a voyage where all was beauty. The day might have been selected for the occasion; a fine blue breeze tempered by pervading sunshine, and wooded Winandermere never appeared more to merit its title of Queen of Lakes then when the first steamer broke its transparent waters into foam on Tuesday last.

Proceeding onwards through the broadest part of

The launch of the **Dragonfly**, 18th November 1850.

the lake, Calgarth, navelled in woods, Low Wood Inn and Dove's Nest were successively passed on the right, and on the left Wray Castle, a superb mansion not yet completed, but presenting a fine model of baronial castles of old times. On her return the steamer passed between Belle Isle and her cluster of islets and the western shore of the lake, to the Ferry Inn, after which she rounded again and returned to Bowness Bay, where she cast anchor about one o'clock.

Lunch with toasts was taken on board, and crowds gathered on deck when Mr Fell presented Mr Ashburner with an inscribed silver snuffbox as thanks for building the boat. The box cost 7s and was inscribed *'Presented to Mr Richard Ashburner, by the Windermere Steam Packet Company, as an acknowledgement of the satisfactory manner in which he has fulfilled the contract for building the Lady of the Lake steam yacht. Lake Windermere, July, 1845'.* Lady of the Lake continued to the foot of the lake passing Storrs, Graythwaite and Town Head, whilst the Kendal Cavalry Band, in regimental dress,

Lady of the Lake and **Dragonfly** in Bowness between 1858 and 1865.

Lady of the Lake at Bowness, c1860.

provided music for dancing. Coal was taken at the foot of the lake before returning to Bowness for around 6 pm. So the first complete circuit of the lake by a mechanically powered vessel was accomplished.

Public services started on Thursday 24th July 1845 with Lieutenant Lambe at the helm. Dredging work had to be carried out and posts positioned along the River Leven, marked the safe channel. The vessel slowed down for the fords at Landing How and Fell Foot. A weir was built at Newby Bridge around this time to raise the height of the lake to accommodate her more easily.

The steamer had a mixed reception around the shores of Windermere. Many locals were opposed, *'so annoyed were they that their darling lake should be disturbed by the revolutions of the paddle, or their clear atmosphere contaminated by the smoke of a funnel'.* One Esthwaite resident, upon first glancing the boat belching black smoke, was reported to have said, *'It may come up Cunsey Beck, but it'll nin git under Dubs Bridge – so we can ga hame saef enough'.* Some locals refused to accept parcels brought by the '*Lady*' and even severed ties with friends and acquaintances that had travelled on her. But many tourists travelled as the steamer cut the full around-the-lake journey time from 9¼ hours with Gibson and White, to around 3 hours.

Lady of the Lake soon settled into her daily routine; leaving Newby Bridge at 8.30 am and 2.30 pm, and Waterhead at 10 am and 4 pm, with a service speed of nine miles an hour. Calls were made at the Ferry Inn, Bowness and Low Wood and the steamer would pick up passengers from small boats put out from Town Head, Graythwaite and Belle Grange. Coach connections at Newby Bridge conveyed passengers to Ulverston and Bardsea for the link to Fleetwood. Connections were made at Bowness with a coach that left the Commercial Inn, Kendal at 8.30 am. It returned to Kendal from the Royal Hotel at 5 pm, allowing passengers time to enjoy a full lake cruise.

The return fare from Ambleside to Newby Bridge was

2s, or 3s in the saloon. Fares were reduced to match Gibson and White in an attempt to put them out of business. Gibson and White had an advantage as exclusive through tickets could be purchased to Ulverston, Fleetwood and Lancaster, but it would not take long for the steamer to make its mark.

The Reverend Chas. Mackay, a visitor to the area in 1845, wrote an account of his trip;

On arriving (at Waterhead) we saw the little steam boat, the Lady of the Lake, which has lately been introduced on this quiet mere, ploughing its way towards Bowness, which made us regret that we had not been in time to avail ourselves of its more rapid conveyance. Remembering Mr Wordsworth's printed denunciation of steam and the opposition that this elegant little boat encountered on its first introduction, we were led to make enquiries about it and learned that it was very ill-supported. Tourists, to whom it is a very great convenience, had no prejudice against it, but the very reverse; and by them during the season, it was very well patronised. The inhabitants, however, of Bowness, Lowwood, Ambleside, and generally the gentry of the neighbourhood set their faces against it and would not use it, we were informed, even for the conveyance of a parcel-so annoyed were they that their darling lake should be disturbed by revolution of the paddle, or their dear atmosphere contaminated by the smoke of a funnel. It seemed sheer pride and aristocratic feeling that was at the bottom of the ill-will, for the boatmen, as far as we could learn, did not regard it with any particular jealousy...

On Windermere, the boatmen are gentlemen in comparison with those on Loch Katrine, and seem to harbour no resentment against steam in general, or against the Lady of the Lake in particular – a fact which I was glad to hear, although it impressed still more vividly upon my mind the uncharitable and foolish exclusiveness of the wealthier classes.

By October 1845, *Lady of the Lake* had carried over

5,000 passengers, prompting a continued service for her first winter. This started at Bowness heading for Ambleside at 8.30 am, sailing to Newby Bridge and back to Ambleside, then returning to Bowness to finish at 3.30 pm. However the service soon reverted to seasonal operation.

Her first winter brought a few complaints, one from an incensed man left waiting at Ambleside after the 'Lady' was two hours late towing a coal barge up the lake. The owner of the barge was a minor shareholder, but also their supplier of coals. As the gentleman wrote in his letter to the 'proprietors of the Windermere Steamer'; 'I believe the same individual supplies coals or coke for the steamers consumption, so that it is probable he has got the oyster and you the shell'.

Success prompted an approach to Richard Ashburner in October 1845 to build a slightly larger vessel for the 1846 season. On 28th March the Westmorland Gazette gave a progress update;

The work is rapidly progressing under the able superintendency of Mr Ashburner, of Greenodd. It is expected that she will be launched about Easter. Not withstanding the obstinate, yet ludicrous, opposition that has been got up by many of the gentlemen residing on the banks of the Windermere Lake, against the Windermere Steam Yacht Company, to prevent them from putting their steamers on the lake, their work has proved abortive, which must be gratifying to those persons who appreciate such acts of enterprise as have been shown by the Steam Yacht Company.

Messer's George Forrest & Co of Liverpool provided the engines for the new vessel. Named Lord of the Isles, she was launched at Newby Bridge on Wednesday 29th April. The Kendal Mercury reported on 2nd May; On Wednesday last, at one o'clock, this launch took place on the quay, at Newby Bridge. It being a lovely day, groups of fashionables had assembled themselves together from Kendal, Ulverston and the intermediate neighbourhood, to witness the sight of launching the 'Lord of the Isles'........

.....The yachts were in full uniform-flags flying, pennants with their names, the Ulverston brass band playing at intervals.....

.....Mrs Rawlinson, of Graythwaite Hall, had the honour of christening the 'Lord of the Isles'. A bottle of wine was suspended from the bow of the yacht, by a small rope yarn. The word to strike the blow was given -the bottle was broken, and thrown with precision and force- off the vessel glided in gallant style into the lake.

Lunch for sixty was served on board the Lady of the Lake during a return cruise to Ambleside and food for 100 was provided in the Swan Hotel. The name Lord of the Isles was, in the words of the Kendal Mercury, 'an appropriate name, we think, because the Earl of Lonsdale is the Lord of the Lake and the islands thereon'. The Earl of Lonsdale charged annual rent of £1 for each lake steamer.

The Lord of the Isles was the same length as her sister but four feet wider and weighed three tons more. She had large square windows lining her lower deck and

was heavier built with oversized paddle boxes marked with the star of the company. She was pressed into service alongside her sister enabling more departures during the height of the season; the 'Lady' usually operated the schedule whilst the 'Lord' handled private parties.

Atkinson's coaches left Ulverston at 7 am and 2.30 pm and arrived at Newby Bridge for connections at 8 am and 3.30 pm before continuing to Milnthorpe on the Lancaster & Carlisle Railway for rail connections. The return journey left at 7.30 pm, arriving at Newby Bridge at 9.30 pm.

Parties leaving London at 10 am, Leeds at 12 pm, Liverpool and Manchester at 3 pm, Edinburgh at 5 am, and Carlisle at 3 am, are at Milnthorpe station in time for the Coach, and will have the advantage at Newby Bridge of the first Steamer up the Lake early next morning.

American author Nathanial Hawthorne recorded what he saw at Newby Bridge from his room on a rainy day in July 1855; We are still at Newby Bridge, and nothing has occurred of remarkable interest.....Two days have been rainy, and today there is more rain. We watch all arrivals and other events from our parlour window, — a stage-coach driving up four times in the twenty-four hours, with its forlorn outsiders, all saturated with rain; the steamer, from the head of the lake, landing a crowd of passengers, who stroll up to the hotel, drink a glass of ale, lean over the parapet of the bridge, gaze at the flat stones which pave the bottom of the River, and then hurry back to the steamer again....

Timetables for the 'Lord' and 'Lady' from August 1846 show three full-lake return sailings were provided from Ambleside at 6.45 am, 11 am and 3 pm, reducing to two from October when she left the head of the lake at 7 am and finished at 5.30 pm after an extended break for coaling at Newby Bridge on the second run. As both timetables depict a one-boat service it is assumed that the second vessel would offer extra trips and charters, both boats being employed in full service during the high season.

On 24th August 1846 the FR reached Dalton from Barrow, whence coaches for Newby Bridge started at Dalton instead of Ulverston. The railway reached Ulverston in April 1854 and opened to passengers in June.

The railway arrives from Kendal

On 22nd September 1846 the railway opened from Lancaster to Kendal, connecting by coach from the Kings Arms in Kendal to the piers at Bowness. This operated for a year, as in 1847 the railway from Kendal reached Birthwaite, opening on 21st April.

In 1848 the River Leven was dredged again to allow the steamers to continue to Newby Bridge; an advert dated April was hopeful that the service would be navigating the river by June. The steamer company financed the works with Mr White of the Swan Hotel, as it was to his advantage if the steamers berthed there. When the River Leven was low the steamers would berth at Kellett's Landing (or Harrison's Landing) just north of the present Lakeside pier. Passengers would be ushered into Kellett's Quay House Inn to await the omnibus from the Swan Hotel, although it was not allowed on Kellett's property. The journey to Newby Bridge could be continued by omnibus or rowing boat. An early guide book shows Kellett's Landing as a request stop for the locals, even when the river was navigable.

Advertisements for the same season show a single vessel timetable maintained by the 'Lady' whilst the 'Lord' took special sailings. Whitsuntide saw special sailings with the 'Lord' taking passengers around the lake for just 1s 6d. An extra shilling was charged to use the cabins. The timetable read;

Windermere Steam Yachts
The Windermere Steam Yachts LORD OF THE ISLES and LADY OF THE LAKE, on and after June 1st, 1848, will ply for the season as under; –
TIMES OF DEPARTURE

	1st Trip.	2nd Trip.	3rd Trip.	4th Trip.
From Bowness,	*a.m.*	*p.m.*	*p.m.*	*p.m.*
up the lake......	7 15	11 15	3 15	7 30
From Ambleside,	*a.m.*	*noon*	*p.m.*	*p.m.*
down the lake....	8 0	12 0	4 0	8 15
				To Bowness only.

	a.m.	*p.m.*	*p.m.*
From Bowness, down the lake......	8 45	12 45	4 45
From Newby Bridge, up the lake......	*a.m.* 10 0	*p.m.* 2 0	*p.m.* 6 15

WHTSUNTIDE HOLIDAYS
REDUCED FARES!
On Monday 12th, Tuesday 13th, and Wednesday 14th,
THE WINDERMERE STEAM YACHTS
Will ply constantly on the Lake, leaving each Pier about every hour and a half
The first Boat will leave Bowness at....7 15 a.m.
Newby Bridge at…..............8 15 a.m.
Ambleside at….…....8 0 a.m.
FARES,
For the whole length of the lake and back...1s. 6d.
For half the length …...........1s. 0d.
N.B. – One of the steamers will adhere to the ordinary Trips.
(By Order,)
J.Y. GREENWOOD, Secretary.
June 2nd, 1848.

The 1848 season ended on 18th October.

The following year unseasoned timbers were found in *Lady of the Lake*'s hull. Taken out of service for repair, her tall masts were probably removed at the same time, as they frequently tangled with trees on the River Leven. A temporary slip was built at Ecclerigg Bay probably in the enclave left by the quarrying for stone for Wray

Castle. *Lord of the Isles* also used this slip occasionally.

The Windermere Iron Steamboat Company

With the railway reaching Birthwaite trade for the steamers increased rapidly and the two vessels struggled to cope with demand. Anticipating potential extra custom from rail passengers, a rival Windermere Iron Steamboat Company was formed in 1848. With plans for an iron-hulled boat contracted to McConochie and Claude Engineers of Liverpool, they intended to be ready for the 1849 season, announcing their plans for a new boat in March 1849.

Sections of the boat were brought by rail to Windermere, and taken to Low Wood, where construction started in March. *Firefly* was finally launched by Mrs Claude on 1st August 1849 – a day that didn't go to plan. Launch was timed for 1 pm, but the blacksmith was still working so the boilers couldn't be lit. She was launched in the late afternoon and steam was raised by 9 pm. *Firefly* took a short cruise to the Ferry and back confirming that she was the fastest vessel on the lake by attaining twelve miles an hour. Firefly was also cheaper to operate, consuming half the coal and requiring half the crew. After internal fitment, she started service on a five round-trip timetable Monday to Saturday, starting at 7 am, with two round trips on Sundays; the first public sailings on Windermere on the Sabbath.

The Windermere Iron Steamboat Company soon encountered problems. In September the *Firefly* left passengers stranded by repeatedly taking private charters in the afternoons, ignoring her timetable.

The pheasant shooting season started on Monday 1st October and a humorous reference to the steamers appeared in the Westmorland Gazette on 6th October;

The Windermere Steamers Pheasant Shooting

On Monday, the first day of pheasant shooting, a fine bird had been frightened from the woods about Brathay, and flying over the higher end of the lake, alighted on the water; and the steamers having nothing more interesting to do, went off in pursuit. Away like lightning dashed the Firefly, fleet as an arrow the Lady of the Lake, furious as an earthquake the Lord of the Isles, and the whole making a din equal to ten thousand Etna's in full operation. To particularise the scene would be superfluous. Enough it is, that the object of all this commotion was captured and carried by the omnibus driver to Ambleside in triumph. Does it require license for steamers to hunt pheasants?

For the last month of her 1849 season *Firefly* operated a more relaxed timetable with Thomas Mattix at the helm. Leaving Bowness at 8.30 am she made two full lake trips and one extra return to Ambleside, ending back at Bowness at 6 pm. This season finished on 20th October, while the 'Lord' and 'Lady' continued to the 28th. This first short season was celebrated by laying on free cruises for local school children from Ambleside,

Bowness, Winster, Staveley, Backbarrow and Finsthwaite. Three days cruising ensured every child had a sail.

The 1850 season saw the two companies seeking to undercut and out-perform each other. When the Windermere Iron Steamboat Company altered its timetable on 4th July to match the times of the *Lady of the Lake*, it created bedlam. Touts coaxed potential customers to *their* steamer and posters were plastered everywhere. With simultaneous departures, the scene resembled the racing then common on the Clyde, and the inevitable collision occurred on 15th July. Vessels came into contact whilst trying to obstruct each other, but no serious damage or injuries occurred. Luckily a head on collision was avoided, as the '*Lady*' would not have fared well if the larger heavier iron vessel had ploughed into her wooden hull. The rivalry continued and in the last weeks of the season the '*Lady*' was advertised to sail around the lake for a maximum fare of 6d inside, or 3d outside, including a free bottle of porter. The Iron Steamboat Company replied by making their sailings free. Neither strategy seemed likely to generate profit.

On 6th February 1850 the Windermere Iron Steamboat Company decided that a second vessel should be built ready for May, named *British Queen*. McConochie and Claude again won the commission for a larger *Firefly* – now nearly a hundred feet in length and double-ended to ease navigation of the River Leven, as the *Firefly's* traditional stern necessitated tight manoeuvres at Newby Bridge. In March the Westmorland Gazette reported that McConochie and Claude '*have obtained the order and she is now in hands*'.

Three steamers commenced plying on the lake from Whit Monday 1850, '*but were not so crowded as on former occasions, people preferring the small craft (rowing boats) instead*'.

Burning of the *Lord of the Isles*

After a refit and repaint costing £200 *Lord of the Isles* re-entered service alongside her fleet mate for the summer season, but was gutted by fire while lying at Bowness on the night of 31st July. After concluding her duties that day, she was moored alongside the *Lady of the Lake*, which in turn was tied to the company's works pier. The boats were moored near the present Old England Hotel, not the steamer pier, to keep this clear for the vessels of the rival company.

The Westmorland Gazette from 3rd August 1850 continues the story;

About one on Thursday morning, Oliver Haydock, who has charge of the boats at night, and was sleeping on board the Lady of the Lake, was awoke by the blowing off of the steam from the vessel alongside. Feeling at once that something was wrong, for the fire had been raked out of the furnace and water thrown on, and everything left with the impression that all was safe, he jumped out of bed in great alarm, ran on deck, and found the after part of the Lord of the Isles on fire. He instantly started off to the village, with nothing on but his shirt, to give the alarm, and roused the

inhabitants. Mr Searle, Mr Martin, of the Stags Head, Mr Brownrigg, joiner, and Captain Mattix of the rival steamer, the Firefly, were the first to give assistance, and exerted themselves most strenuously to extinguish the flames. The first operation was to remove the burning Lord from the endangered Lady by cutting the rope which connected them, and drawing the latter to a place of safety. The assistants then mounting upon the Lord of the Isles, kept a constant stream of water upon the interior of the after part, by means of buckets. In this labour the bystanders, with very few exceptions, joined heartily. For some time the fire raged furiously and threatened to set all efforts to extinguish it at defiance. The flames took complete possession of the best cabin and roared out of the windows and cabin entrance nearly as high as the funnel of the vessel, the coal bunkers being one mass of fire in the engine room, and the boilers red hot. The effect of the conflagration flashing upon the bright calm waters of the lake and the foliage of the trees, and lighting up the beautiful bay and the islands with a strange glare was very striking. The fire was visible as far as Ambleside, the lake being illuminated almost from one end to another. After about two hours exertion the fire was got under, but not before the interior of the after-cabin had been completely destroyed, the beams being almost burnt through, and of course every article of furniture and decoration ruined. One of the most active persons in saving the little that was preserved from the after cabin was Mrs Searle, the stewardess, who took a boat from the bay and employed herself in removing all that it was possible to carry to a place of safety. Mr John Robinson, of Oak Bank, near Ambleside the secretary, arrived about five o'clock, and gave the necessary directions for clearing the vessel of the water...... As proof of her soundness of timber, it may be stated that a hasty effort was made to scuttle her, but the wood was so strong that the attempt was abandoned. The weight of water thrown into her to extinguish the fire had almost sunk her, but this having been got out of her, by Thursday night she was again afloat....... As to the origin of the fire we can learn nothing definite. A boy who was on board the Lady of the Lake when the Lord of the Isles came in for the night states he saw what looked like a fire in the vessel alongside and mentioned it to another boy, but no further notice was taken of the circumstance.

The fire-boys of the '*Lord*' and '*Lady*', James Hiley (17) and William Jackson Archer (20) were charged with arson, appearing before Kendal magistrates twice before being taken to Appleby jail for the assizes. On Friday 23rd February 1851 they appeared before Mr Baron Platt. Hiley, serving on the '*Lord*', alerted the Captain that he could smell fire on the last trip of the day. After searching the vessel they found no flames so she was tied up as usual alongside the '*Lady*'. The prosecution alleged that Hiley had made up this fire to '*allay suspicion against himself, and to prepare the Captain for what happened afterwards*'.

Lady of the Lake, Lord of the Isles and **Firefly** seen at Bowness in a very early view from 1850.

Hiley and Archer remained on board until the engine fires were fully out. Oliver Haydock was the night watchman, sleeping on board the '*Lady*' overnight. He headed up to Bowness village for supper, and on returning met Archer disembarking from the '*Lady*' to head home. After a brief conversation it was clear that Hiley was still on board the '*Lord*', so Haydock boarded the '*Lady*' and crossed to the '*Lord*'. Shouting for Hiley there was no reply, but Haydock heard movement as someone disembarked from the '*Lady*', which he assumed was Hiley. Neither of the boys came to help after Haydock raised the alarm, although many local residents did respond; Archer refused to leave his bed after being told about the fire.

When questioned, Hiley denied hearing the calls, then said he had. Archer said they had been smoking in the engine room when Hiley pointed out a red streak in the coal bunker, but this was dismissed as the bunker could not be seen from the engine room. Towards the end of the hearing the magistrate was told the fire must have been set deliberately due to the course it took. A summary of the facts was read out;

All these facts combined, the pretend alarm of fire on the voyage home, the conduct of Archer on board the vessel when the watchman called to him, the refusal of the prisoners to assist in extinguishing it, and the improbability of the story that they saw a fire in the coal bunker… all points to the prisoners as the guilty parties.

In conclusion Baron Platt was '*at a loss to conceive what motive could actuate the prisoner*'. The case was based on suspicion '*of the slightest kind*', and he thought the prisoners would not be '*burning themselves out of situations*'. There was no evidence that the person Mr Haydock had heard on the '*Lady*' was Hiley. The prosecution could carry the case no further and the boys were both acquitted, but they had spent over four months in Appleby jail.

After meeting aboard the '*Lady*' at Newby Bridge on 2nd October 1850, the Windermere Steam Yacht Company decided not to replace the '*Lord*'. They had made sufficient profit to secure a dividend of 7% for shareholders and fares were set for the 1851 season at a maximum of 3d or 6d for outside or inside accommodation. The burnt out hull of the *Lord of the Isles* remained in Bowness for some time, being photographed by JWG Gutch in July 1855, in remarkably good condition with her paddle wheels and boxes still intact. A later photograph – from around 1860 – shows the *Lady of the Lake* alongside the pier and the burnt vessel on its side against the shore. This time the paddle boxes and wheels are gone, but she seems to be used as a workshop or store, as timber is stacked on the deck.

Launch of a new steamer

Work on the new steamer continued at Low Wood, but was suspended when the *Firefly*, skippered by Captain Mattix, damaged a hull plate near Low Wood, and was run ashore. Once repaired, work on the new steamer recommenced. The short timescale for the build was unachievable and the new iron steamboat, now named *Dragonfly*, was launched nearly six months late on Monday 18th November by the wife of the company secretary, Mrs Rigg. The launch was from Low Wood, complete with engines and steam already up. Once afloat she made a special cruise around Low Wood Bay. On 31st December *Dragonfly*, with a capacity for 250 passengers, made a special trip to the Newby Bridge steeplechases, before being officially handed over to her new owners in April 1851.

The Windermere Iron Steamboat Company issued no timetables for the 1851 season, with customers referred to handbills issued for the '*Lady*', and told that their steamers would apply also. Thus the rivals were again operating at the same times; leaving Bowness at 7.30 am and doing three full circuits around the lake back to Bowness, before a final return to Ambleside, finishing at Bowness at 8.50 pm. Whenever the faster iron boats passed the '*Lady*' the band would play 'The Girl I Left Behind' to antagonise passengers on the slower vessel.

The Ulverston Advertiser noticed the rivalry; '*three steamers are now plying daily, and strong opposition prevails among these splendid rivals*'. In a later edition it described the confusion at Bowness; *Queer scenes take place sometimes at the different stations but especially at Bowness, in the scramble for passengers. Stewards, skippers and busmen display amazing activity, while 'This way for Ambleside'; 'This way for Newby Bridge' salutes the ears of the bystanders. Then amid the roar of steam and smoke, the vessels on their trips begin to ruffle the pellucid water. They boil and wheel and foam and thunder through.*

The Windermere Iron Steamboat Company employed a man on the Ulverston side of the River Leven at Newby Bridge to ring a bell continuously to attract passengers. If levels were low, and landing was made at Kellett's Landing they operated free trips by rowing boat along the River Leven.

An old stunt was reported in the Lancaster Gazette in early June; *On Whit-Monday and Tuesday the Lady of the Lake steamer carried her passengers for 6d and 3d, the whole length of the lake and back. The Firefly's fare was 1s 6d or 1s. The Lady was much thronged. The Firefly company intend giving the public a treat on the same scale of charges, and each to have a glass of porter in the bargain. Several half-barrels of double XX have been purchased separately for the occasion. It puts us in mind of the opposition coaching which took place prior to the railways commencing. The public reap the benefit while the shareholders receive very small return for their outlay. As we said last year- 'Too many cooks spoil the broth'.*

An advert from October 1852 shows both the *Firefly* and *Dragonfly* based at Bowness, making two trips around the lake in opposite directions, giving four departures from both Ambleside and Newby Bridge. They started at Bowness at 8.30 am or 8.45 am and finished there at 7.30 pm.

The 1853 summer timetable offered six sailings from

Newby Bridge each day, and seven from Ambleside; the boats started at Bowness at 7 am (*Firefly*) or 8 am (*Dragonfly*) and finished at 7.30 pm or 9 pm respectively. Omnibuses from the Royal and Crown Hotels met trains at Windermere and connected with steamers at Bowness; at Waterhead coaches for the Salutation, Commercial and White Lion hotels met the boats, as well as an omnibus for Brown's Hotel in Grasmere. This became the pattern for subsequent years, with only slight alterations.

1853 saw one of the companies fined £2,500 for carrying a large quantity of gunpowder destined for the African coast. The fine was 2s per pound of powder but it is not recorded which company received the fine.

A trip around the lake in the early 1850s

Harriet Martineau's Guide to Windermere published in 1853 gives a good description of a tour around the lake using the steamers;

The next thing to do is to take a survey of the whole lake by a steamboat trip. During the summer two steamers make six trips each; so that the stranger can choose his own hour, and go down or up first, as he pleases. In accordance with the rule of lake approach, we should recommend his going down first. He embarks at the pier at Bowness, and is carried straight across to the Ferry, where the boats touch. Then the course is southwards, with the lake narrowing, and the hills sinking till the scenery becomes merely pretty. The water is very shallow towards the foot, and the practicable channel is marked out by posts. The best work that the whole neighbourhood could undertake would be the deepening of the lake at this part, and of the river which carries off the overflow……..

……..The Swan Inn at Newby Bridge is exceedingly comfortable. Now the stranger calls for lunch or tea, during the stopping of the steamer; and then he is

off again, up the lake. After the Ferry and Bowness, the next call is at Lowwood Inn, where there are sure to be passengers landing or embarking. Between Bowness and Lowwood Inn, Rayrigg has been seen, beside the little bay; and then Ecclerigg, with its overshadowing trees, and pretty pier. It is inhabited by Richard Luther Watson, Esq., nephew of the late Bishop of Llandaff. Just above Lowwood, high up on the wooded side of Wansfell, will be seen Dove Nest, once the abode of Mrs Hemans, when its appearance was more primitive and less pretty than it is now,- improved as it has been by its present resident, her then young friend, the Rev. Robert Percival Graves. Next comes Wansfell Holme, inhabited by the Rev. James J Hornby. This is another choice situation. On the opposite shore is Wray Castle, erected by James Dawson Esq.,- a most defensible-looking place for so peaceful a region; but an enviable residence, both from its interior beauty and the views it commands. Just above it, Pull Wyke Bay, where lily of the valley is found, runs far into the land; and overlooking it is seen Pull Cottage, the residence of Major Rogers. Next, the sweet, tranquil Brathay valley opens, with Mr Redmayne's mansion of Brathay Hall, on a green slope above the lake; and just behind, on a wooded knoll in the gorge of the valley, the little church, called Brathay Chapel, built by Mr Redmayne.

The steamer sweeps round to the piers at Waterhead, where there is a cluster of dwellings, the most imposing of which is the large grey stone house called Wanlas Howe, the property of Alexander C. Benchley, Esq. Omnibuses are waiting here, from Ambleside and Grasmere – the one distant one mile; and the other, between five and six. Our tourist, will, however, complete the circuit of the lake, by returning to Bowness.

She goes on to warn anyone intent of taking a boat out on the lake alone; *There are plenty of boats to be*

Dragonfly loading at Ambleside, c1880, with David MacIver's **Wagtail** at a mooring. Note the many horses waiting at the head of the pier.

had at Waterhead and Bowness, and watermen who are practiced and skilful. The stranger should be warned, however, against two dangers which it is rash to encounter. Nothing should induce him to sail on Windermere, or on any lake surrounded by mountains. There is no calculating on, or accounting for, the gusts that come down between he hills; and no skill or practice obtained by boating on rivers or the waters of a flat country are any sure protection here. And nothing should induce him to go out in one of the little skiffs which are too easily attainable here, and too tempting, from the ease of rowing them. The surface may become rough at any minute, and those skiffs are unsafe in all water but the calmest. The long lists of deaths occasioned this way,- deaths both of residents and strangers,- should have put an end to these light skiffs, long ago. The larger boats are safe enough, and most skilfully managed by their rowers; and the stranger can enjoy no better treat than gliding along, for hours of the summer day, peeping into the coves and bays, coasting the islands, and lying cool in the shadows of the woods.

A new slipway – the 'Lady Slip' – was built on the south side of Cockshott Point for the *Lady of the Lake* in the early 1850s. It had limited use, but proved invaluable in 1854 when the *Lady of the Lake* was re-planked by Ulverston ship builders E. J. Shollick, making her *'greatly improved in speed and beautified in appearance'*. *Lady of the Lake* was re-launched on Tuesday 23rd May *'in the presence of a considerable number of spectators, who seemed to enjoy the sight of their favourite old boat again floating on the lake in serviceable condition'*. The Windermere Iron Steamboat Company's steamers were also overhauled prior to the season.

Some spares for the *Lady of the Lake* disappeared from the slip at Bowness in May, and a reward of £10 was offered for their return. On 11th September they were spotted on the Bowness Bay lakebed and retrieved, but foul play was suspected. Other spares for the *'Lady'* failed to arrive, or arrived late; it was suspected but never proved that the Iron Steamboat Company was in league with the Kendal and Windermere Railway, purposely 'losing' parcels intended for the wooden steamer.

Local adverts saw the two companies vying for trade, but in October 1854 a letter to the Westmorland Gazette did the Iron Steam Boat Company few favours. An anonymous writer boarded the *Firefly* at Bowness at 8.30 am travelling to Ambleside for breakfast before getting the 11.30 am coach to Keswick. After conversation with the mate he was persuaded to leave Bowness on the *Firefly* at 10.30 am for Newby Bridge before reaching Ambleside in time for the 3 pm coach to Keswick. However the traveller discovered that the coach had been discontinued three weeks before, *'and as this mate of the Fire Fly must necessarily be well acquainted with this, as he will be asked daily for similar information, I can arrive at no other conclusion than he purposefully deceived me, and caused me*

considerable inconvenience, for the sake of taking 2s. 6d. instead of a one shilling fare from me; and I feel certain his employers would not so instruct their servants to mislead the public'.

The Declaration of Peace for the Crimean War in March 1856 was cause for celebration, and Mr Duking Astley, a director of the Iron Steam Boat Company, arranged a grand display with fireworks and a bonfire. The steamers came out of winter hibernation to support the event and were said to have done *'good business'*.

Competition was wasteful, and it was evident that co-operation would benefit all involved. Sailing bills for April 1856 were undersigned with *'The Windermere Iron Steam Yachts'*, and on 6th May both companies issued special timetables for Whit week, one for the *Lady of the Lake* and one for the *Dragonfly*, showing complementary services. Both started in Bowness and did three full tours of the lake. The *'Lady'* heading first to Newby Bridge at 7.30 am finishing at 8 pm, whilst the *Dragonfly* left for Ambleside at 8 am and finished at 8 pm. Both boats charged the same fare of 1s for a full lake tour.

From the 15th May, an advert signed *'By Order of the Directors of the Windermere Steam Yacht Company and Iron Steam Boat Company'* stated that the companies were working in co-operation. This was clearly advantageous to lake users as three steamers could offer a comprehensive service, instead of following each other around the lake.

A grand sailing regatta was held on Thursday 10th July 1856 starting from the Ferry Inn. The *Dragonfly* left Bowness at 9 pm to see the end of the sailing race, and did not arrive back until after fireworks finished at 1 am. Great credit was given to the crew of the steamer for their *'endeavours for the safety of their passengers in the midnight darkness'.*

Firefly struck the bottom of the lake near Storrs Hall when operating the 3 pm sailing from Newby Bridge in July 1857 on the day of the Windermere regatta. The funnel fell forward onto the badly damaged bow section due to the force of the impact, but luckily no one was injured. *Firefly* limped to the pier at the Ferry Inn where passengers landed to continue their journey on another steamer. The incident was covered in the Westmorland Gazette on the 18th July; *as it* (Firefly) *approached the shallows a little way below the ferry, the man at the helm was engaged in conversation by several of the passengers about the regatta and that he suddenly lost sight of a buoy which marks a rock called Bull Head, and as suddenly struck upon it, when by the sudden concussion the chimney top was thrown down upon the deck, as well as several of the passengers, who created great commotion by their cries to the boats which were out in great numbers and not too far distant; however the boat never stopped and the man very coolly, and with no little nerve, steered right forward to the Ferry….*

Once the *Firefly* had transferred her passengers she was beached at Harrowslack Farm as she was taking in water to the forward cabin. After temporary repairs she was removed for more substantial work to be done.

The Windermere United Steam Yacht Company

In April 1858 the amalgamation became official with the creation of The Windermere United Steam Yacht Company. The directors comprised John Hudson and J. Rawlinson from the Windermere Steam Yacht Company and E Garnett, James Birkett and Robert Pickthall representing the Windermere Iron Steam Boat Company.

Their first meeting on 5th May 1858 included an agenda item to consider the re-introduction of winter sailings, operating six days a week. The summer timetables showed a two-boat service, operating seven days a week, using the *Firefly* and the *Dragonfly*. Both were based at Bowness with *Dragonfly* starting at 8.30 am, doing three trips around the lake heading first to Waterhead and finishing at Bowness at 6.30 pm. The *Firefly* headed to Newby Bridge at 7.30 am before doing four return trips from Bowness to Waterhead, two of which were extended to the Ferry Inn. The *Lady of the Lake* covered charters, overhaul periods and breakdowns, as well as providing extra services.

Two separate timetables were issued for the 1859 season, one for *Lady of the Lake* the other for *Firefly* and *Dragonfly*. Surviving timetables for *Lady of the Lake* are from the peak season, implying that she was used to complement the other steamers. A one-boat service was timetabled for May and June, with literature showing *Lady of the Lake* sailing alone between May 30th and June 11th. This allowed *Firefly* and *Dragonfly* to be prepared for the two-boat service.

The winter sailings were unsuccessful and a notice in the Lancaster Gazette stated that steamers would cease to ply on 29th October 1859, with no winter sailings offered that year or the next, when sailings ceased on 20th October. A service operated at short notice for winter 1861-62 but regular winter services were not re-introduced until the late 1860s. Vessels remained at the calmer waters of Newby Bridge during the off-season, and were brought to Bowness in March for painting and repairs before starting the season.

In December 1860 the company was successfully sued by an Ambleside tailor Mr John Love, for loss of time and expense incurred by a refusal to take him on-board at Waterhead for Bowness during the previous summer season. Running late, the master had decided not to pick up the only passenger waiting on the pier. Mr Love was awarded 7s.

May 1861 saw *Lady of the Lake* grounded near Belle Grange after springing a leak. She left a busy Bowness at 12.15 pm for Ambleside with a (roughly!) estimated 200 – 400 passengers on board, far more than legally allowed. As the '*Lady*' turned leaving Bowness, she leaned over from side to side and had barely gone a mile before water entered the cabin. Passengers rushed to the upper decks and panicked with shouts of '*We're sinking*' being discernible from the screaming. The Captain ran the '*Lady*' ashore just south of Belle Grange on the western shore, making the confusion worse with many passengers injuring themselves by jumping into the water to escape the stricken vessel. The passengers

remained on the shore until rescued by the steamer returning from Ambleside, summoned by repeated blowing of the ship's steam whistle. With engines submerged and fire doused, a great volume of steam was let off, making a plume to be seen from afar. Once repaired she was hastily returned to service.

The Windermere United Steam Yacht Company contemplated selling the '*Lady*' in 1863, but kept her going for at least another season. She was probably withdrawn at the end of 1865 when a new vessel was ordered for the following season.

Another accident occurred in 1864 when Mr G.A. Aufrere of the Windermere Sailing Club brought action against the company after a steamer sank his yacht, moored in Bowness Bay.

The two-boat service remained similar for a few years, but the steamers were now out-dated despite their young age. Ship design evolved rapidly from the 1840s driven by intense competition between shipbuilders and between steamer companies. Engine design evolved with steeple engines being replaced by oscillating engines, with increasing numbers of cylinders. A boat of the 1840s could be out of date by the 1860s. Welsh anthracite coal was used in the 1860s to prolong the life of machinery in the vessels, improve performance and reduce smut emitting from the funnels.

Winter sailings were still not operational in 1864. In October a letter to the Westmorland Gazette claimed a service would be viable if it connected with trains and coaches;

Peter Allen, at Lindale, has for some years run an omnibus or other conveyance between Grange and Newby Bridge all the year round, and has made it pay...........Will the gentlemen of the Windermere Steam Navigation Company meet the requirements of the people?

The FR moves in

The Windermere United Steam Boat Company had a very successful 1865 season. Extensive reserve funds, which had a 12.5% dividend, were distributed amongst the shareholders and a new vessel was ordered from the Lune Iron Shipbuilding Company of Lancaster. Designed by Liverpool naval architect Douglas Hebson of the Inman Steam Company, sections of her iron hull were transported '*by land carriage*' to Newby Bridge for assembly on the slip above the Swan Hotel. She was the final vessel to be built there, and the last paddle steamer to be built for public use on the lake.

Rothay was launched without a funnel or engines on Wednesday 6th June 1866. Many of the company directors attended, departing from Bowness on a service steamer at 12.20 pm and arriving at Newby Bridge at 1.00 pm. Sunny weather encouraged a large crowd to gather, '*under plentiful supply of flags, which contrasted prettily with the well wooded-hills around*'. The Lancaster Gazette carried the story of the launch on 9th June; *On Wednesday afternoon a new steamer, belonging to the Windermere United Steam Yacht Company (Limited), was launched at Newby Bridge. It is called 'The Rothay'........ All being prepared, the wedges were knocked away, and as the steamer glided beautifully into the lake, amid the reiterated cheers of the assemblage, the interesting ceremony of naming the new craft was performed by Miss Crewdson, daughter of G. B. Crewdson, esq., of the Wood, Windermere, who wished Success to the Rothay.*

As the boat slid down the cradle at about 1.30 pm, the company's band played 'Rule Britannia' and 'God Save the Queen' from the vessel. The launch was celebrated with a meal for over fifty guests at the Swan Hotel, with appropriate speeches and toasts being given. The Reverend E Townley offered *'Success to the Rothay'* and then went on to say *'Those individuals who came from the murky towns of South Lancashire would be charmed with the scenery of the district'*. The guests boarded the *Rothay* and were towed to Bowness by Major Ridehalgh's yacht *Fairy Queen* in around fifty minutes. After fitting of engines she commenced her passenger service in August.

Rothay was 105 feet long with a beam of fifteen feet, and for the first time offered both first and second class cabins. Each about sixteen feet in length, the best had seats of polished East India Teak covered in velvet cushions, whilst the second class also had teak, which was extensively used in the deck fittings. She had a central wheel, and was steerable from both ends, being equipped with rudders at each extremity to aid navigation of the River Leven. To aid visibility and reduce windage, the decks were lowered slightly at either end or, as the Westmorland Gazette put it, *'There are two bows which are sterns, and two sterns that are bows'*.

There was talk of sister vessels being ordered from the same builder – the *Brathay* to be followed by a *Leven* and a *Troutbeck* but circumstances were to

Rothay at Bowness with **Esperance** behind in the bay, c1885.

conspire against this. Timetables from September 1866 still show a two-boat service despite the arrival of the *Rothay*, with *Firefly*'s sailings marked, as in previous years, with a star. However, it is probable that the timetables had been printed before the *Rothay*'s launch.

With no winter sailings in 1866, a letter to the Kendal Mercury in September complained bitterly about the lack of a service, and insisted that the new iron steamer was well fitted out for winter sailings. These were eventually re-instated before 1870, when the Westmorland Gazette reported that a steamer had become stuck in ice.

As aids to navigation during the short days, large light buoys lit by paraffin were positioned at two points around the lake – Hartley Wife in Bowness Bay, and the Mid-Water Shallows between the Nab Ferry and Storrs Hall. Captains must have been skilled as there would only have been limited light lining the shore. Evening navigation, especially during the winter months must have been challenging.

A disturbing event took place to the *Dragonfly* on Bank Holiday Monday 1867, with parallels to the *Lady of the Lake* incident of 1861. The vessel was overcrowded with 400 passengers aboard (her passenger limit was 250), and was grounded after water entered the cabin windows. Passengers were transferred to the *Rothay*, and the stricken vessel was towed to deeper water to right her before being taken for repairs. Timetables again made for interesting reading; one showed a two-boat service with *Firefly* sailings starred. The other vessel was presumably the *Rothay*, as separate timetables were released in May for sailings of the *Dragonfly*.

The band of the Windermere United Steam Yacht Company was rarely mentioned in the press, but on

Saturday 31st August 1867 they played a concert at the Grand Bazaar building in Bowness, which was a huge success with *'most of the wealthy families of the neighbourhood represented'*. Over the years there were a number of 'Steamer Bands', the best remembered being the 'Bijou Band' and 'Bateson's Orchestral Band'. As well as playing on the vessels, concerts were held at lake-side hotels and at local events.

A Railway to Lakeside

The FR had been expanding its network from its hub in Barrow in Furness and in 1866 obtained an Act of Parliament to extend a line from Greenodd to the field where the *Rothay* had been launched at Newby Bridge (not the present day halt). The Act included permission to build a new pier, and to take shares in the steamboat company. Construction proceeded quickly, but before completion the Directors decided to extend a further mile to near Kellett's Quay House Inn. The route through Newby Bridge was realigned behind the hotel, missing the steamer quay. The FR perhaps already planned to take over the lake steamers and introduce larger vessels, but a major restricting factor was the ability to navigate the shallow and narrow waters of the River Leven. More powerful, deeper-draughted, screw vessels could be accommodated further up the lake, so a new terminus was built incorporating a steamer berth. It was built by William Gradwell of Barrow.

The pier was 633 feet long, capable of handling all three steamers if the need arose. There were three platforms, sidings capable of storing excursion trains and an engine shed complemented by a 46-foot turntable. Running along the front of the pier was a narrow gauge track to assist fuelling of the steamers. Coal was stored near the front of the station and pushed in hand propelled trolleys along the track to the waiting steamer. Swill baskets were used to transfer coal to the vessel.

The new station incorporated substantial passenger facilities, leading to some shareholders questioning the scale of investment and the opulence of the structure. The cost for the complex was £4,461, but extra income was gained by charging 1s for each passenger boarding a non-company vessel.

Offices were provided at the north of the station, and a two-storey veranda covered the lake-side frontage, with restaurant and refreshment room facilities at the upper level. The building was constructed of *'patent white bricks'* supplied from Leeds, with horizontal lines of vitrified purple-black stretchers, and red brick and sandstone quoits. A light shone from a tower in the station building to assist steamers approaching in the dark.

The veranda restaurant was publicised as *'commanding magnificent views of Lake Windermere'*. Spiers and Ponds of London, who already managed the Furness Abbey Hotel and other catering services for the FR, provided catering. By 1906 a fifty-foot extension was provided at the northern end. Diners could enjoy musical accompaniment from Bateson's Orchestral Band during lunch and tea on summer weekdays. Bateson's were contracted by the FR between 1859 and 1915, when war intervened; they also played on *Britannia* and the cross-bay steamers.

The complex included a large slipway capable of pulling steamers out of the water. During final preparations for opening, a new screw steamer was assembled on the slip, having arrived in kit form by rail from the Clyde. Ordered by the Windermere United Steam Yacht Company, and no doubt influenced by the FR, the *Swan* (I) was designed by Douglas Hebson. This set the standard for the next three passenger steamers.

Swan (I) was a twin-screw iron steamer built on the Clyde by T. B. Seath & Co of Rutherglen for £4,000. Her length was 147 feet and she was seventeen feet wide with a draught of just over three feet. Weighing in at 120 tons she could carry 485 passengers. Her two twin cylinder steam engines developed twenty horsepower each and the local papers described the vessel as a *'gondola'*, so different was she to previous company vessels. A defining feature was a large carved swan on the bow. An early master of the *Swan* (I) was Mr Thomas Metcalfe Thompson who relocated to Pooley Bridge in the 1870s to become master of the *Enterprise* on Ullswater.

Below: **Esperance** at her dedicated berth at the Ferry Hotel. This is the landing now used by the Cross Lakes Shuttle. Rowing boats were available to hire here until the mid-1960s.

Bottom: Looking north from the Ferry Hotel, over **Esperance**, through the islands to Wansfell. **Esperance** ran an hourly service to Bowness from the hotel between 1891 and 1914.

Near the Ferry   Windermere

She was scheduled for launch on 5th June at 2.30 pm. Over 2,000 people gathered at Kellett's Steamer Hotel – renamed to reflect where steamers now berthed – whilst Mrs Ramsden did the honours. The Barrow Herald recorded the launch; *The hammers of the workmen displaced the stays and a flutter of excitement ran through the crowd. She stirred not, however, and almost breathless silence prevailed for a few moments whilst a little pressure was brought to bear upon the bows, upon which she began, almost imperceptibly at first, but every instant increasing momentum, to glide towards the water amidst the hearty cheers of all present, the firing of artillery and the strains of 'Rule Britannia' from the band. Just as she began to move the Mayoress broke the bottle on her bow…..*

Colonel Ridehalgh celebrated by firing a salute from his steam yacht *Fairy Queen*, before towing the *Swan* (I) to Lakeside pier, where invited guests

boarded to admire the sumptuous fittings and enjoy lunch in the saloon. Fitting out took a month and a trial trip reached Storrs Hall before returning to Lakeside. Then *Swan* (I) took a private party on a cruise to Waterhead before entering service in July under the command of Captain Thompson as the flagship of the fleet, which otherwise consisted of *Firefly*, *Dragonfly* and *Rothay*. It was reputed that she could travel at eighteen miles per hour, considerably faster than the older steamers.

Summer Sunday sailings, which had operated since the launch of the *Firefly*, were withdrawn in 1869 under pressure from the Bowness Local Board. In the same year the *Esperance* was launched for Mr Henry Schneider of Belsfield, Bowness. Possibly the first twin-screw vessel in the world, she was certainly the first on Lloyds Yacht Register. Although not then a public vessel, and never owned by the FR, she would later come into public use.

S.Y. "SWAN" ARRIVING AT AMBLESIDE PIER

WINDERMERE STEAM YACHT "SWAN"

By now the FR was the majority shareholder in the Windermere United Steam Yacht Company after purchasing £10,000 worth of shares. In February 1871 it was agreed that the FR buy out the whole concern, provided a perpetual dividend of 10% was paid. This was confirmed by an 1872 Act of Parliament *'for authorizing the FR Company to provide and use Steam and other Vessels on Windermere Lake and Coniston Lake; and for other Purposes'*. This brought the Windermere steamers into railway ownership for the next century.

Seaths next provided the company with a cargo steamer in 1871. She was transported in sections to Lakeside for assembly and launch at a final cost of £1,400. Named the *Raven* she was designed to supply the lakeshore settlements. The Company's only single screw steamer on Windermere was launched without ceremony. A barge steered with a 'rib tickler' tiller at the stern, her engine was provided with steam from a deck-mounted donkey boiler and she had a steam-operated crane to aid loading and unloading cargo. She was seventy-one feet long and a touch under fifteen feet wide with a draught of four feet. Crew comfort was not a priority; the stokehold was so cramped that the fireman could not straighten his back, and the engineer and skipper stood on the open deck. During tight turns two men were needed to move her heavy tiller.

Raven sailed from Lakeside, berthing at the northern end of the pier, where the waterbuses land today. Her year-round timetable saw Mondays, Wednesdays and Fridays spent loading very varied cargo; timber for boat builders of Bowness, animal feeds for lake-side farmsteads, coal, lime, salt, beer barrels along with heavy goods and mail were carried up the lake, as well as general cargo for railway warehouses at Bowness and Ambleside. Saltpetre and sulphur were carried for the Elterwater gunpowder works on Langdale Beck.

Tuesdays, Thursdays and Saturdays were delivery days; *Raven* would slowly head up the lake calling at the small piers including Storrs and High Cunsey, where cargo would unload for Hawkshead to avoid the steep hill of Briars Brow. Prickly Borage – a non-native blue flower – grew here having been introduced from south Lancashire in coal sacks delivered by the steamer. *Raven* called at the Ferry to discharge cargo including sacks of flour, coal, beer and other commodities, using a dedicated cargo berth in Mitchell Wyke, around the back of the hotel. At Bowness goods were discharged into the Company's 1881 warehouse – cargo previously being left on the wharf in the open. The facilities were only for railway cargoes, other boats discharged goods at the public wharf south of the steamer pier. Goods landed here had to be removed within 48 hours.

Raven would next discharge goods at Low Wood, and saltpetre for the gunpowder works was unloaded at Pull Wyke; the sulphur was kept separately at Waterhead. Goods for Ambleside, Grasmere and Langdale were stored in the warehouse at Waterhead pier for collection. On her return, Raven occasionally

carried gunpowder, as well as general cargo for onward shipping throughout the rail network. By the 1920s her trips had been reduced to one a week as road transport became more economical, and she was taken out of service at the end of 1922.

Raven was also used as an icebreaker; she would depart shortly before the passenger vessel, clearing a path as she went. Another use was as a tug – in August 1876 she towed the private steam launch *Wyvern* to Lakeside where it was planned to remove her to Barrow.

Not long after the launch of the *Raven*, the Curwen family, owners of the pier at the Ferry Inn, prohibited passenger steamer calls. Geoffrey Dixon, lessee of the steam ferry crossing to Ferry Nab, thought the steamer company was running in opposition to Bowness from the Ferry Inn and taking his trade. Calls were resumed in May 1872 and the steamers continued to call, but the matter ended up in the courts.

August 1877 was a busy time on the lake which saw the *Dragonfly* involved in a tragic incident. A party of six men from Huddersfield hired a rowing boat and were off Belle Grange when the steamer passed creating a considerable swell. The men were unfamiliar with boats and the wake created alarm, causing them to capsize. All six drowned despite the efforts of Stephen Carr who rushed to their aid whilst rowing a party around the lake.

A year later on 5th December 1878 the *Firefly* was involved in an accident whilst heading from Lakeside to Bowness. A man named Tomlinson was rowing from Bowness to Cunsey around 4.50 pm and was hit by the steamer just north of the Ferry Hotel. It's unlikely either boat would have been displaying lights, and Mr Tomlinson became entangled in the paddle wheels and was killed instantly.

Railway companies were now offering reduced fares, especially at fair weekends and holidays, leading to a big increase in passenger numbers. Much to the disdain of the wealthy, working class families could afford day trips

Swan (I) coming alongside at Bowness in the 1890s.

Raven in October 1979 near the Steamboat Museum. (George Woods)

Raven after restoration by the Windermere Steamboat Museum.

to the Lake District. Special rail excursions were laid on, and by the 1870s working class accommodation began to appear in Bowness. What had once been the exclusive playground of the rich became more accessible to all.

By 1879, *Firefly* and *Dragonfly* were in need of replacement as the Lakes Chronicle's edition of 24th May illustarted;

On Thursday morning, through an accident to a portion of the mechanism of the engine, the steamer timed to start for Ambleside (from Bowness) at 7-45 did not go, and as it was doubtful whether she would be competent to make the journey to Lakeside passengers were not booked for the first journey south. She, however, succeeded in paddling slowly down to Lakeside where she was anchored, and her place taken by the 'Rothay,' gay as new paint could make her, and on entering Bowness Bay……..she seemed almost to glide proudly up to the pier amid the strains of her old friends of the steamer band; and being on her deck was a pleasant change from the bumping and thumping and jumping of the old 'Firefly' and 'Dragonfly' which have been plying during the past long and severe winter. But we hope we have seen the last of the two flies, for we understand one, if not both, of the two new screw steamers, which

are to be named 'Teal' and 'Signet,' were to be launched at Barrow during the high tides of yesterday and to-day (Friday), and that they will be ready to ply on the lake on Whit-Monday.

The Barrow Shipbuilding Company built these larger steamers for £3,500 each, the first wholly owned railway vessels to ply on Windermere and the first steel vessels for the company. Each was a hundred feet long and could carry 336 passengers; they had first and second-class saloons and carvings on their bows of the birds after which they were named, respectively *Cygnet* and *Teal* (I). *Cygnet* was launched on 22nd May and *Teal* (I) followed on 5th June. The railway was singled under bridges to improve clearance and carry the vessels from Barrow to Lakeside. They were transported in near complete condition, and launched in quick succession by Mrs Wadham, wife of an FR director. One advanced feature was an engine control system direct from the deck; alongside the steering wheel were reversing levers and stop valves (also fitted to *Swan* (I) and *Tern* for a time), which led the way for more sophisticated bridge controls in future vessels.

Firefly was quickly broken up but *Dragonfly* may have been retained as a spare vessel. Photographs by Henry Herbert and Frances Frith show her at Waterhead and Bowness in 1885, consistent with Herbert's move to Windermere in the 1880s, so evidently *Dragonfly* lasted until at least then.

On 24th June 1879, Colonel Ridehalgh of Fell Foot launched his private steam yacht *Britannia,* assembled by T.B. Seath & Co at Lakeside for £12,000. Launched in quick succession to the *Cygnet* and *Teal* (I) she also was delivered in a near complete state by rail. Despite being a private steamer she could carry 122 passengers, and was 102 feet long, with a raked copper funnel. She was lit by gas and internally heated using steam, and in 1887 fired a twenty-one gun salute to celebrate Queen Victoria's jubilee while moored in Bowness Bay. She eventually came into railway ownership in 1908.

The winter of 1879-80 was so bad that ice affected the schedules, and in January steamer sailings were suspended as the lake froze. Bad weather struck again in September 1888 when *Swan* (I) ran aground in foggy conditions on Ramp Holme island near the ferry crossing, while on her way to Lakeside. She was not significantly damaged and sounded her whistle to summon assistance. The Ferry Hotel sent out rowing boats and passengers were put up for the night in the hotel. The next morning *Swan* (I) was re-floated and the passengers continued their journey to Lakeside, on which steamer is not recorded. The master of *Swan* (I) was criticised in the Westmorland Gazette the following week for sailing when the *Teal* (I) stayed at Bowness.

In 1887 Henry Schneider died, and his vessel *Esperance* was laid up for sale just south of Cockshott Point, possibly on the old slip used by *Lady of the Lake.* She was acquired in 1891 by Bruce Logan of the Ferry Hotel, and placed on an hourly run to Bowness at a fare of 2d. In her first year she had a minor mishap recorded in the local newspaper;

Three persons had a narrow escape from being

Left: **Teal** (I) leaving Bowness for the Ferry, Storrs and Lakeside, viewed from the stern of the **Swan** (I).

Middle: **Teal** (I) leaving Lakeside.

Bottom left: **Cygnet** or **Teal** (I) closing on the Ferry Hotel pier. The lake's eastern shore is still lacking development in this view from the 1890s.

Bottom right: **Tern** is seen leaving Lakeside, whilst the **Swan** (I) strains at her ropes. Both are photographed from the bow of the **Teal** (I).

Lakeside Station and Boat Landing, Windermere, E.L.D.

Cygnet leaving Lakeside. On the far shore Colonel Ridehalgh's Fell Foot residence can be seen. Also the front façade of the Lakeside Station complex is show to advantage here.

drowned in Lake Windermere on Monday evening. The small screw steamer Esperance was plying frequently between Bowness Bay and the Ferry. A small pleasure boat had been engaged by two gentlemen and a lady, and on turning a corner off Cockshott Point the boat and the steamer came into collision. The little boat was cut in two and the occupants thrown into the lake, and for a time it looked as if their lives would be lost. The captain of the steamer, without any preparation, jumped overboard, and seizing the lady was able to place her on board, amid the hearty cheers of those who had witnessed the accident. The two gentlemen could evidently swim, and being assisted by life buoys were able to scramble on deck.

On Sundays she sailed to Wray Castle boathouse to allow hotel guests to attend service at Wray Church. Her engineer was George Stuart. *Esperance* operated for the Ferry Hotel until the outbreak of World War One, when she became a houseboat. She is still on the lake in the care of the Windermere Steamboat Museum.

During the 1880s the main timetable utilised three boats, with extras as required; eight round-the-lake trips were offered in addition to three shorter cruises between Bowness and Ambleside. The paddle steamer *Rothay* was brought into service during busy periods but became increasingly out-dated. She was slower and less economical than the screw steamers, so the FR ordered another screw vessel to update the fleet. Forrestt & Son of Wyvenhoe in Essex were approached for the new ship, to *'replace the Rothay which is no longer fit for navigation'*. Forrestt's submitted the lowest tender of £4,800, but ultimately the new vessel cost £5,200. As before, she was transported by rail to Lakeside and assembled on the slip from sections. The

Westmorland Gazette reported a week before the launch, on 20th June;

New Steamer for Windermere
A large number of men from the firm of Messrs. Forrest (sic) & Company, of London, have arrived at Lakeside, and are busily engaged in constructing the hull of the new steamer which is to be added to the Windermere Lake service. The new vessel is to be built on similar lines to those of the Swan, which at present is the finest boat plying between Lakeside and Ambleside.

The work of construction is proceeding on the stocks at Lakeside Station, the materials being brought from Wyvenhoe by rail. It is expected that the new steamer will be ready about the end of June. It will be a twin-screw propeller, and will be able to cover the length of the lake, eleven miles, in about 45 minutes. The engines are being built by Messrs. Westray, Copeland, & Co., of Barrow-in-Furness. The vessel, when complete, will be quite an acquisition to Lake Windermere, and will be named the Swallow.

The new steamer was intended to be named *Swallow*, but a last minute change saw her slide down the slip on 27th of June 1891 as the *Tern*. Her engines, provided by Barrow engineering firm Westray and Copeland, consumed an economical 0.29 tons of coal per mile, from a hold capacity of around 4 tons. She had a locomotive boiler supplying steam to the engines, with the engine on the port side driving the starboard shaft and vice-versa. The engines used one and a half tons of coal a day, and ran at very low speed – between 135 and a 140 revolutions per minute; the propellers were, and still are, correspondingly large giving her a very small wake.

One of *Tern*'s remaining defining features is her Canadian canoe-shaped bow embossed with an image of a tern. The steel vessel measures 145 feet long with a breadth of eighteen feet and a draught of four feet. As built she could carry 633 passengers and as a two-class ship, those using the forward saloon and foredeck

Cygnet approaching Low Wood from Ambleside.

paid the first class fare. She was built with two masts and an exposed steering position just forward of the funnel amidships. With the *Tern* in service the *Rothay* was withdrawn and broken up. At this time the Railway Company paid the Earl of Lonsdale, who owned the lakebed, £5 per year for every steamer on the lake.

A month later, the conversion of Storrs Hall from a private residence to a hotel, which had started in 1890, was completed. The hotel boasted a large steamer pier just north of Storrs Temple. The Westmorland Gazette noted on 4th July; *'the Railway Company announce that the Windermere steam yachts will call on request at the Hydropathic'*.

Now there were six steamer piers in use on the lake; after leaving Lakeside, Storrs Hall was reached after twenty-five minutes. Five more minutes saw the steamer alongside the Ferry Hotel, and a further five saw her reach Bowness. The boat reached Low Wood twenty minutes later, and Waterhead ten minutes after that. The piers at Storrs Hall, the Ferry Hotel and the Low Wood were request stops. In 1896, for the first time since the FR takeover, Sunday excursion trains connected with steamers and a seven-day service has operated ever since, at least during peacetime summer months. In the winter one vessel ran from Ambleside at 8.40 am, made three round trips of the lake and finished at Ambleside at 5.20 pm. Winter sailings were provided primarily as a service for locals.

A letter of protest was sent to the FR in 1891 regarding the disposal of ashes in the lake. It had been the practice to dispose of ashes ashore, as to dump it in the lake was in contradiction of the Public Health Amendment Act. Anyone throwing ashes in the lake could be summoned to see the Bowness Local Board. Quite why this changed is not recorded, nor is the reaction to the letter.

On 18th November 1893 strong northerly gales swept north Lancashire, and sailings were cancelled with *Swan* (I) and *Tern* moored in the middle of the lake, just off Lakeside. Both were subjected to the onslaught of the wind and waves, eventually succumbing and sinking at a depth of around 100 feet. Divers were sent down to assess the situation and found the boats deeply embedded in mud and clay, so many buoys and pontoons were gathered to raise them. Once raised and restored, the boats returned to service for the 1894 season.

The Great Freeze of 1894-5 stopped sailings for six weeks. In November 1894 the prevailing southwesterly winds shifted northerly and by mid-January the lake was frozen from end to end; although the steamers were cancelled, tourism boomed. One Saturday over 7,000 came by train to Windermere and another 3,000 arrived at Lakeside. A huge lamp illuminated Bowness Bay from the gardens of the Old England Hotel, and a band was positioned on Hen Holme with drinks available; chairs were fitted with skates for any who couldn't skate. Ice yachts fitted with steel runners attained speeds of over thirty-eight miles per hour – by far the fastest on the lake to that date. The ice claimed two lives; John Wade and James Studholme who fell through into the freezing water between Storrs and Beech Hill. The coal merchants

Cygnet departs Ambleside, as Teal (I) arrives.

of Bowness used the ice to their advantage by utilising carts on the lake – far easier than lugging it on and off the cargo boats. Thawing started on March 20th, but it was a while before the steamers could sail again.

Kaiser Wilhelm II, Emperor of Germany, visited in August 1895, staying with the Earl of Lonsdale and cruising along Ullswater before travelling over Kirkstone Pass for a trip on the steam launch *Maru*. He left by coach to Keswick before returning to Penrith.

1897 proved a successful season with 156,161 passengers carried on the steamers – not including through tickets booked at railway stations. 255 bicycles were carried in whit week alone, and during the summer the first boat left Waterhead at 7.20 am, the last finishing there at 7.55 pm. A one-boat timetable was again provided through the winter.

Threats to navigation made by the FR

These larger steamers required larger piers to accommodate them. Bowness Pier became partially unusable at low water due to silting at the shore end, so in 1896 the FR sought permission to extend the pier by 90 feet. The Company may already have been considering plans for the *Swift*, to be launched in 1900; the longest steamer on the lake at 150 feet. The original pier had been extended around 1869 to accommodate

The FR produced a range of postcards, illustrating trains, ships and key locations around their network. **Cygnet** is depicted here arriving at Lakeside.

Above: **Britannia** berthed at the Ferry Hotel in 1887. The festivities were for Queen Victoria's Jubilee.

Right: The plush interior of the **Britannia**.

Below: **Britannia** at Waterhead for Queen Victoria Jubilee celebrations. She is pictured firing a 21 gun salute. (Reproduced by courtesy of the Museum of Lakeland Life and Industry, Kendal, Cumbria)

the *Swan* (I), which originally lay fully against the structure but now hung off due to the shallowness of the water near the shore. The Council refused permission for the extension and offered to financially assist the Company with construction of a new pier to the south of Bowness Bay nearer to Cockshott Point. They envisaged a promenade with a grand view of the lake, not split in two by a huge pier.

The FR announced in December that they would continue without permission, and on 11th February 1897 brought a pile-driving machine to Bowness to start construction. This infuriated the Council who took out an injunction to prevent work starting.

A description of the bay at the time would not go amiss. North of the steamer pier were public landings, where present day rowing boats are hired. There were two small piers with rowing boats and small steam launches available for hire. South of the steamer pier was the sixty foot long wharf used by Mr Pattinson's barges for unloading sand and gravel, then the Esperance pier co-owned by Bruce Logan of the Ferry Hotel and Mr Bridson, and another small jetty. Other private steam launches, of which there were nearly forty at the time, could use these two piers with prior permission of the owners. Further round the bay was Colonel Steble's boathouse with more boathouses lining the shoreline to Cockshott Point.

In June the case came before Mr Justice Gainsford Bruce at the Westmorland Assizes in Appleby. Bowness Urban District Council and the Attorney General were the plaintiffs represented by Mr Pickford and Mr Sanderson, while the Railway Company were the defendants represented by Mr Dankwerts, Mr Page and Mr Granet. The case took four days. Mr Pickford opened by raising two main points about the proposed extension; that the pier was a trespass upon grounds in possession of the county, and that it was an obstruction of a public highway. Bowness Urban District Council leased the lakebed in Bowness Bay from the Earl of Lonsdale who owned the bed of the entire lake. The water though, was a public highway to which there were no restrictions.

Prior to 1867, when the Bowness Local Board was formed, there had been the Windermere Steam Yacht Company, who had a number of steamers plying on the lake, and built a small pier on the site of the present one. In 1870 the steamers of that company were bought by the defendants, and in 1871-2 they obtained an Act to carry on the business of steamship owners. They at that time proposed to increase the size of the pier which had been built by the old private company, but were opposed by the Local Board, and when action was threatened, the parties came to an arrangement, by which the pier was extended to its present size.

The Railway Company had '*made a rod for their own back by building bigger and bigger boats and it was not the fault of the Council and other lake users that they had done this in pursuit of profit*'. The Council had designated another possible site for a pier, but the FR would have to '*buy land at the Southern*

end of the existing pier in order to build a landing stage'. The Railway Company believed a new pier was too expensive, and would be an inconvenience for the tradesmen and hotelkeepers of Bowness.

On the second day, Mr Dankwerts opened for the railway observing that the proposed pier was '*outside land leased by the District Council, and the present pier was to be used as a gangway to approach the new pier*'. His witnesses included boat owners, solicitors, and residents. Concerned that an extension would hinder navigation, they noted that Bowness Bay was already overcrowded and this would make matters worse. Hire boats leaving the public landings would have to leave in single file, creating chaos. There were seven public landings on the lake, approachable from all directions. The new pier would not allow such a varied approach to existing public facilities in Bowness Bay.

Continuing on day three, Mr Dankwerts argued that just because people use the lake as a right of way, does not make it such, and that in '*other pleasure resorts, the local authorities and railway companies worked together for the purpose of enhancing the convenience of the people frequenting the place*'. He thought that '*the Bowness Council would have been only too glad to do everything they could to attract passengers to the place. The people using the company's steamers were as much to be considered as those using the rowing boats*'. Witnesses for the proposal then testified. Alfred Aslett of the FR, Frank Stileman, engineer for the company, steamer masters, pier masters, members of the Windermere Yacht Club and others all supported the extension.

Summarising, the Council thought the new pier would be an eyesore and would obstruct navigation to the busiest part of the lake. Sand barges and steam launches would have difficulties gaining their berths and Colonel Steble's boathouse would be cut off. Local boatmen agreed: inexperienced trippers hiring rowing boats could be swamped by the wash from the large vessels. The FR thought the site of the present pier was the only suitable one. A landing parallel to the shore, like Lakeside, would not be practical in strong winds, and the proposed site at Cockshott was too far from the town for convenience.

On day four, the jury decided that the pier would

Britannia off Lakeside.

On 7th September 2014, the last two flying Lancaster Bombers, one from Canada and one from the UK, staged a flyover of Windermere to celebrate the 100th birthday of Archie Johnstone. He was a navigator in the 617 Squadron of the RAF. Unfortunately he passed away a few months before his centenary. They are seen here flying over the **Tern**.

hinder navigation along the right of way, and found in favour of the plaintiff and the public. Mr Justice Bruce said that he *'should, with some hesitation, enter a verdict for the plaintiff, but the case must go to the Court of Appeal'*. The Carlisle Patriot reported on 17th September that; *'THE FR COMPANY, has given notice of appeal against the recent decision at Appleby Assizes in the Bowness pier case'*.

On 14th January 1898, the appeal was heard at Appleby in front of Mr Justice Wills, and also lasted four days. The same representatives returned and The Westmorland Gazette reported. Day one commenced with Mr Pickford outlining the history of the case and the previous trial. He mentioned that the Council *'were anxious to do everything they could to meet the company, but came to the conclusion that the pier, erected where intended and as proposed, would be such an interference with the rights of way that they could not consent to its erection'*. The Railway Company responded *'either we will have our pier as proposed or we will have nothing'*.

The plaintiffs and defendants reprised their previous arguments. Then a counter argument was put forward; *'Assume the case of a sailing boat going from Bowness Bay northwards against a north wind. The boat could not go in a straight line or track, like a horse upon a road, but it would have to beat backwards and forwards'*. It was agreed that the only limits placed on a marine right of way could be the shores of the lake.

Mr Justice Bruce wanted to see the location, so Mr Dankwerts promised the FR would lay a special train on for him on Sunday.

Witnesses were called against the extension. Mr Gatey an Ambleside solicitor and clerk for Bowness Urban District Council told how *'the landings were so crowded that the local authority could not provide accommodation for the private steam-launches to land, and by permission they used the Esperance Pier'*.

The court resumed after Mr Justice Wills had visited Bowness. Several witnesses opposed the extension. Sir William Forwood of Liverpool said he *'had spent every summer during the last 34 years at Windermere… ..and….owned a steam launch, three sailing yachts, and a number of small boats on Windermere…… .There had been absolute freedom in passing over the lake, and no limits could be fixed to its navigation. The effect of the proposed extension would be to add great risk to the pleasure boats, and be a very serious inconvenience to steam launches and rowing boats'*.

The defence argued that the extension would shorten time spent by steamers at the pier; by using two gangways simultaneously the time at the pier for a full steamer could be reduced by twelve minutes, thereby benefiting passengers. Mr Woolgar, senior master, and Nicholas Herd of the *Tern* both described the difficulties in approaching the pier on busy days, and Herd mentioned that it sometimes took twenty minutes to leave the pier at Bowness. Boat owners and proprietors from Bowness with small launches or hired-out rowing boats, gave evidence about how the area had changed over the years, emphasising that the extension would cut off the inner part of the bay.

On Tuesday Mr Dankwerts argued that if people were using the lake for pleasure, they were not exercising their right of way, and the Company represented private and

Top: **Tern** in the late 1950s after her conversion to a motor ship.

Above: Early in her career, and still sporting two masts, **Tern** leaves Lakeside for all stops north.

Bottom: **Tern** is seen here departing Bowness for the Ferry, Storrs and Lakeside.

Swan (I) leaves Lakeside with **Tern** and **Swift** moored together, and **Teal** (I) or **Cygnet** to the right hand side. The coal store is in the enclosure behind the latter vessel.

public interests as they carried large numbers of passengers. Supporters including Dixon Cloudsdale, Alfred Aslett and John Fell, testified before the case discussed the Earl of Lonsdale's interest in the Lake.

After closing speeches on Wednesday, the Judge told the jury to base their decision on the threat to navigation on the lake. After two and a half hours they found in favour of the plaintiff. The FR set upon another course of action starting proceedings to obtain an Act of Parliament to allow them to extend the pier. The Council wondered what powers this would give the Company, and what else they could go on to build. Whilst the FR Bill was being considered in 1899, a letter was sent to both the Houses of Parliament suggesting that an enlarged pier would be *'nothing less than a national calamity, which is never likely to be remedied'*.

The Railway Company received their Act giving powers to remove the old piers at Bowness and Waterhead and replace them with new structures extended by 70 feet and 60 feet respectively. But the

powers were never exercised as agreement was reached at a meeting in Bowness in March 1899. A new shorter pier – 168 feet long and 24 feet wide – was permitted to remain in Bowness Bay as long as it did not exceed the arranged limits, but no hotel or other building could be built without written consent from the Council – a permission unlikely to be forthcoming. A structure of these precise dimensions was built, just in time for the arrival of the next steamer. This pier is still in use today, albeit with minor modifications

Mr Justice Bruce presided over another court hearing in July 1898. A father claimed damages when his three-year-old son broke his arm, crushed between the *Swan* (I) and the pier. The master, Isaac Fell, told the parents to look after their child but a lapse of attention saw the incident occur. The jury found in favour of the defendants. One wonders if the case would have the same outcome today.

A Final Steamship

The last decade of the nineteenth century was the busiest on record and the Postmaster General required the boats to carry mails. Despite having four screw ships in service – excluding *Raven* – the FR commissioned in 1900 their longest passenger steamer for the lake from T.B. Seath & Co.

The paper carried a short piece about the journey of the vessel to Lakeside; *During the week-end a new steamer, which has been built at Rutherglen for the Windermere Lake service, was shipped at Barrow, and carried from that town to Lakeside by rail, where she will be put together and be ready for service on the lake in four or five weeks' time, and will be on her station for the Whitsuntide traffic.*

Seath's assembled the *Swift* on the slip at Lakeside and Mrs Percy Hibbert launched her at 1.30 pm on Saturday 21st July 1900. Costing £9,500 she was powered by two twin cylinder compound steam engines

Tern loads for a busy trip up the lake. A horse and carriage wait outside the station while **Raven** is berthed for her next turn of duty.

Lakeside Station   Windermere

using a locomotive type boiler, each providing over sixty-three horsepower. She was the last steam powered public pleasure boat ordered for the lake. Her engines, supplied by Fishers of Paisley, pushed her along at a sufficient fifteen knots. She was 150 feet long with a breadth of twenty one feet and a draught of four feet, and as built could carry 781 passengers. Flush decked she was distinguished from previous screw steamers with their lower decks at the bow and stern and raised centre areas. She was also much wider, helping make room for the many bicycles carried at the time. Seath's also constructed *Sir Walter Scott* for Loch Katrine at the same time, and she bears more than a passing resemblance to her Windermere sister.

On Saturday 7th September 1901 the *Swan* (I) and *Tern* made contact at 8.15 pm near Storrs Hall pier. The Westmorland Gazette carried the story on the 14th; *On Saturday evening a collision took place on Lake Windermere, off Storrs, between the 'Swan' and the 'Tern', two of the five lake steam yachts belonging to the FR Company. The yachts were on their last journeys of the day, the 'Tern' being on its way northwards and the 'Swan' going southwards to Lakeside. Darkness had set in by the time they reached Storrs; the 'Tern', which will carry 532 passengers, left Lakeside a good deal late, having been delayed waiting for trains, and at the time had on it about 50 passengers and was the first to arrive at and leave the pier at Storrs Hall. As the 'Tern' was leaving the pier the 'Swan' approached it, about half full speed. The night was dark, though clear, and each vessel carried the customary blue and green lights. By some means, to be hereafter revealed, the two came into collision at a point about 200 yards north of the pier. The bow of*

the 'Tern' cut through the 'Swan' to the foot of the fore-saloon stairs. Captain Fell was in charge of the 'Tern' and the 'Swan' was captained by Angus McNeil. It was immediately evident to those on the 'Swan' that the vessel was hopelessly disabled. Captain Fell kept the engines of the 'Tern' moving slowly forwards, and thus kept his bow within the cleft in the 'Swan's side, and the 'Swan' was thus given sufficient length of time to enable the passengers, over 50 in number, to be lifted up on to the deck of the 'Tern', which was no easy task. The ladies were taken on first, and the men and crew quickly followed, the greater part of the luggage was also removed, including some bicycles. The last man to leave the ship was McNeil, the captain. The 'Tern' was then reversed and withdrew itself from the wreck and the 'Swan' drifted towards mid-lake, and within 5 minutes went down'.

The paper failed to note that the *Swan* (I)'s engineer opened the boiler valves to let off as much steam as possible, to let in cold water and prevent an explosion as she sank. *Swan* (I) lay in forty feet of water, while *Tern*, despite slight damage, backed up to Storrs Hall pier to offload passengers from the sunken vessel, before continuing to Bowness and Ambleside. A coach and horses was sent from the Old England Hotel to Storrs Pier to collect those from the *Swan* (I) proceeding to Lakeside. The paper carried accounts from people who were on board the vessels. Mr Brocklehurst was on the *Swan* (I); *Captain McNeil gave the order to board the 'Tern', 'ladies first'. There were only a few lady passengers, and they were assisted to the 'Tern' in a not very ceremonious manner, for the deck of the 'Tern' was some six feet above that of the 'Swan'.*

A letter, signed JWB, from Bowness had a thorough

Tern seen in her present condition passing the site of **Raven**'s pier at High Cunsey. In 1954 a decision was taken to replace **Tern** and **Swift** with three 250 passenger motor vessels which would compete with the launch operations. Tenders were received in 1956 ranging from £178,350 to £194,080 but this was too much, and the vessels were converted to motor ships instead.

account of the accident; *You will be surprised to see me dating my letter from Bowness but the reason will be apparent when you read this. I took the opportunity of a fine Saturday afternoon to take a trip to Windermere, intending to return on Saturday evening. Accordingly I left Bowness at 7.50 p.m. in the Swan steamboat for Lakeside. The last glimmer of twilight was fading as we left and in a few minutes darkness spread over the lake.*

As we approached Storrs, we saw the return steamer leaving Storrs pier. It appeared to be passing us on our right, but by some fateful mis-calculation, before anything could be done, the steamer Tern crashed into our boat amidships, cutting us nearly in two. The shock threw many people on their backs. At a glance, and also by the noise of water rushing into our hold, it was apparent that our boat was hopelessly disabled and sinking in mid-lake. Fortunately the Tern was not clear of our wreckage and ropes were thrown to aid us in boarding her.

The Captain called 'ladies first' and I can assure you they were pushed and hauled over the bulkwark of the Tern in quick time. The men needed no invitation to follow, though the deck of the Tern was six feet above our deck. In a very few minutes, all passengers and crew were on the Tern and then she backed out of the wrecked Swan. A few minutes later we saw the Swan disappear into the depths of the lake.

The *Tern* was withdrawn for re-plating the five-foot long two feet deep gash in her bow but returned to service later the next week. Divers assessed the damage to *Swan* (I), and evaluated how best to raise her. Pontoons arrived from Barrow, via sea to Greenodd and rail to Lakeside, whence they were towed into position

to commence operation on 17th October; *Four pairs of windlasses attached to wire ropes passed under the keel were placed on a superstructure of timber resting on four pontoons. After an hour's winding, first the funnel and then the bow appeared above the water, the vessel being meanwhile hauled shorewards by men with ropes.*

Swan (I) was patched up at Storrs Hall and towed to Lakeside by the *Tern* for full repairs and refurbishment, before re-entering service for the 1902 season. As a result of the collision, navigation lights were introduced to the lake steamers. The report to the Board of Trade recommended that the company should apply to the King in Council to frame rules under the Merchant Shipping Act of 1894, section 421, requiring inland vessels to operate to the same rules as sea going vessels. These passed entirely to the lake, so henceforth steam gave way to sail, and vessels passed port to port.

The winter of 1901-02 was another poor one. On Monday 10th February the *Cygnet,* due at Bowness at 9 am from Ambleside, was more than an hour late having got lost in fog off the north end of Belle Isle. She forced her way through ice over an inch thick, but tied up at Bowness and passengers were forwarded by coach to Lakeside.

In February 1904 The Lakes Chronicle outlined how an additional light buoy was brought to the lake. It was brought to Lakeside on two railway wagons and placed on a shallow between Bowness and Ambleside. An oil tank that could provide illumination for several days and nights fuelled the buoy.

The private steam yacht *Britannia* came onto the market in 1907 and the FR purchased her in 1908 for a remarkable £350 – considering she was built in 1879 for £12,000; the sale included two small boats, equipment and ten tons of lead ballast. She had been offered to the company in 1898 for £1,200 but that offer was declined.

Britannia could carry 122 passengers but wasn't used on service runs, except on rare occasions as high season relief. She was used for private charters costing between five and ten guineas for eight hours – depending how many were on board – and could be booked at half a day's notice. Her panelled saloon was adorned with leather seats and mirrors, while her spacious deck was garnished with carvings of eagles and lions. *Britannia* was moored at Lakeside and was eventually withdrawn in 1915, being offered for sale in 1918. When the directors contemplated sale it was revealed that she had never been profitable, nor was she ever likely to be. No bids were received so she was scrapped in 1919. Some of her named crockery is at the Windermere Steamboat Museum, and the aft staircase was put in the garden of the Barrow Station Master's house until destroyed by a German bomb in May 1941.

On 27th September 1909 *Swan* (I) ran aground in thick fog around 7.15 pm off Belle Grange; as usual the Westmorland Gazette recorded the event; *On Monday evening, the FR company's Windermere steam-yacht 'Swan' ran aground near Belle Grange, a remotely-situated spot on the western shore of the lake. The steam-yacht left Ambleside at 7.15pm. The journey* *being intended to terminate at Bowness though up to Saturday last the journey extended to Lakeside. After calling at Low Wood the steamer grounded about 200 yards north of Belle Grange. There were only seven passengers on board. The shock caused by the contact of the vessel with shore, which was fortunately not of a rocky nature there, made the vessel sway about a good deal, and one of the passengers, Mrs. Johnson of Ellerthwaite Road, Windermere who was in the cabin, was thrown off her feet, but without receiving bodily injury. The men in charge of the steamer went ashore, and after a rather prolonged search for help from the only habitation anywhere near, and obtained a ladder from Belle Grange, and with its aid, the distressed passengers were got off the steamer. Afterwards, in company of the captain, they were obliged to walk southwards to the Ferry Hotel, a distance of more than two miles. There they were taken indoors and given some refreshments, after which they were taken across to the Ferry Nab in two rowing-boats, and thence walked through the rectory fields to Bowness pier, and it was after ten o'clock when they reached their homes, their discomfort being increased by the pouring rain. They spoke of the coolness and watchfulness, in trying circumstances, of Capt. Eccles and crew and the kindness of Mr Logan the proprietor of the hotel.*

A claim was paid to a lady, presumably Mrs Johnson, which cost the company £10 with £1 11s 6d costs added. *Swan* (I) was re-floated on the 29th with the help of the *Tern* and *Swift*. She was involved in another incident on the 22nd June 1910 running into a rowing boat in Bowness Bay and drowning two lady workers from the Old England Hotel. The coroners inquest declared the vessel's design unsatisfactory as the Captain had no elevated view over the bow; they suggested a lookout be placed at the bow in busy parts of the lake and when approaching piers, but whether the company followed this advice is unknown.

Steamers still entered the bay past Cockshott Point at speed with blatant disregard for safety, despite protests from the Council. In the confines of the bay they created a significant wash, occasionally swamping

Opposite top: **Swift** at Lakeside in the first decade of the twentieth century. The narrow gauge tracks in the foreground came from the coal store. Hand-propelled trolleys were pushed along to fuel the ships. These have now been removed.

Opposite middle: **Swift** sets sail, leaving **Tern** and **Raven** at Lakeside.

Opposite bottom: Seen here after her conversion to a motor ship in the 1950s, **Swift** is arriving at Waterhead, Ambleside.

Swift bow in at Ambleside.

small boats and soaking the occupants. To round off a decade of bad luck, on 30th August 1910 *Tern* caught fire whilst berthed at Ambleside, causing £74 damage to the deck and fittings. She was withdrawn for refitting, with other vessels filling her place in the timetable.

1913 was a bumper year and over 179,000 passengers were carried. Although 1914 saw the outbreak of war, the services ran seven days a week with a minimum of three vessels needed Monday to Saturday, and two on Sundays. W. Cliffe was fourteen in 1914 and worked that season on the *Tern*. He wrote a letter about his experience to Cumbria Magazine many years later, illustrating how crews worked back then; *Captain Holmes was then in charge of the Tern. Bob Roskell, who lived in Lake Road, Ambleside, was the engineer, Bill Harrison was fireman and Albert Bayliffe, Bob Hiller, J. Harrison were deckhands. Mr. Tyson was stationmaster at Lakeside. Tern was based at Ambleside and made the first run from Ambleside to Lakeside, where she was coaled and washed down before the next run back. She made the last run from Lakeside to Ambleside in the evening. We had a seven day week, starting at 12 noon on Sundays, others at eight. It was a twelve hour day. My pay was 12s.6d per week. Many of the passengers in those days were wealthy Americans on holiday in the Lakes. I was sent from Arnside by the FR Company to work on the Tern, and I had to live in Ambleside with a family in Smithy Brow. They were busy days, as the Tern stopped at all landing stages such as Hows Wood (Low Wood), Ferry and Storrs Hall, if requested. I well remember the sooty spots, and many a lady started with a white blouse and finished with a black-spotted one.*

They were happy days. I always try and see Tern when visiting the Lakes.

After the 1914 season services, and the connecting Fleetwood – Barrow steamers, ceased. For the rest of the War the vessels remained tied up at the piers, but the FR still issued a cross-bay timetable in 1915 with *'DEFERRED UNTIL FURTHER NOTICE'* printed across it. Services resumed in 1919, and when the season finished the FR, probably on an economy drive, considered installing oil fired engines in the *Tern*, but this was never carried out.

Winter sailings were withdrawn in 1920 due to high cost of wages and fuel, explained in a letter to the Council. The Railway Company proposed to operate a local bus service, leaving Ulverston twice a day to connect with trains and head up to Lakeside, and along the east shore to Bowness and Ambleside. A Model T Ford omnibus was purchased in 1921 for £370, replacing a hired vehicle, and was kept in Ulverston goods yard. It operated at a loss but was a saving for the company, as the winter steamer operating deficit had been £1,063 (for the 1919-20 winter), whereas the bus only lost £510 and £260 in 1920-21 and 1921-22 respectively. For the 1922-23 winter season the bus service was operated by the Lake District Road Traffic Company on the condition that they would *'undertake the road motor passenger service and receive all proceeds on being indemnified against loss not exceeding £100'*.

The withdrawal of the winter service marked a watershed in the history of lake services. Winter sailings had been provided primarily for residents, so the service went from being part of the local transport network to becoming a holiday attraction. Locals still used the services in summer, but the early trips provided from the 19th century for residents to get to appointments and markets were withdrawn. Now the first trip departed Lakeside at 9.50 am.

The heyday for the Windermere steamers was in peacetime between 1880 and 1920, but the increased tourism still put a few local noses out of joint. Two quotes from the period give a flavour of the opposing views. Cowper a resident of Hawkshead noted;

A crowded train arrives at Lakeside, and the steamer, packed with trippers so densely that they can hardly stir, whirls them away to the discordant sounds of the concertina, past the Ferry Hotel, to Bowness or Ambleside, where they are landed, and regaled by brass bands and nigger troupes; and where, perhaps, meeting the tide of another cheap trip, brought by the London and North Western Company to Windermere Station, they contrive to turn this unfortunate district into a perfect pandemonium.

Hermann Prior, a tourist wrote;

There are pleasant things in life, with all its drawbacks; and a sail on Winander-Mere is, or ought to be, one of them. It exhilarates one to think of it. What suggestions of bright skies and flashing waters; of rock-tower and jutting headland, fern-brake and shadowy glade and mossy meadow; of banks decked with fairy-like homesteads; the light boats skimming the lake beneath them, peopling its echoes with merriment; glen and valley tempting the wanderer's steps in the distance; overhead, the mountains, gazing down silently through a summer haze!

The Piers

The passenger steamers used many different landing stages over the years. This was part of the attraction and success of the system for tourists, as a trip was short enough not to become dull. No sooner had one pier been left astern than the next came into view. Between 1891 and 1923 when six piers were in use, the longest sail was 25 minutes between Lakeside and Storrs. Of the nine piers or wharfs in use over the 170 years of service, only three are still in regular service, with one used occasionally.

The southernmost pier was Newby Bridge, situated one mile along the River Leven from Lakeside, and terminus of the lake passenger services until 1869. Originally a ford with stepping-stones to cross the River Leven, the first wooden bridge was built around 1622, and replaced in 1652 by a five-arched stone structure. The weir downstream of the bridge submerged the original stepping-stones.

The Swan Hotel still stands on the northern side of the river, and American author Nathanial Hawthorne described the bustle surrounding the inn in July 1855;

Twice a day the stage coach passes from

Milnthorpe towards Ulverston, and twice returns, and three times a little steamer passes to and fro between our hotel and the head of the lake.........

............Young ladies in broad-rimmed hats, stroll about, or row in the river in light shallops (a small boat), of which there are abundance; sportsmen sit on the benches under the windows of the hotel, arranging their fishing tackle; phaetons and post-chaises, with postillions in scarlet jackets and white breeches, dash up to the door. Morning and night comes the stagecoach, and we inspect the outside passengers, almost face to face with us, from our parlor –windows, up one pair of stairs.

The pier lay upstream of the Swan Hotel, which was ideally located for thirsty travellers. The slipway where the *Lady of the Lake*, *Lord of the Isles* and *Rothay* were constructed and launched is nearby. No images or engravings of the landing have come to light; the narrowness of the river suggests it was a quay running along the riverbank. The shallow river caused problems and a deep water location was needed, but it was not until 1869 that the terminus at Lakeside was built. Before then if the water was too low to allow navigation to Newby Bridge, steamers terminated at The Landing.

This name was ancient, from the days of the St Nicholas Clerks collecting the tolls for the ford. The first Ordnance Survey maps date from the early 1860s and show a 'Quay' in roughly the same location as the present Lakeside pier – presumably The Landing. A 'Landing Place' was located around the first bend in the River Leven, but steamers unable to navigate to Newby Bridge could not have reached this point through Fell Foot. The Landing was also known as either 'Kellett's Landing', after the

Kellett family's nearby inn, or 'Harrison's Landing' as the land belonged to Myles Harrison.

James Gibson gave a description of the landing in 1843 in his guide to the scenery of the lake; *A new Inn, called Harrison's Landing, is erected at this spot, on the west side of the Lake, and has an excellent wharf for loading and unloading goods, as yet they have only obtained to it a beer license, but expect to obtain license for spirits and wine soon.*

Here was a quay capable at least of handling cargo vessels. A small wall allowed rowing boats to come alongside; and the first pier was just a cart pushed into the lake from this wall, half submerged, with a plank laid across the gap. The steamers brought a more permanent structure to permit landing when Newby Bridge was inaccessible. 'A Guide to the English Lake

The location of the steamer pier at Newby Bridge. This now forms part of the Swan Hotel marina.

The River Leven at Newby Bridge. The steamer pier was located where the jetty in the centre of the image is. The Swan Hotel is just out of the image to the left.

Clappersgate Slate Wharf,
John Harden 1810.

District, intended principally for pedestrians', implies that The Landing was also used as a request stop for nearby residents. The 1863 edition suggests; *After leaving the Ferry Hotel, the steamer does not again stop, except by signal at the Landing, until it arrives at Newby Bridge, the end of the lake...... The Landing is a station used almost solely by people residing in the neighbourhood. After passing the Landing, the lake rapidly diminishes in breadth, till it is not so wide as many of our larger rivers, the narrow passage which is thus left for the steamer necessitating careful and accurate steering.*

Passengers were unloaded next to Kellett's Quay House Inn (a renamed Harrison's Landing Inn) for refreshment before continuing by rowing boat or omnibus to Newby Bridge. Two stagecoaches ran on to Ulverston station, one owned by Mr Kellett, the other by Mr White of the Swan Hotel. The Kellett family had a long association with boats, George Kellett became skipper of the *Tern* in the 1950s-60s and his brother in law W McGarr, was skipper of the *Swift*. At the same time another Kellet partnered Joe Huddleston running *Have a Go*, a small wooden launch from Lakeside.

The site became the Lakeside station complex in 1869 when the FR reached here from Ulverston. A large hotel was built, now the present Lakeside Hotel. The Kellett family renamed their Quay House Inn the Steamer Hotel, and in the 1960s the family still had a café near the pier. The slipway was constructed at the same time as the station, and all the steamers since 1869 have been launched there, arriving to the site by rail. Today the *Tern*, *Teal* (II), and *Swan* (II) are still hauled out here for their winter maintenance. The *Raven's* cargo berth was at the northern end of the quay near the hotel; the waterbuses now use the *Raven's* berth.

The next stop up the lake was originally the Ferry, but in 1891 Storrs Hall was added. Storrs Hall was built in 1790 for the MP John Legard who sold it in 1804 to David Pike Watts, whose nephew was the painter Constable. In 1806 the house was sold to John Bolton who made his fortune trading slaves from the West Indies. Bolton employed Joseph Michael Gandy, an architect from Liverpool who had designed Storrs Temple and boathouse for Legard, to complete extensions to the east and west of the building, which were completed in 1811.

John Bolton's widow put his cedar barge at the disposal of the dowager Queen Adelaide after his death, and it took the Queen to Millerground on 26th July 1840. Queen Adelaide's hill commemorates this occasion. The barge was sold in 1888 in such good condition that it was rebuilt into rowing boats. Storrs Hall was sold at auction in 1889 to Benjamin Townson of Barrow, who set about converting the building into a first class hotel that opened in 1891. The steamer pier was situated just north of Storrs Temple, a monument and registered war memorial for four admirals from the Napoleonic Wars.

An advert for the hotel dating from 1895 mentions the steamer service; *'A PRIVATE PIER has been erected about 50 yards from the mansion, at which all steamers will make their first call after leaving Lakeside, and at which sailing and other boats, and yachts, will be readily obtainable. There is extensive stabling, with accommodation for over 20 horses'.* Access to Storrs pier was allowed through the grounds for locals living nearby. Those on the western shore near Cunsey often found it more convenient to cross by rowing boat to Storrs to catch the steamer to Bowness than to walk to the Ferry Hotel and wait for the irregularly timed chain ferry.

The pier was 'T' shaped and the steamers would berth alongside in a north-south direction. A railway signal was positioned on the end of the pier which was raised to summon the steamer as Storrs Hall was a request stop. The call was retained after the LMS took over, and a Handbill from 1938 detailing a tour of Windermere and Coniston includes a small commentary that mentions *'Storrs Hall Pier is the first calling place'.* The following year the hotel was marked on LMS network maps and tour bills. Storrs Hall Hotel did not feature in literature after 1939.

An early important call from the first days of the *Lady of the Lake* was the Ferry Inn where a pier was built in 1845. It was equally important in the pre-steam days when Gibson and White exchanged their passengers here. Connections could be made with coaches to Hawkshead and Coniston, and the ferry across the lake to Ferry Nab. In 1869 when the FR took control of the sailings, the Ferry Inn became a request call and a signal was erected on the end of the pier. There were three piers at the Ferry Inn designed for larger boats; the main pier was used by the railway steamers, *Esperance* used a pier opposite Crow Holme, and the *Raven* berthed at a pier in Mitchell Wyke to the rear of the hotel. Maintenance of the pier was disputed between the Railway Company and the Curwen Family who owned the Ferry Inn. The pier fell into disrepair and became dangerous, but when Richard Borwick became tenant of the hotel he placed an advert in the Westmorland Gazette in June 1870 for the construction of a new pier;

New Pier at the Ferry Hotel,
Windermere
TENDERS are wanted for the ERECTION of a NEW PIER at the FERRY HOTEL, WINDERMERE. Particulars will be given on application to Mr. Borwick, Ferry Hotel, Windermere, where a Plan of the Pier may be seen. The Tenders may be either for the erection in Stone, Wood, or Iron. Tenders will be received up to July 5th, and the taker will be declared immediately after.

The introduction of the first steam chain ferry in 1870 created problems for the steamers.

In timetables the call was referred to as 'FERRY' and it was dropped from the timetable in 1925 after the LMS takeover, as the pier was again in a dilapidated condition. The Curwens had not carried out repairs – which were estimated to cost in the region of £400 –

so the steamers simply stopped calling. Unlike the 1870s, the call was never resumed. There was an outcry, but the LMS proclaimed that it was not bound to call at any pier on the lake. The Ferry Hotel was sold in 1948, and after a variety of uses is now private apartments. The building is now known as the Ferry House.

After the Ferry the next call for the steamers was in the wide bay of Bowness, well sheltered by Belle Isle. This was always a busy area and as far back as the reign of Queen Elizabeth I, there were three piers in Bowness Bay, licensed by the Earl of Lonsdale's predecessors for the use of fishermen.

In 1786 Gilpin described Bowness in his guide as '*a capital port town, the great mart for fish and charcoal*'.

When the passage boats of Gibson and White called they made do with existing jetties, but a small steamer pier was built following the launch of *Lady of the Lake* in 1845. Twelve feet wide and eighty feet in length it was not much longer than the '*Lady*' herself. The following year it was recorded that alongside the steamer pier three small stone jetties were still in use, one belonging to the Crown, and another to Mr Ullock. Mr Bellasis owned the steamer pier from the late 1840s until the Railway Company's involvement. In the 1860s goods were handled south of Bowness Pier. General cargo for the lake-side settlements was brought in and out of the area by the steamers, and timber and sand were deposited here too.

As the steamers lengthened so the piers had to evolve and the steamer pier was extended in March 1870. Although permission was granted for a 25 feet extension, the pier was extended by 50 feet by Barrow contractor Mr Strongitharm to accommodate the newly launched *Swan* (I). In 1871 the distinctive Paley and Austin designed booking office was opened at the head of the pier and Bowness became an 'issuing station' for the first time. The smaller jetties were modernised in wood in 1872 to avoid scratching the highly varnished steam launches. *Esperance* had its own pier, south of the steamer pier, although other private launches could call there if they were not in the way of the *Esperance*.

The steamer pier was further extended to 148 feet, and in 1881 a warehouse was built to the south of the booking office to handle the *Raven's* cargo. 1889 saw the addition of the covered walkway through the booking office onto the pier. The beach north of the steamer pier was raised in 1892 to match the entrance to the pier concourse, removing the steps down to the beach. A dedicated sand wharf was also built in the bay south of the steamer pier in the 1890s to cater for the dredging boats.

During 1898 there were over forty steam yachts on the lake with private vessels still using the Esperance pier, whilst the hire fleet used the public landings. The same year the Bowness Pier Case put a stop to a proposed lengthening of the steamer pier by a further forty feet, but a more modest extension was built.

A large pavilion – a refreshment stall with a shingle floor – stood where the grassy area is now in front of Pier 2. On 30th September 1911 it was sold and removed to facilitate major improvements to the lake frontage in 1912. The line of planking of the promenade was removed and rebuilt from stone. The Belsfield Hotel's grounds were pushed back from the lakeshore – where public access to the lake was allowed along an old cart track – to the present boundary. Tom Storey's, and other boat builders' sheds were removed along and the sand wharf moved even further south. The improvements added gardens near where Pier 3 is today, and railings along the lake frontage. The beach was cleared of private boats and two cushion huts were built next to the goods warehouse. Thus only hire boats were moored at the jetties or pulled up the beach between the Cushion Huts and the beach south of the Esperance pier. Eventually the small launch piers were removed and upgraded structures built south of the Esperance pier. In 1921 the sand wharf was moved to the site of the Windermere Steamboat Museum when the promenade was extended yet again.

Modifications were made to the pier as the steamers grew, but no further extensions. The launch piers were

The 1915 Ferry crossing to Ferry Nab. The Ferry Hotel steamer pier is visible on the right.

Bowness between 1894 and 1898.

Bowness in the 1880s.

Storrs Hall Hotel on Lake Windemere

P.8040A.

Top left: Storrs Hall seen from the air. The hotel is in the trees, and Storrs Temple is on the end of the pier to the right.

Left: The pier at Low Wood. Note the railway semaphore signal on the end, used to inform steamers whether a landing was necessary. The Ferry Hotel, and Storrs Hall also had signals.

Top right: **Tern** at Waterhead dwarfed by Todd Crag. The River Rothay from Grasmere, joins the Brathay and they flow in at Waterhead, as seen here.

Above: **Teal** (II) at Waterhead in LMS days. **Raven's** old berth is in the foreground. Note the Hovis advert.

Waterhead again, showing Raven's berth to advantage. The large building to the right is now a Youth Hostel.

Windermere viewed from Brant Fell.

Tern is pictured carrying the Olympic Flame from Waterhead to Bowness on 21st June 2012.

A private steamer waits at Lakeside. Note the coal baskets piled up on the trolley, ready to fuel the steamers for the next working day. The Lakeside Hotel is in the background.

visitor centre, which opened in June 1969. The wooden launches and waterbuses began calling at a small wooden jetty at Brockhole, facing northwest from the northernmost point of the grounds.

Brockhole pier was the first new steamer pier built on the lake for over 120 years. Work commenced in late 2010 and launches started calling from May 2011. *Teal* (II) was the first steamer to land there on 25th July. Launches and waterbuses now operate to the lake's only floating steamer pier, with steamers calling in for special occasions such as the Great North Swim each June, or the Royal Visit of 2013 when the Queen landed from the *Teal* (II).

Low Wood pier was built and owned by the hotel, a feature of the lakeshore from at least 1702. It was on the itinerary of many early tourists and by 1832 boats were available for hire, and '*a cannon is kept for the purpose of gratifying visiters with those extraordinary reverberations which follow its discharge in these romantic districts'.* Steamers called regularly from 1845 and the present hotel building dates from 1859. At first a guaranteed call it became a request stop sometime between 1869 and 1882. As with other piers there was a signal to attract the steamer. Regular calls at Low Wood ceased in 1936 with the introduction of the *Teal* (II) that was too large to use the pier.

May 1986 saw the *Tern* call to pick up a charter – the first steamer visit in fifty years. She has returned a handful of times since. A scheduled service once again links the hotel with other piers around the lake, as since 2001 wooden launches from Brockhole have called at Low Wood several times each day.

rebuilt to accommodate waterbuses and today in Bowness there are three piers used for waterbuses and wooden launches, and one for steamers. The self-drive and rowing boats for hire have three further piers.

Brockhole, the National Park visitor centre, was a large estate built in 1899 for Henry Gaddum who purchased land by the lakeshore in 1895. Dan Gibson designed the mansion, and Thomas Mawson laid out the ornate gardens. From 1945 the house was used as a convalescent home. In 1968 the estate was purchased by the Lake District National Park and converted into a

WINDERMERE. LAKE SIDE HOTEL.

The northern terminus is Waterhead, commonly referred to as Ambleside. The early wherries of Gibson and White probably set off from the beach or a small wooden jetty. The first large pier lay to the south of the Wateredge Inn, with buildings on the north side for handling of goods; behind the pier complex was the tollhouse. At the time of the *Lady of the Lake* the road between Kendal and Grasmere had five tollgates and passengers between Windermere and Ambleside may have found it cheaper by steamer than toll road. By the 1880s tolls had been abolished.

A substantial pier replaced the older structure for *Swan* (I) around 1870, and a cargo berth was built for the *Raven*. Perpendicular to the main pier, *Raven*'s berth ran alongside the store yard, now the car park. A large crane assisted cargo handling, and goods were stored in the warehouse. The crane survived into the early 1960s although long out of use, and the warehouse became the present day café. The old cargo berth at Waterhead was used for occasional lay up of *Swift* or *Tern* as late as the 1960s, despite the poor condition of the structure.

The 1890s row of terraced houses just south of the pier, now one of the largest Youth Hostels in Britain, is known as The Esplanade. The steamer pier at Waterhead is now a modern structure using concrete and wood. Unlike the pier at Bowness, it has steps on the north side for loading waterbuses at any level of the lake. Two further wooden piers serve the waterbuses and launches.

Clappersgate is worthy of mention. It was the original northern hub although no scheduled passenger services operated here. Rowing boats with boatman were available from the early 18th Century, but it remained primarily a cargo destination. Clappersgate was used until the arrival of the deeper-draughted *Raven* in the 1870s, when services transferred to Waterhead. Once an important port for Langdale, Ambleside and

Silverholme calls at Brockhole while deputising on the Green Cruise from Ambleside and Wray Castle.

Tern calls at Low Wood. This shows how the request stops of Storrs, the Ferry Hotel and Low Wood differed from the main piers. Instead of berthing the whole ship alongside the pier, the vessel would touch along the end, in the direction of travel. This meant that a minimum of time was spent making the call. Confusingly, the 1939 timetable specified calls at Low Wood and Storrs were provided, but only on sailings taken by the older vessels – but did not mark which sailings these would be!

MOTOR BUS SERVICE

BETWEEN

AMBLESIDE
AND
LAKE SIDE

IN CONNECTION WITH TRAINS.

Commencing Nov. 1st, 1920,

UNTIL FURTHER NOTICE.

ON WEEK DAYS.

FOR CONDITIONS UNDER WHICH THE
SERVICE IS RUN SEE BACK.

L. SPEAKMAN,
General Manager.

Barrow-in-Furness,
October, 1920.

"Guardian" Printing Works, Barrow.

The first timetable for the bus which replaced the winter steamer services, commencing on the 1st November 1920.

Grasmere, Clappersgate is now a rural village between Ambleside and Hawkshead.

London Midland & Scottish Railway

In 1923 the FR and the lake steamers were incorporated into the London Midland & Scottish Railway. With the new takeover an old FR tradition ceased. The steamers flew the White Ensign, normally reserved for serving naval vessels. Reginald Fletcher complained about this in 1910, but Alfred Aslett replied that the Admiralty *'have no jurisdiction over inland waterways'*. The Admiralty wrote to the FR in September 1913 declaring that they *'did not consider it proper for vessels on inland waterways to wear a flag they would not be permitted to fly if they were on the high seas'*. This practice was only stopped when the LMS took over.

The LMS reduced the service to two boats Monday to Saturday and one on Sundays, making two tours of the lake. Timetables also advertised Coniston services as *Gondola* and *Lady of the Lake* were now under the control of the LMS.

Cygnet was converted from steam in 1924, following installation of two Parsons paraffin engines. The new engines vibrated badly, so she was seldom used. One traveller wrote;

Instead of the soft rhythm and impulses of the steam engine one had to endure the most appalling racket, noise and stench of fuel oil, and to try and believe that all this was progress in transportation … …for sheer discomfort it would be difficult to find anything worse than Cygnet in her converted condition.

Teal (I) was laid up in 1926 and scrapped a year later.

Raven was withdrawn in 1922, and sold in 1927 to Vickers Sons and Maxim of Barrow, although she remained on the lake. Refitted for testing mine laying equipment she was equipped with rails over the bow to lower mines into the water. Vickers allowed the LMS to use her as a works barge, and although laid up during the Second World War, in 1947 she returned to Bowness to remove two light buoys lit by carbide and water. In the winter of 1956-57 she operated as a repair barge to replace the king piles of Lakeside Pier and was then sold to ship breakers.

Raven was saved by George Pattinson, and towed to the Windermere Steamboat Museum for restoration by the *Esperance*. On 18th October 1971, in her centenary year, she raised steam and is now kept at the Steamboat Museum. She re-visited her launch site at Lakeside for repainting in the late 1970s.

The LMS upgraded its inland fleet in the 1930s using money made available by The Railways (Agreement) Act 1935, which set aside £26.5 million for the big four railway companies. Unemployment was high after the depression of the late 1920s and the money was intended to create work. As well as building inland vessels the company commissioned 369 new locomotives and 270 carriages. *Countess of Breadalbane* was built for the Caledonian Steam Packet services on Loch Awe in Scotland; for Windermere the

LMS approached Vickers-Armstrong for a new motor vessel, with a provisional order for a second, should the first prove satisfactory.

Vickers constructed the new vessel – yard number 715 – at Barrow in Furness, before dismantling her for transportation by rail to Lakeside for re-assembly on the slip. Tracks were laid along the side of the slipway where she was being assembled. Miss Harris, daughter of the LMS Marine Superintendent, launched *Teal* (II), on 4th July 1936. The launch made front page news in the Westmorland Gazette under the headline *'Windermere's Show Boat'*.

A Great Achievement

Exactly two months after the keel was laid Windermere's new L.M.S. motor vessel, Teal, was launched at Lakeside on Saturday, under circumstances which had the happiest of auguries. Precisely at 11 o'clock with a pair of gold handled scissors Miss Harris, daughter of Capt. Harris, superintendent, L.M.S. Railway at Lakeside, snipped the tape, the Chief Engineer called 'One, two, three,' the deep throated contralto of the syren roared its challenge to the whole of Lakeland, drowning the cheers called for by Commander Sir Charles Craven, and in five seconds the handsome boat was fully launched. In five seconds more she was moving to her mooring in Lakeside Bay -a perfect picture- immediately surrounded with a ring of varied craft such as probably no other inland sheet of water in the world can produce at a few moments notice. It was no intention of being flippant that one spontaneously designated it as Windermere's Show Boat. It looks what it is –a pleasure steamer- and its homely and alluring design immediately invites company.

It is really a remarkable performance for a vessel of this dimension to be launched practically completely finished, two months after the laying of its keel, but it is just what could be reasonably expected from such an efficient firm as Vickers Armstrong, of Barrow. Here the parts were made, and they were assembled on the cradle at Lakeside. The last vessel of similar character took twelve months to construct.

At 251 tons, 142 feet long and 25 feet wide with a draught of 4 feet she was the largest (in tonnage) vessel yet built for Windermere and could carry 867 passengers over three decks. She was powered with twin Gleniffer diesel engines giving a total of 320 horsepower and a service speed of eleven knots. Her two-class accommodation included first class saloons towards the bow with oak fittings and greyish-blue velvet upholstery; mahogany was used in second-class areas. As built it was possible to walk around the saloon on the middle deck, and there was no roof over the top deck.

Her inaugural sailing on Friday 17th July 1936 left Lakeside at 3.05 pm for Bowness, arriving at 3.40 pm. Ten minutes later she departed for Ambleside arriving at 4.15 pm. After leaving Ambleside at 4.30 pm she returned to Lakeside at 5.45 pm. From Sunday 19th July she joined the other vessels in public service.

The 1936 and 1937 seasons were a huge success with 492,668 passengers carried during the latter season. The *Teal* (II) proved its worth, so the LMS confirmed their repeat order. The new vessel arrived in Lakeside on Sunday 10th April, taking two months to assemble on the Lakeside slipway.

Swan (II) was built to near identical specification to *Teal* (II) and launched on 10th June 1938 by Miss Joyce Davies, daughter of LMS Chief Commercial Manager Mr Ashton Davies. Amongst the crowd was Miss C. Robinson who had attended the launch of the *Swan* (I) in 1869. Miss Davies cut the blue ribbon that held back a bottle of wine at 11 am, and said '*I name this ship the 'Swan''*. The bottle didn't break against the hull so an official completed the job. As the *Swan* (II) slid down the slip, her sixty-nine year old namesake was loading at the quayside for her sailing up the lake. After the launch *Swan* (II)'s fitting out was completed and her trials commenced on Monday 20th June.

Like her sister, *Swan* (II) had no funnels, exhaust being let through vents on the lower section of the hull at the aft end. *Teal* (II) carried fifteen tons of ballast whilst the *Swan* (II) did not need any (although this would later change). The newer vessel carried slightly fewer passengers, as her passenger complement was 820. Her first passenger sailing on 24th June carried a group from the Municipal Tramways and Transport Association from Lakeside at 11.30 am to Ambleside. The following day saw her in public service.

The arrival of *Swan* (II) saw *Swan* (I) withdrawn and sold for scrap.

Windermere steamers were laid up during the

Second World War, but *Teal* (II) and *Swan* (II) sailed in the summers of 1939, 1940 and 1941 before being tied up at Lakeside. The *Tern* remained at Bowness as a Sea Scout training vessel, named after destroyer *HMS Undine* which had been adopted by Ambleside and Bowness during the war. A sign on the vessel read;

SEA CADET CORPS
    (Administered by the Navy League on behalf of the Admiralty)
TRAINING SHIP
'UNDINE'
PRE-ENTRY TRAINING FOR THE
ROYAL NAVY, ROYAL MARINES & MERCHANT NAVY PARADE;- {SUNDAYS 10-30 A.M. – 12-30 P.M.
{TUESDAYS & FRIDAYS 7-9 P.M.

Towards the end of the war the rest of the fleet was

Teal (II) and **Swan** (II) berthed at Waterhead.

Teal (II) crosses the ferry line heading for Bowness. In the foreground is a self-drive motor boat.

Right: An unusual view for the present day shows **Teal** (II) bow in at Waterhead. The steamers usually berth stern in here.

Far right: On the first trip of the day, **Teal** (II) is seen approaching Bowness pier, from Lakeside.

Right: **Teal** (II) heading north from Bowness, for Waterhead.

Far right: **Teal** (II) arriving at Lakeside with enclosed sides, but still in Sealink colours.

Below left: **Teal** (II) leaving Lakeside whilst in her Sealink colours. Perspex dodgers are visible at the front of the upper deck, and an awning has been placed overall.

Below right: Awaiting her first turn of duty for the day, **Teal** (II) is seen alongside at Lakeside in her present condition.

Bottom left: **Teal** (II) and **Swan** (II) cross paths off Storrs. The Blackwell Arts and Craft centre is prominent on the hill behind.

Bottom right: **Teal** (II) landing at Brockhole on 25th July 2011.

moored at Lakeside, and Alf Mawson of Newby Bridge was employed to 'turn the engines' to keep them free.

Post war services resumed on 16th July 1945 when *Teal* (II) and *Swan* (II) commenced a short season. 1946 saw resumption of a two boat schedule, and in 1947 *Teal* (II) and *Swan* (II) operated daily, while *Cygnet* sailed on Sundays, Tuesdays, Wednesdays and Thursday, leaving steam vessels *Tern* and *Swift* tied up at Lakeside due to a coal shortage.

Tourism boomed after the wartime restrictions, and the boats often left people behind during the high season; on one occasion the *Tern* left trippers at Ambleside on her last sailing, and the stranded tourists had to wait for the *Swift* to come from Lakeside and collect them – even though *Tern*'s passenger complement was 677 compared to today's 350.

Liveries through the years

The Windermere fleets exhibited a variety of liveries over the years. In times of rivalry this enabled easy identification by potential customers, or under one operating company, provided uniformity between different ships.

Lady of the Lake and *Lord of the Isles* of the Steam Yacht Company were identifiable by their black funnel, a very broad white band on their black painted hulls and a star painted onto the paddle box. Rival vessels of the Iron Steamboat Company, carried a funnel half black from the bottom and white to the top. When amalgamated, the black funnel with large white band and paddle box star was adopted by all the vessels.

In the FR era vessels received a buff funnel with a black boot top, and grey and white hulls. The *Raven* was

Swan (II) with Rawlinson Nab behind in the southern basin of Windermere.

Teal (II) departs on the 10.10 am to Waterhead, leaving Swan (II) to load at Bowness for the 10.30 am for Lakeside.

given a white funnel. The LMS maintained the liveries, although during the 1930s the *Tern* at least had a black hull for a few seasons.

British Railways gave the *Swift* and *Tern* buff yellow funnels with a black rim – a large surface area after their conversion to motor ships. *Swan* (II) and *Teal* (II) retained white hulls for most of their career, but British Railways placed grey canvas buffers around their upper decks. Sealink painted hulls white, with a slim blue line above the main deck windows. Above this was the BR logo, also in blue. Later the sisters had blue hulls, from waterline to the bottom of the saloon windows, and the logo was replaced with 'Sealink' in large letters along the upper deck. Sealink painted *Tern* and *Swift's* funnels in standard orange with black rim, with the Sealink logo over the orange, although for at least one season they sported blue funnels with black boot top.

Sea Containers painted *Tern's* funnel white with a green boot top, and on the white section printed the logo of the Windermere Iron Steamboat Company. The two larger sisters were painted white apart from the woodwork. They still carry this livery today with the addition of dark green lines along the deck divisions and green boot tops to their funnels.

In 1991 the *Tern* received a green dummy steam funnel – yellow for 1996 at least. Today *Tern's* funnel is white and her hull is the same colour, but with a green underside.

Today's waterbuses are painted blue and white.

British Railways Days

1948 saw the 'big four' railway companies nationalised to form British Railways, controlled by the British Transport Commission. The Windermere fleet had been nationalised.

The Windermere Motorboat Racing Club was formed in 1925, headquartered in Bowness. In 1951 they moved to Broad Leys, south of Storrs Hall. Club members raced around a course at high speeds until the 10 knot speed limit was introduced in 2005. For around 20 years until around 1968, when the World Championships were held on the lake, *Teal* (II) and *Swan* (II) were used as grandstands, moored in the middle of the course. They were secured using their bow anchor and stern ropes tied to buoys attached to permanent anchors. These huge anchors were from Heysham and kept on the lakebed – they are probably still there.

For the 1952 season, two boats were used from 4th – 17th June but between 18th June and 23rd September three or four boats were needed. *Teal* (II) and *Swan* (II) operated full-lake cruises, while the *Tern* and *Swift* came from Lakeside in the morning and sailed between Bowness and Ambleside during the day before heading back in the evening.

Cygnet was largely laid up, covering breakdowns and charters. She sailed her last season in 1953 and was sold to Lake District Estates Company Limited, who sold her in 1955 to Sir Wavell Wakefield, who had a controlling

Opposite: **Teal** (II) is left at Lakeside ready for the 10.20 am departure for Bowness. **Swan** (II) is leaving on the 09.20 am.

Below: The view up the lake from Lakeside. Taken from the wheelhouse of **Swan** (II). **Venture** is seen returning from a cruise, ahead of the steamer.

Swan (II) arriving at Waterhead.

Swan (II) reversing out of Bowness on a balmy summers day.

interest in the Ullswater steamers. *Cygnet* was to move to Ullswater and was painted in the new company's colours at Lakeside. She received a new funnel in 1956, but never left Windermere, probably due to difficulties in transporting her to Ullswater. The intended route was to take her via Kendal and Shap. She was sold in 1957 to Lake Windermere Properties Limited for conversion into a houseboat. Moored near Lakeside, she sank on 17th May 1962, became a total loss and was broken up in 1964.

From the mid-1950s full size leaflets were issued to attract tourists, with colourful covers and details of the history and scenic splendours of the landscape, alongside the older handbills. This coincided with a shift in society as disposable income increased, and holidays abroad became cheaper. It was hoped that this literature would entice more to remain in the UK for their holidays.

The Queen and Duke of Edinburgh sailed on the *Teal* (II) from Ambleside to Bowness on Saturday 11th August 1956, and glass windscreens were fitted along the upper deck for the occasion. Invited guests accompanied the Royals and departure from Waterhead was scheduled for 11.50 am although *Teal* (II), skippered by Jimmy Jackson, departed fifteen minutes late. Her Majesty was saluted by forty-seven boys in fourteen boats from the Brathay Hall Centre, and ex fleet member *Cygnet* was filled with Sea Cadets who cheered as the *Teal* (II) passed. She was escorted from Ambleside to Belle Grange by twelve motorboats from the Windermere Motor Boat Racing Club. At Belle Grange they peeled off to be replaced by yachts from the Royal Windermere Yacht Club. The *Swan* (II) became a floating grandstand, coming from Lakeside with 88 special guests on board.

On Friday 26th July 1957 a plaque was unveiled on the *Teal* (II) commemorating the Royal visit. Alongside the plaque were hung signed portraits of Her Majesty and Prince Philip. In 1990 the Queen re-signed the photograph on board the vessel and in 2013 again sailed on the *Teal* (II), fifty seven years after her first visit.

During the mid-1950s *Swift* was only used for six weeks of the high season on Bowness to Ambleside sailings with *Tern*, as she had a temperamental boiler. The two veterans lacked covered accommodation and in 1956 *Tern* had a canvas awning placed over her rear deck – which has been retained to the present day. *Swift*'s boiler failed halfway through the 1956 season and she was withdrawn. The two steam boats were earmarked for conversion to diesel and in the winter of 1956-7 *Swift* had two six cylinder Gleniffer diesel engines fitted, each providing 150 horsepower. *Tern*

followed the next winter and her steam engines were removed on 29th December 1957. She returned on 18th May 1958, with updated décor. Both boats lost their 'Woodbine' steam funnels, receiving smaller squat funnels. Despite the gleaming diesel engines, bridge controls were not installed and the old telegraphs remained in use. Although no longer steam, we will continue to refer to the vessels as steamers to distinguish from the waterbuses and launches.

Whilst *Tern* and *Swift* were unreliable, the timetable showed only a three-boat service. From 1958 all four boats were rostered during the summer with the two older vessels used primarily between Bowness and Ambleside and the newer twins operating full lake cruises. This pattern remained with minor alterations until the end of the 1981 season, so that a steamer departed Bowness for Ambleside every half hour, and vice versa.

Swift would leave Lakeside at around 10.45 am before undertaking five return sailings between Bowness and Ambleside, finishing back at Lakeside at 6.25 pm. *Tern* would leave Lakeside at 11.45 am, do four returns from Bowness to Ambleside and finish back at Lakeside at 6.55 pm. The next day the ships would switch rosters. Other timetables were issued for Easter and early season periods, and usually one steamer rested on a Saturday and a three boat service operated, reducing to two from the mid-1970s, each running the length of the lake. During the Barrow holiday fortnight in 1959 nearly 48,000 people passed through Lakeside. Although holidays abroad were becoming more popular – in 1962 2.4 million Britons holidayed abroad – the Windermere services remained well patronised.

The 1960s saw further improvements to all four

vessels, each receiving enclosed wheelhouses keeping masters dry and warm in inclement weather. *Swan* (II) and *Teal* (II) had canvas awnings placed over upper decks, and perspex wind buffers at the forward end of their upper decks to increase passenger comfort.

Management of the Windermere operation was from regional offices at Heysham, with a smaller office at Lakeside station. Passenger figures continued to rise, as they had since the 1930s. Whilst in 1937 492,500 passengers were carried, 453,240 was the average for the 1950s, but 1964 saw record carryings of 500,000.

Excursion trains waned in the post-war period as more people used cars, and by 1964 only 10% of passengers on the lake arrived through Lakeside station. The coach tour took trade away from the railways and became increasingly popular. A trip on the lake allowed

Swan (II) seen in 1979 at Lakeside.

Swan (II) at Brockhole, the National Park Visitor Centre. **Miss Cumbria IV** passes en route for Ambleside.

passengers a lunch and toilet break, and let the driver rest before continuing to the next destination.

In 1969 *Teal* (II) played host to The Spinners folk band. The vessel was moored off Lakeside using anchors, and a film crew placed on the upper concourse of the station looking down and across to the steamer. Whilst setting the bow anchor the weight was lowered and the chain allowed to run through. The anchors were rarely used, and the chain had not been re-shackled to the boat – so the helpless crew watched the chain slide into the water. Luckily a diver lived locally, and within an hour the chain had been located and the boat secured for filming to commence. The band performed on board the vessel and the programme was shown on national television the following week. Original copies of the film – which showed a lot of the boat – have been lost, although a few scenes were saved.

During the 1960s and 1970s when the final steamer of the season left Ambleside it would take the gangways and ropes from the pier. Once departed, Mr Tyson of the Wateredge Inn would sound his hunting horn, to which the steamer would reply with blasts from her horn. Once berthed at Lakeside the overhaul season began. Each boat received a thorough overhaul and, as regulations dictated that a vessel must have its propeller shafts examined every four years, an inspector came every year to view one of the ships, as they were pulled up the slip in turn. Throughout the 1960s ten permanent staff were employed as masters, mates and engineers, who turned their hands to maintenance during the winter, supplemented by seasonal crews.

For the 1969 centenary of railway operation, Sealink sponsored a Lady of the Lake competition. Young ladies who wanted to work as a hostess on the steamer during summer were encouraged to enter, and the prize also included a two-week cruise around the Mediterranean. The following year the boats carried a record 634,000 passengers, a record broken again in 1972 when 640,000 passengers enjoyed a cruise on the lake.

Around this time the delicate matter of waste water was raised. A local magazine in 1971 reported;

'The organisers of the service, anxious to prevent any sort of pollution to the lake, are arranging for large tanks to be fitted to the craft to take liquid waste'.

The same magazine had a rather humorous tale regarding the boats registration; *The service goes out of its way to be helpful to visitors, though one lady tried the patience of the staff when she sat on the boat at Waterhead and insisted on being taken direct to Barrow-in-Furness. Several times it was explained that the steamer went to Lakeside only and that there was no handy transport connection beyond this point. She would have to take a bus from the eastern side of the lake. But it says it goes to Barrow, insisted the lady. She was asked to elaborate, and she took the officials round to the stern of the craft. There was the vessel's name and the port of registration – Barrow!*

Teal (II) received a major upgrade in 1974, gaining a larger saloon whilst removing passenger access around the outside of the main deck. The toilets were moved downstairs and the engine room entrance moved aft. *Swan* (II) followed for the 1975 season; by 1979 both had a solid roof over the top deck replacing canvas awnings, and allowing more passengers to stay dry in bad weather.

The main station building at Lakeside fell into disrepair and in 1978 the clock tower and main building were demolished.

On 1st January 1979, Sealink UK Ltd took control of the steamers as a wholly owned subsidiary of the British Railway Board.

On Sunday 6th September 1981 *Swift* made her final voyage on Windermere and was moored up at Lakeside after eighty-one years service. The timetable was amended with *Teal* (II) and *Swan* (II) sailing the full lake and *Tern* operating between Bowness and Ambleside. *Swift's* retirement ended the half-hourly Ambleside trips, and *Tern* only operated during June, July and August. It was intended to bring *Swift* back from retirement for the 1985 season to enable *Tern* to be available for charters, but she remained mothballed at Lakeside, her future uncertain. In 1989 she became a floating museum, telling the story of Donald Campbell and his world water speed record attempts.

On 27th July 1984 Sealink was privatised, with Sea Containers taking the operation into non-railway hands for the first time since 1869. James Sherwood, known for the restoration and operation of the Orient Express, promised investment across the Group. Sea Containers purchased a small wooden fishing boat from Arnside for a service between Lakeside and Fell Foot, the old residence of Colonel Ridehalgh. *Cygnet* was limited to twelve passengers and was later superseded by *Sunflower II* in the 1990s – *Cygnet* is still in use as a workboat.

In 1986 the company revived the name of the 1848 company, and rebranded as the Windermere Iron Steam Boat Company, becoming part of Orient Express Hotels for administrative purposes.

1987 saw the introduction of forty-five minute non-landing mini-cruises from Bowness, operated by *Tern* to compete with the Bowness Bay Boating Company's

Swan (II) landing at Lakeside in July 1989. (George Woods)

Islands Cruise. They headed south to Storrs Hall then north to Troutbeck and back; for the first year of their operation seven departures were provided each day. *Tern* berthed at Ambleside overnight to provide an earlier sailing to Bowness, saving passengers having to wait for the *Swan* (II) or *Teal* (II) coming up from Lakeside.

In 1989 *Tern* again found herself on round the lake cruises, based at Lakeside, but mini-cruises of varying durations were slotted into her timetable in the afternoon, before her final trip back to Lakeside. A larger steamer berthed overnight at Ambleside, except on Sundays and Wednesdays when it returned to Bowness to do two more late mini-cruises. The following year the mini-cruises were dropped and *Tern* sailed round the lake in the high season, complementing her larger sisters.

Teal (II) was upgraded again in 1990, when the lower saloon was revamped and fitted with a bar and toilets. 1991 was *Tern*'s centenary and to celebrate she was totally refurbished on the slip at Lakeside over the winter of 1990-91. She received a dummy steam funnel on top of her motor funnel and her bridge was moved forward near to the bow and power steering was fitted. In recognition of her century of service a plaque was unveiled on the 27th June by the Right Honourable The Viscount Whitelaw whilst on board a special cruise. This is still displayed on the port side of the vessel under the funnel. During *Tern*'s centenary year 280,000 passengers were carried, considerably less than a couple of decades earlier. Daily sailings continued during November using one boat from Monday to Saturday and two on a Sunday. In December a weekend service was provided using just one boat. For large groups the steamer could be seen out in January, February or March.

On 24th May 1993 the Bowness Bay Boating Company purchased the Windermere Iron Steam Boat Company bringing all the passenger boats on the lake, apart from the car ferry, under common ownership. The new operation became known as Windermere Lake Cruises and introduced combined publicity for the steamer and the smaller launches.

The smaller operations

An abundance of small watercraft offered trips on the lake in addition to the steamer operation, mainly from Bowness but also from Lakeside, Ambleside and the various hotels. The small launches and rowing boats of Bowness could head around the main group of islands on the lake, where steamers couldn't go, and with many more launches than steamers, departures were more frequent.

Rowing Boats and Self Drives

From the late 18th century rowing boats were available to hire – with or without a boatman – and one traveller noted how he hired a boat at Ambleside as early as the 1770s. Rowing boats were popular in Bowness, although in the 1840s that there were only about a dozen boats for hire; Bowness had yet to be 'discovered' by the masses. Later, hotels gathered their own hire fleets, and independent boatmen took over the hiring.

James Branker built a small pier in the 1840s on the

Swan (II) seen in October 1979, the first year of Sealink UK Ltd operations. (George Woods)

Swan (II) in Bowness Bay.

Below: A few well-dressed adventurers prepare to hire a rowing boat from Bowness. (Reproduced by courtesy of the Museum of Lakeland Life and Industry)

south-eastern side of Hen Holme. He also created a large marble table, with seats, for visitors to picnic. The island was seldom empty of people, unlike today. The table supports are still there, hidden by rhododendron.

Another tradition was to row a loved one behind Belle Isle and pick the lilies which grew on the islands. The two small islands of Small Holme and Ing Holme were known collectively as the Lilies of the Valley from the mid-18th Century – they have retained their altered name, but the flowers no longer grow there due to over picking.

Belle Isle was owned by the Curwen family until the late 20th Century. They allowed visitors to the island and sold tickets from Bowness hotels for the privilege of landing. This continued until the Curwens leased Belle Isle to Mr Bridson in 1884. He forbade unauthorised visits and since then landing has been prohibited.

On 1st June 1850 the Lancaster Gazette reported; *Windermere Lake now presents a gay appearance. There are more than one hundred small pleasure boats in the bay, exclusive of large pleasure boats and steamers. To see so many small craft riding at anchor is a very pleasant sight.*

Bowness Bay was cleaned up in March 1868. The lake shore had become a tip and was an eyesore compared to remoter parts of the lake. The Bowness Local Board instructed the owners of boats and timber lying along the shore to remove them within a week or they would be sold. This action was for *'the purpose of providing a pleasure ground for the inhabitants and visitors of Bowness and of regulating the pleasure boats and Vessels at Bowness'.*

In autumn 1869 the cushion huts were moved to the north end of Bowness Bay, where the road heads up into the village. These were offices for boat owners, and places where plush cushions, oars, fishing tackle, bait and anchors were kept for rowing boats. They had previously been dotted along the lake shore taking up valuable room, and this was now a perfect location, the first thing most tourists would see as they headed for the lake. An image from the 1870s shows the cushion hut – owning families of Dixon, Campbell, Lancaster,

Robinson, Holmes, Tebay, Mason, Taylor, and others which are indecipherable. Other families known to be hiring were the Hodgson, Fleming, Bispham, Briscoe, Braithwaite, Atkinson, Fawcett and Leak families. They were among the first generation boatmen in Bowness.

The cushion huts have been rebuilt to the original design, and now house a lake information centre although that nearest the lake maintains the tradition of hiring out rowing boats. Old images show cushion huts along Myley Birk now the Aquarius beach, but these were later removed probably with the promenade alterations of 1912.

'The Saturday Review of Politics, Literature, Science and Art' was particularly patronising and scathing regarding the Windermere boatmen in 1866;

The lake boatmen, it should be observed, seem ignorant of the rudimentary principles of rowing; not, probably, can correct form be attained with their pivot-sculls and oars, which make 'feathering' impossible. The London Rowing Club might advantageously hold a provincial retreat at Windermere, and diffuse the correct principles of their art. It is a pity to see fine broad-chested Lancashire men fumbling at their paddles like so many old women.

Although Sunday steamer sailings were withdrawn in 1869, Bowness boatmen continued to hire-out seven days a week. The 1869 'Bye-laws on the Regulation of Pleasure Boats' stipulated; -

• Each boatman had to be licensed.
• All touting was prohibited.
• An annual license of ten shillings to hire out on the Sabbath (equivalent to £250 today).
• A restriction to the maximum number of non-residents hiring out a boat of any size to six.
• The lake-side should be kept clean and free from litter.

The penultimate byelaw was introduced to reduce the *'dangerous antics of excursionists'*. Boatmen clubbed together to oppose this change, considering licensing ludicrous for a family trade practiced for generations. In

1871 the Board withdrew the new byelaws excepting those forbidding touting and enforcing cleanliness. A lower licence fee was imposed, but some refused to get licenses and others applied but declined to pay.

The banning of touting was a blow as it was relied upon to attract customers. The boatmen competed with each other and sometimes customers were blocked from passing or grabbed and 'escorted' to the boats. Some boatmen fished on the side, but the job of a Bowness boatman was a full time summer occupation. The touting byelaw was disregarded, and luckily for the boatmen the Bowness Local Board did not enforce it.

Two quotes provide differing opinions about the touting. The first is from the 1880s;

Scores of pleasure-boats lie waiting for hire, and by the side of which stand the boatmen in the sun, not ready to tear you in pieces among them, as in less peaceful regions, but civilly requesting a patronage you will scarcely withhold.

On the other hand a guide book from 1890 recorded; *Anyone presenting the appearance of an excursionist at Bowness is beset immediately on his entrance to the village by a curiously importunate trade of men, who stick like leeches to their victims, dinning their ears by –'a boat today sir?' 'A sail on the Lake?' &c. Those peculiar individuals are the boatmen, among whom there is such uncalled-for rivalry, that their continual solicitations for employment have of late become a thorough nuisance to the inhabitants.*

Touts still work for the pleasure cruisers and rowing boats today, but their methods are more customer-orientated!

With restrictions on Sunday hire, one way around paying the extra fees was to hire it out during the week and hide it away for use on the Sabbath. Fishing was also banned on Sundays.

Boats were hired from three stone piers north of the steamer pier. The central one was for the embarkation of passengers, the other two for public use, although the boatmen ignored this rule as there were too many boats for just one pier. In 1873 the Windermere Pleasure Boat Company was told not to monopolise the public landings. By 1882-83 the three small piers were replaced with two longer wooden structures. Today's two wooden piers are descendants of these and the northernmost pier is a floating jetty allowing access at all water levels.

The Windermere Pleasure Boat Company comprised a collection of boat proprietors operating from the lake-side but it is not recorded how formal this association was. In 1885 Bowness boat proprietors included William Begbie, John Braithwaite, George Brockbank, John Campbell, Stephen Carr, John Fawcett, Richard Hayton, William Kirkbride, Joseph Lamb, Robert Millray, William Robinson, Thomas Storey, James Walker, Thomas Walker and Harry Woodend.

Rowing boats were locally built from 3/8 inch larch hulls with rudders to aid steering; the average length of a boat being 18 feet. These sturdy little craft were, and still are, well built and often completed with mahogany fittings, oak stems, and keels made from larch, oak or pitch pine. Brass screws and copper nails are used to prevent rust, and the planks are placed around a wooden mould and steamed into place. Screws and nails are fitted and the mould removed. Originally rowing boats were built using six planks, counting from the keel, but from the 1960s they were built using seven. Boats are usually built in three sizes; two, four or six people, although some cater for eight, so groups can go out together.

Early boats were built in Bowness and Windermere and carted down to the lake, but construction moved to the lake-side as boathouses sprang up along Bowness Bay. They were clinker built as this is a more sturdy design than carvel, and can be dragged up rough beaches or islands. Oars were originally made from silver spruce and placed in 'tholes' (grooves) set into the gunwale. They could be feathered when rowing to reduce windage. Many tourists couldn't operate oars through the tholes as they could pop out, or 'catch a crab' (when the oar catches the water unexpectedly whilst pulling back for the stroke). Inexperienced rowers could also catch their thumbs between the oars as they rowed.

Many tourists preferred to hire a skilled boatman to convey them on a tour, until Tom Hayton of Bowness designed the offset rowlock. These were metal frames in a triangular shape set into the side of the boat that moved the pivot point 3-4 inches away from the gunwale. The oar is placed in a pin at the end of the triangular frame. Oars were modified – by having holes bored through them – to sit on the pin. This simple mechanism reduced lost oars and avoided the dreaded thumb smash. Now even the most inexperienced rower has a fighting chance of getting around Belle Isle and back. The offset rowlock revolutionised rowing on the lake, but Tom Hayton never patented the design and didn't benefit from the widespread adoption.

Cushions added value to the experience and the boats were designed to cater for all takers.

In 1898, there were more than 240 rowing boats available for hire from Bowness. The Bowness boatmen

Bowness, showing the Cushion Huts. See how each Cushion Hut has the name board of the proprietor. (Reproduced by courtesy of the Museum of Lakeland Life and Industry, Kendal, Cumbria)

each owned a few, some more than ten; John Braithwaite alone had nineteen.

One way of creating trade was enticing customers with the prospect of seeing a rare mammal unique to Windermere. The Tizzie Whizie, (Erinaceus volans), an animal with the body of a hedgehog, the tail of a fox and the wings of a bee, not to mention antennae, was first spotted around 1900 by some inebriated boatmen. They recounted their tale at the nearest pub, the Stag's Head, no doubt in exchange for more beer! The Tizzie Whizie is unique to Bowness; one was captured in 1906 and photographed in Louis Herbert's Photographic Studio, but flew out of an open window. A search was made for another specimen, but as soon as one was sighted it flew off so fast it was just a blur.

Boatmen cashed in and organised hunts, creating healthy queues for rowing boats. Tourists were told by boatmen that a Tizzie Whizie had just flown past heading for Belle Isle, and boats were hired with a guide to hunt for the beast. Inevitably the creature proved just too elusive and the tourists returned to shore out of pocket and disappointed. One American offered a reward of £5 for a specimen, dead or alive. Postcards of the only picture of the animal gave Louis Herbert plenty of business, and the boatmen kept up the story for many years.

Another ploy played on potential fishing parties was to throw a handful of pebbles into the lake when they weren't looking. These simulated fish surfacing to feed and the boatman would shout 'they're rising!' and the boat would be hired there and then.

A byelaw of 1909 stipulated that all boatmen should wear a 'Windermere Boatman' badge. They naturally objected and a deputation went to the Council to be informed that badges need only be worn when rowing people on the lake. In 1911 there were 297 licensed rowing boats for hire on the lake with 35 boat proprietors and 59 licensed boatmen in Bowness alone. They did good business in the lead up to the First World War and even the 1915 season proved successful because 'there have been no prosecutions, or complaints against proprietors or boatmen, and their conduct generally has been quite satisfactory in every respect'.

The boatmen worked closely together, leading to the formation of the Bowness Bay Boating Company in 1934. Boats in Bowness were hired from Myley Birk until the 1980s and the beaches between the launch jetties, as well as the beach where they can still be hired. Boats were repaired and varnished in lake-side boathouses during the winter, but in 1968 the Bowness Old Laundry was purchased and the boats moved there. Sometimes in winter the lake rises sufficiently to cover the piers; one tourist asked a boatman where the piers had gone and was informed that they had been taken in with the boats for winter storage!

William Robinson, known locally as Aggy Billy, set up the Promenade Café in the early 1920s to complement his boat hire business and create jobs for his family, even though water was carried to the café by hand. It remained in his family until the 1950s.

During the Second World War the rowing boats were very busy. Fuel rationing stopped motor launches sailing, and the steamers ceased too. In the summer the rowing boats were as busy as the halcyon days of the 1890s when people thronged the beach. The rowing boats were given names such as *Dolly*, *Comet*, *Alice*, *Avril* and each boatman had his 'series' of boats. In 1964 there were still 150 rowing boats available for hire at Bowness. *Jessie*, built in 1896 was still hired in the 1980s, and a couple who honeymooned aboard her in the 1920s were delighted to see her still afloat fifty years later.

Small petrol-engined motor boats began to appear between the two World Wars, although some had their origins in the previous century. One such, the *Ailsa* is still available for hire; built as a pinnace for the Royal Windermere Yacht Club in the 1890s, she may originally have been steam powered. Traditional hire boats powered with Stuart Turner engines were made for the lake until the 1960s. Most were open boats but those with cabins were more appealing in inclement weather. Many were named and *Bee*, *Vivena*, *Mayfly*, *Helen*, *May*, *Gay*, *June* and *Carol* still operate, amongst others. Apart from *Ailsa* which is carvel, they are all clinker built with engines amidships. Early boats were steered with tillers at the stern, but throttle controls were on the engine so steering whilst adjusting power required long arms.

In the 1970s Brockbanks boat builders built small fibreglass motorboats, also using Stuart Turner engines. Some have been converted to use silent electric motors making the experience more enjoyable. These have sliding canopies and are steered using a wheel instead of a tiller. Six new self-drive boats were introduced in 2015 at Ambleside. Using silent electric motors, the Mystic type vessels have a ten hour battery life. Today there are still three companies hiring out self-drives in Bowness Bay; Windermere Lake Cruises, Shepherds and Aquatics. There are still over fifty rowing boats, fifteen traditional motor boats and twenty fibreglass motor boats available for hire from Bowness and Ambleside. From Lakeside, Joe Huddleston and Mr Kellett hired rowing boats until their retirement in the early 1970s. Rowing boats are still hired at Fell Foot although these fibreglass vessels are not a traditional design.

Rowing boats were probably first hired at the Ferry Inn when the Curwens took over in the 1780s and Mr Hodgson – who operated the Ferry Bay Café – continued to hire in Mitchel Wyke until the mid-1960s. At Millerground the Baines family hired rowing boats from the 1880s until 1947, and hiring here continued until the mid-1960s. Brockhole has fibreglass rowing boats for hire, and at Ambleside rowing boats have been available since the late eighteenth century. Early twentieth century boatmen included Forrest and Robinson, and the Hardy family. Robert Clarke had a small fleet of rowing boats here too, but he later relocated to Coniston Water.

The Bowness Bay Boating Company sold rowing boats to Derwentwater, where they remain for hire on the foreshore, whilst others left for a new career on the Thames at Windsor in the 1980s.

Opposite: In 1774 Thomas English commissioned John Plaw to design a residence for him on Long Holme. The Round House seen here from Cockshott Point was duly completed in 1778, but unfortunately gained much local opposition, not least from William Wordsworth who said the house reminded him of a Pepper Pot. In 1781 English sold the island to Miss Isabella Curwen of Workington Hall. She married John Christian (cousin of Fletcher Christian of Mutiny on the Bounty fame), who renamed the island after his wife, hence the name Belle Isle.

BOAT LANDINGS, LAKESIDE ON WINDERMERE

Top left: Very early launches in Bowness Bay including **Flo**.

Top right: **Mayflower** (II) arriving at Low Wood.

Middle: **Fleurette** with the Langdale Pikes behind. She was owned by, and operated from, the Langdale Chase Hotel.

Right: The well-travelled **Iris** owned by the Ambleside Motor Launch Company, and Huddlestone & Kellet's **Have a Go** at the Lakeside Hotel.

The legendary, rarely-seen Tizzie-Whizie.

Top: **Iris** and possibly **Bee** at Waterhead.

Middle: **Iris** reversing from the Ambleside Motor Launch Company's piers at Waterhead.

Bottom: A busy 1950s scene at Waterhead with (closest to furthest) **Mayflower** (II), **Princess of the Lake**, **Spray** and **Swan** (II) at Waterhead.

Launch Operations

Launch operations started in the later nineteenth century. Colonel Ridehalgh's *Fairy Queen* ran occasional trips from Bowness from 1866, and *Cygnet* was operating from the Swan Hotel at Newby Bridge about 1871. It was recorded in 1873 that; '*On Windermere tiny steam yachts are now to be hired by the hour like rowing boats, and we may expect to see this sort of craft indefinitely multiplied*'.

Boatmen – each with their own boat – competed from the Bowness promenade, and in 1898 there were around six steam launches operating from the Esperance pier. 46 electric and steam launches were recorded regularly visiting Bowness, with some of these available for hire. Berths became scarce, and vessels started operating from the public piers north of the steamer pier.

The first motor boat on Windermere was launched in 1899. A private boat, she was quickly joined by others and soon motor launches were operating from Bowness. Cruises became properly established in the years leading up to the First World War. Sometimes rowing boats filled with people were towed by steam launches but the Council quickly stopped this practice.

A standard cruise developed around the islands in the central part of the lake. Originally called the 'Eight Mile Cruise' it involved travelling north to Millerground and Belle Grange via Fallbarrow, around Belle Isle, before heading down to the Ferry Hotel and returning to Bowness via Parsonage Wyke and Cockshott Point. An alternative missed out Millerground and Belle Grange heading straight around Belle Isle, allowing boats to reach Grass Holme opposite the Beech Hill Hotel, before returning to Bowness. This has evolved into today's Islands Cruise. These cruises offered views of the north and south basins of the lake and the islands in a short space of time, usually 45-60 minutes. This cruise competed well with the steamers as with fewer passengers the skipper could offer a local commentary and answer questions.

Gradually steam launches gave way to motor launches as steam was impractical for the nature of work from Bowness. Getting up steam took a couple of hours and trips ran on demand, so vessels could be waiting with steam but no passengers, or passengers but no steam. Motor launches took minutes to get ready starting up with petrol and switching to burn TVO (Tractor Vaporising Oil). Petrol tanks only held enough to warm the engine up, so timing of the switch was crucial. Many were later converted to diesel.

Motor boats were of similar design to steam boats with a cabin aft and open bow. They were smaller, often carrying 12 passengers, but with some up to 30 and a few even more. The Windermere Motor Launch Company Limited, formed in 1913 by boat proprietors from Bowness and directors from Borwicks, used two large launches *Mayflower* (II) and *Sunflower* (I). In 1913 there were 8 motor boats licensed for hire from Bowness. Just two years later there were 21.

In the early 1920s the *Sunflower* (I) and *Mayflower*

Bowness in the late 1950s. **Tern** leaves Bowness for the north. Among the many launches visible are **Shamrock, Dolly, August Moon** and **Sunflower II**.

(I) were sold to Loch Lomond where they operated for many decades. The *Mayflower* (I) was notably smaller than *Sunflower* (I) so probably operated at Bowness for a private operator carrying 30 passengers compared to *Sunflower* (I)'s capacity of around 50.

The number of launches at Bowness dramatically increased after the First World War, causing capacity problems as they competed for mooring space with rowing boats. When the promenade was altered in 1921, they moved to the Esperance pier, and in 1922 Borwicks built another pier further south of the Esperance pier for exclusive use by the launches. Launches for hire were then banned from the rowing boat piers.

Rivalry between boatmen was intense but friendly, although 'stealing' trade from steamers was a bonus. Rules made competition fairer between launches, restricting them to remain at the pier no longer than 20 minutes, to avoid blocking another boat from loading passengers.

Touting was key to procuring passengers for one's boat. Each proprietor usually had one or two men whose job was to coax tourists over for a trip. Each theoretically took turns to approach customers; some going to Windermere station to catch people right off the train. When Henry Segrave made his water speed record attempt in 1930, touts littered the station to attract camera crews and newspaper reporters.

Omnibus tours started in the 1920s, bringing people right to the lake shore. Efficient touts could get the group onto the lake before a steamer had been sighted. Invariably rail passengers travelled by steamers, but motor car or coach visitors took the launches.

A 1932 leaflet for the Motor Launch Company offered cruises to Ambleside and the Lakeside Hotel piers, taking passengers down the River Leven to Newby Bridge if requested. They had three motor launches that year, *Mayflower* (II), *Sunflower* (II), and *Muriel*.

Intense rivalry was detrimental to profits for all concerned, so in 1934 John Bispham formed the Bowness Bay Boating Company (BBBC), bringing together boatmen and the Motor Launch Company to pool resources and operate as one. Twenty members offered their boats to the company and with so many launches available, one was always ready to depart. The fleet included amongst others, *August Moon*, *Fairy Queen*, *Osprey*, *Pastime*, *Shamrock*, and *Waterlily*. Known launches are recorded in the fleet lists. Some were built for the company, but others were purchased from private individuals, including *Osprey* and *Shamrock*, converted from steam to motor boats by the company.

Private boatmen struggled to compete with the new concern and gradually the BBBC became the major proprietor. As they expanded, trips were offered to Ambleside and Lakeside, landing at the public piers at either end. These became increasingly popular as they allowed time ashore. A contemporary handbill offered cruises to Newby Bridge for 1s. 6d. leaving at 10.45 am, returning at 1.00 pm, to Ambleside departing at 11.00 am and returning at 12.45 pm for 1s. and an evening

trip at 8.45 pm for an hour at 1s 6d. These supplemented the Eight Mile Cruise. The trip to Ambleside was called 'Ambleside via the Islands' whereas the Ambleside Motor Launch Company offered the reverse entitled 'Bowness via the Islands'.

Small shallow-draughted motor launches reinstated services *'down t'beck'* to Newby Bridge in the early 1930s, usually once daily until the mid-1950s, and the Swan Hotel benefitted significantly. This kept the channel dredged but the river has returned to being very shallow, leaving boats in the marina by the hotel with restricted access to the lake.

Bus tours became increasingly popular prior to the Second World War and larger launches like *Muriel II*

A lovely colourful late 1960s scene at Bowness with **Venture, Waterlily, Penguin, Silver Gleam** and **Fairy Queen**. Note the café across the bay.

The company's present work boat, **Cygnet**, was built as a fishing boat which worked from Arnside. She was purchased to inaugurate a ferry between Lakeside, where she is seen here complete with dummy steam funnel, and Fell Foot.

Below: **Fairy Queen** seen in 1971. The Calgarth pumping station is being built in the background. (Peter Morison)

Bottom: **Iris** with Wray Castle behind. (Peter Morison)

were built. Dating from 1936 she could carry 60 passengers, cover being provided by an awning over the stern, which was removed in good weather. Fuel rationing during the War stopped launch operations and the building of pleasure boats, but after the conflict people returned in their 1930s numbers.

The introduction of coaches with larger seating capacity prompted the launches to adapt. *Sunflower II* was launched in 1950 with a large passenger complement and a permanent cabin with drop down windows; *Muriel II* and *Mayflower* (II) were soon adjusted to match. These deeper draughted launches shortened the Newby Bridge cruise back to the Lakeside Hotel piers.

The precursor to today's Commentary Guidebook was published in the mid-1950s. 'Lake Windermere by a Local Boatman' by Walter Lees, owner of the *Waterlily* with the BBBC, told the story of the lake and provided a history of points of interest seen during a trip.

At the start of the 1960s many small twelve-seat launches, suitable for small groups and private families, filled the bay. Demand dropped off and the smallest launches were disposed of. Family groups were lured by the self-drive boat – why pay for a six person cruise when for a similar price they could drive themselves? For many it was their first opportunity to handle a boat. This prompted the demise of small launches in Bowness Bay. Some have survived in private hands, like the *Dorothy* which, after a well-travelled 40 years is back on the lake in tip-top condition.

In 1966 a small fibreglass waterbus named *Venture*, built in Windermere by Youdell & Brockbank, was launched. She marked a weather-proof change in the launch fleet, with no outside seating. Her Eight Mile Cruise fare was increased for cruising on a modern launch. She was instantly popular after her maiden voyage on Easter Sunday 1966, being perceived as a modern vessel. Five decades later she is still regularly in service, as a relief vessel covering the wooden launch routes the large waterbuses can't get into, from Lakeside to Fell Foot, Bowness to Ferry House, and Ambleside to Wray Castle and Brockhole.

From Lakeside Joe Huddleston and Mr Kellett took passengers on short cruises around the south basin in *Have a Go*, also seen regularly in Bowness Bay, or berthed at Waterhead.

A similar pattern developed at Waterhead. James Robinson was a boatman and hirer in the 1840s. Early twentieth century hirers included Robinson and Forrest, but later Fran and Tom Hardy worked the beach with rowing boats and launches. At the same time Jack Thompson and Robert Clarke had rowing boats, and they formed the Ambleside Motor Launch Company (AML) using small launches operating from jetties north of the steamer pier. The AML ordered *Queen of the Lake* and *Princess of the Lake* from Watercraft of Molesey in 1949 and 1950 respectively; the two largest wooden launches on the lake, each carrying over eighty passengers. They supplemented a fleet comprising *Iris, Spray, Lotus* and *Bee*. Robert Clarke left the company in 1960 taking his fleet of rowing boats to Coniston Water.

The AML offered short cruises around the northern end of the lake and two longer trips. A twice-daily 90 minute cruise went around the islands and touched in at Bowness. A longer cruise left Waterhead at 2.00 pm for the Lakeside Hotel piers returning to Waterhead after a stay of 90 minutes to arrive at 6.00 pm. *Iris* usually took the Lakeside cruises leaving *Princess* and *Queen* to operate the busier trips. By the late 1960s there was little at Lakeside when the boats arrived, although a small café belonging to a descendant of the Kellett family who had the steamer hotel in the 1850s remained open; the skipper received 3d for every customer brought to the café so boatmen worked hard to promote it!

Longer cruises called at public piers in Bowness to pick up disembarked passengers from earlier sailings – the same location today as they were in the 1960s. These were built in winter 1950 on Glebe Road, replacing the one lost when Bowness promenade was upgraded. The public pier at Waterhead was built at the same time.

For many years on Sundays a launch left Ambleside for Wray Castle at 10.15 am to allow passengers to attend service at Wray church. The return departed at 12.15 pm.

In 1968 the BBBC and AML amalgamated, becoming known as the Bowness Bay Boating Company Limited. The former brought 100 rowing boats and fourteen launches whilst the latter contributed five wooden launches and thirty rowing boats. A combined half hourly schedule was advertised between Bowness and Ambleside. From 1973, cruises were offered from Bowness to Belle Isle, after Mr Curwen allowed access. A brochure was published for landing passengers and the cruise lasted until 1993, when the island changed hands and access was withdrawn.

'Princess' and 'Queen' were moved to Bowness after the amalgamation, and more waterbuses were planned. The *Wynander* and *Belle Isle* – small enclosed vessels capable of carrying around 50 people, built by Cheverton on the Isle of Wight – were introduced in 1971 and 1972 respectively. In 1973 the second-hand 1934 built waterbus *Ladyholme* was added; having worked in Ireland as *Harbour Princess*, she acquired the nickname of the 'HP Sauce boat'. As the fleet modernised so the smallest wooden launches were sold or broken up; the *Waterlily* was sold in 1973.

Bowness Boatmen in the 1960s and 1970s passed a test organised by the Lake Wardens who issued a local license. Today the Boatmasters licence is gained following testing by the Maritime Coastguard Agency.

The waterbuses became victims of their own success and larger vessels were needed to accommodate bigger coach parties and bus trips. *Miss Cumbria*, a steel launch built in Holland at Molenaars Scheepswerf shipyard in Zaandam, arrived in 1974. Launched on 16th May 1974 she was much larger than previous waterbuses, with top deck seating and toilets, which became standard for all subsequent boats. Passengers boarded at the rear into a well deck to head through to the saloon with rows of bus style seats, or up steep steps to the top deck.

Skipper Peter Nock and Director Jim Fleming wrote the first colour guide in 1976, giving more in depth knowledge of the lake than could be gained from a commentary. Updated versions are still sold on board today. Just north of Bowness in Rayrigg Wyke, the Windermere Steamboat Museum opened in 1977 and operated the *Osprey* on short cruises around Belle Isle to the Nab ferry. Originally part of the BBBC fleet, she was restored to steam by the museum.

Two more waterbus type vessels – *Miss Cumbria II* (1977) and *Miss Cumbria III* (1979) – were supplied from Molenaars, and by 1980 there were seven waterbuses operating. Traditionally a couple of waterbuses operated from Ambleside, with *Ladyholme* being there for most of her career. Second hand *Silver Arrow II*, was purchased in 1982 from the Manchester Ship Canal and renamed *Silverholme,* with an outside top deck added after her first season.

In 1985 a new design of vessel was introduced to the BBBC, catering for wedding charters and large groups. *Miss Lakeland*, another Molenaar product, much larger than the 'Cumbria' class, had a wheelhouse to separate the skipper from the lower saloon, enabling more seating downstairs. A bar was added, and winter sailings again offered. *Miss Westmorland* joined the fleet in 1988, but never gained a wheelhouse, instead

Below: **Swan** (II) arriving at Bowness. Amongst the many launches are **Miss Pat** and **Ousel**.

Bottom: This time it's **Teal** (II) in the background. Launches **Merry Widow**, **Glider**, **Iris**, **Shamrock**, **Merry Maid** and **Kiwi** are tied alongside.

Muriel II getting lifted out of the water at Lakeside to undergo her yearly winter overhaul.

Ambleside sailings the wooden launches provided sailings from Bowness to the Steamboat Museum and Brockhole. Another launch shuttle served Brockhole from Ambleside.

Ladyholme was becoming out-dated and was sold in 1990 followed in 1991 by the smaller wooden launches *Mayflower* (II), *Spray* and *Lotus*. These boats proved surplus to requirements following purchase of a waterbus from the Clyde in April 1991. After fitment of an upper deck she was renamed *Miss Cumbria IV*, and commenced service on Monday 20th May 1991.

1992 saw special cruises provided to a Sunderland Flying Boat – the last to use the lake as a runway – moored just north of Bowness Bay. Passengers were taken around the aircraft in a wooden launch, and could board the Flying Boat before returning to Bowness. A new Lakeland class vessel was launched the same year. *Miss Lakeland II* is an improved *Miss Lakeland* with power steering and wide side decks, she has a different hull design incorporating sealed tanks to ensure buoyancy. *Miss Lakeland II* was the final boat purchased

being fitted with a helm position at the front of the lower saloon. She was built at the Albion Dockyard, Bristol by David Abel Boat builders.

During the late 1980s and early 1990s the boats cruised all parts of the lake, alongside the scheduled

Muriel II leaving Bowness for Ferry House late in the season. She is the mainstay in the short link of the Cross Lakes Shuttle. She crosses to Ferry House 10 times daily.

by the Bowness Bay Boating Company, as in May 1993 they bought the steamer operations from Sea Containers to create a combined fleet of eighteen boats.

Jim Fleming, a late director of the company, summed up the rivalry between the steamers and the Bowness Bay Boating Company, in a 1995 edition of Cumbria magazine; *The railways were a bit blasé. They had nice steamers but before they knew it we had the modern boats. They did sit up and take notice then but still not really enough. We all had a hands-on attitude and worked the boats ourselves so we appreciated what was happening faster than the railway people ever could. We would be chasing people onto our boats before the steamers could get in. Everything we did was looking over our shoulders at the opposition. I don't think they ever did.*

A combined fleet

The 1993 literature was issued before the amalgamation was completed, but after the season had started so

Pleasure launches moored near the Cushion Huts in the early 1900s.

showed two independent operations, but from 1994 an integrated timetable was distributed. One steamer was kept out of service outside the peak season, with the smaller launches covering sailings. From 1995 the steamer fleet sailed all season alongside the launches, which also operated non-landing cruises around the islands. Wooden launches sailed between Ambleside and Brockhole, and waterbuses provided timetabled winter services, with a steamer venturing out at weekends if the weather permitted.

The steamer were upgraded after the BBBC takeover; in 1993 *Teal* (II) was given Kelvin engines and the following year two funnels were fitted at the rear of the top deck of *Teal* (II) and *Swan* (II). All three steamer had bridge controls installed over the next few years and telegraphs became a thing of the past. *Swan* (II) received a set of Cummins engines in 1996, her Gleniffer engines having been thoroughly overhauled in the winter 1989-90.

In the late 1990s the waterbuses were also

Osprey, **Penguin** and **Wynander** in Bowness. (Peter Morison)

Busy times at Wray Castle in 2013. **Princess of the Lake** is operating the Green Cruise from Ambleside to Wray and Brockhole. **Sunflower II** is seen in her guise as the summer Bike-Boat. Both boats were built in 1950.

upgraded. *Miss Cumbria's* seating was replaced with tables and later the well deck was raised. *Miss Cumbria II* and *Miss Cumbria III* later had their well decks altered to match. *Wynander* and *Belle Isle* became surplus to requirements and were laid up in 1996. In late 1998 they were purchased by Mullen's cruises of Loch Lomond.

Lakeside station saw a major upgrade with the addition of the Lakes Aquarium in 1997. Now a thriving attraction, it is connected to the restaurant by a glass roofed walkway, which houses the ticket office for the trains and boats. The same year the *Tern* received a pair of Cummins engines, and a bow thruster.

In 1998 the directors decided to dispose of *Swift* to allow time to maintain the three working passenger steamer. The FR Trust and the Cumbrian Railways Association backed a campaign to 'Save the Swift', and engines were sourced to convert the ninety-eight year old veteran back to steam power. However fundraising took time, and Windermere Lake Cruises needed the pier and slipway space. Another proposal looked to keep *Swift* at Ambleside as a floating exhibition in the *Raven's* old berth, but this came to nothing. After sitting on the Lakeside slipway for three months, the seven-week scrapping of *Swift* commenced on Monday 24th August 1998.

More services were considered in the late 1990s. In 2000 the *Esperance's* route between Bowness and Ferry House was restored and Wray Castle was incorporated into the Waterhead – Brockhole route making it possible to combine a cruise with a walk along the shoreline to Ferry House.

In 2001 Mountain Goat introduced a grandly named 'Cross Lakes Shuttle' service to connect with launches at Ferry House, for Sawrey and Hawkshead.

Over the winter of 2002-3 *Swan* (II) was brought up to modern standards including creating more outside seating by extending the deck forward of the bridge. The next winter *Teal* (II) followed suit, returning to service in June 2004. Modifications made it easier to distinguish between the sisters as the lower bar windows of *Teal* (II) were adjusted to be noticeably different. Both vessels received bow thrusters to aid turning around the piers at Bowness

Princess of the Lake just off Bowness in the 1970s. (Peter Morison)

and Ambleside, and assist in the tight approach to Lakeside pier.

Navigation was aided by the introduction of speed limits and shallow marker buoys. From 2005 a 10 mph speed limit was introduced to the lake as there was no restriction outwith the Bowness Bay area. There were speed limits on the lake for over a century; in 1902, a 6 mph limit was introduced for steam vessels passing east or west of Belle Isle and in 1912 this was raised to 12 mph with boundaries extended to Lady Holme, and the Nab Ferry. Restrictions were proposed for Waterhead and Lakeside, although a 10 mph limit was not imposed until 1958 when the limit in Bowness was reduced to 10 mph, and later 6 mph, as in 1902.

The earliest navigation and shallow water buoys were placed by the FR in Bowness Bay and on the Mid-Water Shallows but not elsewhere, as users were locals who knew it intimately. With the growth in lake users it became imperative to mark danger areas and in 1947 it was recommended that the Council should lay shallow water buoys. In 1948 Shepherds placed twenty markers and these have increased to be now dotted all over the lake. Until 1971 buoys were removed for winter maintenance, with smaller ones in place off-season. Plastic buoys were introduced to remain in position year round. Red markers or red triangles identify shallow areas, yellow markers show fairways and safe channels, and green buoys are for yacht races. There are multiple white markers for moorings.

Since 2008 a regular summer event has been the British Gas Great North Swim. Thousands of competitors descend on the Low Wood to swim a course in the bay for charity. Roads are usually grid locked so the Windermere fleet operates cruises between Bowness

and Ambleside every ten minutes at peak times from as early as 6.15 am through to around 7 pm.

A new service was trialled between 26th July and 30th August 2009 using *Sunflower II* and later *Muriel II*, offering four return sailings daily leaving Ambleside for Bowness, calling at the Low Wood, Brockhole and White Cross Bay. White Cross Bay was dropped after a couple of weeks; at Brockhole the service connected with the service between Ambleside, Wray Castle and the visitor centre. The trial was not repeated.

Devastating flooding in 2009, saw the lake rise nearly ten feet higher than it had ever been before on Friday 20th November. The steamer and launch piers disappeared from view causing untold problems for passenger boats and damaging buildings around the lake-shore. At Lakeside *Swan* (II) was almost floating on the slip, whilst *Miss Westmorland*'s after end was floating in the Ambleside boathouse. The four wooden launches were inches from floating off their trestles on the Lakeside car park and, with the launch piers well underwater, remaining vessels were tied up to the steamer piers which were also submerged. The schedule was cancelled for just two days, but the clean-up operation took months and new precautions are in place, should a repeat ever occur.

On 31st March 2010 the Prince of Wales inspected the recovery works, boarding *Queen of the Lake* at Waterhead for a short cruise with Ian Cormack, the vessel's helmsman for most of his time at Windermere Lake Cruises.

A further upgrade to *Teal* (II) in the winter of 2010-11 created a more open accessible tea bar. Brockhole received a new larger pier to handle steamers – the first such pier to be built since 1891 and part of an

Princess of the Lake about to turn into Wray Castle. The Low Wood is seen in the background.

Right: **Queen of the Lake** ready to head down to the River Thames to take part in the Jubilee Pageant.

Below: **Queen of the Lake** in Pull Bay with Bow Fell and the Langdales in the background.

£800,000 scheme to revamp the visitor centre. This became a scheduled stop for launches on Ambleside cruises, with occasional steamer calls during the summer. Winter sees occasional steamer sailings at weekends until Christmas and from February which call at Brockhole.

Miss Lakeland II, *Miss Cumbria*, *Miss Cumbria II* and *Miss Cumbria III* were extensively refitted between 2011 and 2014, and June 2012 saw two lake vessels in the national limelight.

Queen of the Lake – an historic vessel of 1949, powered by a very rare Gardner 4LW engine – took part in the Jubilee Celebrations Pageant on the Thames in the 'Historic and Service Vessels' category. On the 28th May she was craned onto a lorry at Bowness for her journey to the Thames at Penton Hook Marina near Chertsey, arriving late on the 29th. On the 31st she started to make her way down river through Sunbury Lock later passing her builders at Molesey. That night was spent near Teddington berthed behind *Devon Belle*

a former fleet mate of Ullswater's *Western Belle* when she was in service in Plymouth and on the River Dart.

Queen of the Lake passed through the Teddington Lock onto the tidal part of the river on the 2nd June and made her way to near Hammersmith where she berthed mid river for the night.

Joining the procession on 3rd June at 2.30 pm she passed under Putney Bridge at 2.50 pm and Westminster Bridge at 4 pm. Tower Bridge was reached at 4.32 pm and three minutes later all on board saluted the Royal Barge. The weather was poor with rain dampening the event for most of the day. Berthed overnight in West India Dock on the Isle of Dogs she retraced her steps home on the 4th June.

On Thursday 21st June *Tern* carried the Olympic Torch from Waterhead at 6.51 pm, arriving in Bowness at 7.46 pm as part of the Olympic Games celebrations. She was joined by nearly a hundred boats and escorted into Bowness Bay by dragon boats from the Low Wood Hotel.

2013 saw Wray Castle introduced to some Ambleside to Bowness sailings. In May a 'Bike-Boat' sailed every forty minutes between Brockhole and Wray Castle. *Sunflower II* was converted to carry twelve bikes and connected four times a day with a Mountain Goat service from Wray to Hawkshead, which linked with the Cross Lakes Shuttle. At Brockhole she connected with the Stagecoach 800 Bike Bus between Ambleside and Haverthwaite.

Longer term plans suggested construction of floating pontoons at Bark Barn near Belle Grange, at the YMCA, and at a boathouse on the western shore near Ling Holme. In parallel, Go Lakes developed bike and walking trails along the western shore of the lake.

Queen of the Lake passing Lady Holme inbound for Bowness. At the helm is George Dennison who owned her from new. (Peter Morison)

The Queen sailed on *Teal* (II) on Wednesday 17th July 2013 to celebrate sixty years on the throne, repeating her trip of August 1956. Her Majesty arrived in Bowness from Kendal just after midday, boarding the steamer under the command of Keith Jackson, and took a leisurely sailing to Brockhole, where she disembarked. Whilst on board, she unveiled a plaque commemorating her visit, to accompany that celebrating her previous visit.

The Bark Barn jetty came into operation on 24th May 2014. *Sunflower* (II) commenced a modified Bike-Boat timetable, sailing to Bark Barn from Brockhole seven times daily, with Wray Castle visited twice. The waterbus fleet was also geared up to convey more bicycles. Bike racks were fitted to the rear decks, and *Miss Cumbria IV* had an extension fitted to her small rear deck. Further maintenance to the *Tern* over the last couple of winters have meant that she has been re-decked and had large sections of her hull re-plated, and inside, her saloons have been re-upholstered. The YMCA pier was completed in March 2015, and *Swan* (II) had her tea bar altered to match the *Teal* (II) ready for the new season.

A standard timetable developed when all the boats came under the umbrella of Windermere Lake Cruises. The steamers still operate from Lakeside, and *Tern* starts and finishes there in summer. *Teal* (II) and *Swan* (II) swap rosters daily; one starting at Lakeside and finishing at Bowness, and vice versa. The Bowness-based launches add extra services between the steamer sailings, as well as non-landing circular cruises.

The steamers finish service in early November for overhaul, although one sometimes continues at weekends until the New Year alongside the launches, which operate all winter. The slipway at Lakeside can accommodate one vessel to carry out all manner of work, such as the 2012-13 hull re-plating of *Tern*; sometimes two steamer are accommodated — one before and one after Christmas.

Even the youngest of the larger vessels, *Swan* (II) is now nearly eighty years old, showing the longevity that life in freshwater and regular maintenance provides. All three steamer and four wooden launches are on the National Historic Ships Register.

During the summer two wooden launches and two waterbuses are based at Waterhead. At Lakeside are usually found *Sunflower II* (except when in use for the Bike-Boat), and *Venture*. The remaining waterbuses are Bowness-based along with wooden launch *Muriel II*. Waterbuses are overhauled each winter receiving an out-of-water survey every two years either at the boathouse at Waterhead or for the 'Lakeland' vessels the slip at Lakeside as using Waterhead necessitates removal of the wheelhouse. The wooden launches are craned out of the lake at Lakeside every November and moved into the car park. Maintenance takes place enveloped in a tent, sheltered from the weather.

Queen of the Lake passing White Cross Bay.

Right: **Spray** at Waterhead. (Peter Morison)

Below left: **Sunflower II**, **Muriel II** and **Princess of the Lake** berthed at Bowness. Note the large green shed belonging to Shepherds in the background. (Peter Morison)

Below right: **Sunflower** (I) on a card posted in 1913. She was sold to Loch Lomond in the 1920s where she remained until around 1975.

Bottom: **Waterlily**, owned by Walter Lees. Built in 1926, she is still operational on Loch Awe as the steamboat **Lady Gertrude**.

Above: **Lady Holme** berthed at Bowness. The only red waterbus! Also in shot are **Belle Isle** and **Teal** (II).

Right: **Coventina**, ex **Belle Isle**, sailing down the Tyne. Owned by David and Gill Fozard, she now operates for River Escapes. Her base is next to the Millennium Bridge in Newcastle. Her small size makes her suitable for the 'Quay to City' cruise which takes her under many of the Tyne's bridges.

Above: **Miss Cumbria** on a busy August day with an abundance of watercraft all around.

Below: **Ladyholme** as **Glen Lyon** on Loch Tay in 2005.

Right: **Belle Isle** and **Wynander** when new in 1972. Seen under Claife Heights.

Waterhead Bay.

Miss Cumbria II passes
Holme Crag heading for
Waterhead.

Miss Westmorland heads
between Ferry House and
Crow Holme on the Islands
Cruise, while **Miss Cumbria IV**
waits to pass the other way.

Miss Cumbria III passing Fir
Holme and Belle Isle.

Miss Cumbria III and **Miss Cumbria IV** at Lakeside on an autumn morning with the lake as still as a mill-pond.

Miss Cumbria II leaving Bowness in the gloaming.

Opposite top: **Miss Lakeland** arriving at Waterhead.

Opposite bottom: A wedding meant **Miss Lakeland** made a very rare call at Belle Isle on 27th April 2012.

Left: Snow on a frozen Bowness Bay gave for unusual photographs in January 2013.

Below: Weddings account for most charters during the year, and **Miss Lakeland** is seen here at Storrs Hall dressed for the occasion. Other hotels regularly used include the Beech Hill, Cragwood, Langdale Chase and Low Wood.

Miss Cumbria on August
Bank Holiday weekend 2014.

Miss Cumbria IV with a wintry Claife Heights behind.

Miss Cumbria IV and the Low Wood hotel behind.

Left: **Miss Cumbria IV** passing High Wray Bay in February 2013. Wansfell and the Troutbeck Fells dominate the view which was taken from the summit of Latterbarrow.

Above: **Miss Cumbria IV** at Bowness.

Left: **Miss Cumbria IV** off Lakeside on a still day.

Below: Summer 2014 in Bowness Bay. Viewed from the **Swan** (II) are; **Miss Cumbria IV** (with recent rear deck extension), **Silverholme**, **Miss Lakeland**, **Miss Cumbria** and **Miss Cumbria II**.

Right: **Miss Lakeland** on the slipway at Lakeside.

Far right: **Miss Lakeland** on her delivery journey to Windermere in 1985. She is seen on the M62. (Stubbs)

Below: **Miss Lakeland II** passing Wray Castle with the snowy Langdales behind.

Miss Lakeland II with Calgarth Hall to the right of the image.

Miss Westmorland coming into the Aquarius pier in Bowness, passing the Aquarius building.

Below: **Miss Lakeland II** coming through Windermere village for her launch at Bowness Bay in 1992. (Alex Williamson)

Bottom: **Miss Lakeland** with Rawlinson Nab, Troutbeck Tongue and the Troutbeck valley behind.

Above: **Miss Lakeland II** seen nearing Bowness with the fells looking unusually close behind.

Silver Arrow II being viewed by Jim Fleming at Manchester, 1980. She would become **Silverholme**. (Lee Howson)

Other ventures on Windermere

The Nab Ferries

The ferry service between Ferry Nab and Ferry House dates to the earliest habitation on either shore. This is a natural ferry point roughly halfway along the lake where the water is only ¼ mile wide with two promontories jutting out into the lake. It is probable that a regular ferry provided by boat owners was in existence from the mid-13th Century as Hawkshead became a prosperous centre.

The earliest reference to an organised service dates from 1438 when 3d a year was paid for the right to run one boat of passage on the lake. In 1454 documents relating to a rental agreement of Edmund, Earl of Richmond stated that John Idyll and William Dykenson *'did not answer for any profit forthcoming from the passage of the water of Wynandremer, which is worth 10— per annum.....because Henry Belyngham, farmer of the fishery of said water, claims to have the said passage'.*

Rowing boats were used with two sweeps almost as long as the boat, perhaps capable of conveying a horse. As the crossing's importance grew so did the size of boats. In 1570 the ferry could convey men and horses – loaded facing the centre of the vessel to keep them calm – with owners helping to row. Today's four minute crossing was unimaginable to early ferrymen who allowed up to half an hour for the trip.

Miles Milner was the ferryman in 1570 and the following confirmed his right to ferry within the Middle Cubble; *First wee finde that the Ferryers in the Lowest Cubble is Free to Ferry within the said Cubble to their most advantage, also wee finde that Miles Milner is Free to Ferry within the said middle Cubble both for horse and man or any other Carriage that shall be requested of him or his assigns to Ferry paying the yearly rent to the Lord thereof six shillings eight pence and that noe other Ferryers or Fishers within the said middle cubble doe Ferry but only for their own use upon payment of one shilling three pence unto the Lord thereof......*

In 1574 at the Court Baron of Applethwaite the jurors testified that *'Les Fyrrying of the water of Wyndermyer pay the queen £6 annually'.* 1582 sees reference again in the will of Edward Ridge of Hawkshead. He left £6 for *'erectinge buildinge and setting upp of an howse at the water syde in Swynsnesse'.* This shelter developed into the Ferry Inn over the next two centuries. Traffic between Kendal and Hawkshead grew. A grammar school opened in Hawkshead in 1585, and in 1608 the village was granted its first market charter. On market days local merchants and carriers flocked to the Nab to cross. Ferrying across the narrows was a full time job, crossing many times daily.

On 19th October 1635 the ferry was the scene of tragedy when forty-eight people and seven horses drowned during a crossing. The boat was of substantial size manoeuvring with long sweeps, probably two men to each oar. It was heavily overcrowded; bad weather forcing the ferrymen to take everyone over at once rather than make two journeys. Ferryman Thomas Milner drowned along with his two daughters. Passengers were returning from market day at Hawkshead, and many had attended the wedding of William Sawrey and Thomasin Strickland the previous day.

The level of the lake was high, as on the 18th October Kendal chronologist Wharton recorded that the River Kent had entered the Vestry. The rain was followed by gales which caused the vessel to capsize; no passengers survived. It must have been a terrible event.

Mallard before her 2014 modifications.

Weary passengers huddling in the flat bottomed barge with horses tethered at either end, facing the centre. Once past the shelter of the headland they hit a south westerly gale and as the boat rocked the gunnels slowly heeled over and submerged. Those arriving late at the Ferry Inn stood on shore rooted to the spot in horror. One escaped horse stampeded for almost 4 miles before being reined in.

Some believe there were two boats involved in the accident but the Grasmere Parish Register, which accurately records the names of the deceased, states that they were drowned in 'one boate'. The dead, including the bride's mother and brother, were buried at St Martin's church in Bowness. The newly married couple did not fare well; Thomasin had a still born child the following July and died a few days later, William remarrying in 1638. The tragedy affected the local community for generations and is still spoken of today.

In 1636 'The Fatall Nuptiall', a poem probably written by Richard Braithwaite to commemorate the disaster, was published in London. A single copy of the poem survives at Oxford. Thomas Hoggart of Troutbeck, also known as 'Ald Hoggart' wrote about the disaster in 'Remnants of Rhyme'; *Upon the 19th day of October 1630* (sic) *the great Boat upon Windermeer Water sunk about sun setting, when was drowned fforty seaven persons and eleaven horses; from sudden Death Libera nos.*

There is debate as to whether the Millers Crossing or Nab Ferry was the ferry in question. It is the authors' opinion that at the time of the accident there was no Millerground ferry, as rights to ferry within the Middle Cubble were granted to the lessee of the Nab Ferry since at least 1570. The chance of the Nab Ferry rights holder allowing competition without protest is highly unlikely.

The tragedy was a lesson for local boat builders, and if the *Mary Anne* and the submerged vessel in Mitchell Wyke are anything to go by, subsequent boats were smaller and more manageable.

The ferry lease passed to the Braithwaite family of Braithwaite Fold on the Westmorland side of the lake. Part of their estate where the Ferry Nab is today was appropriately named The Boat. On 13th April 1670 a dispute was settled between the lake's ferrymen and fishermen, and Thomas Braithwaite who took on the lease in 1635. The document names ferrymen in the higher and lower Cubbles; Roger Parke worked the northern end, Rowland Park the Middle Cubble, and William Robinson the Lower Cubble. The dispute concerned the right to ferry in certain areas of the lake, and the jury found; -

(1) That all Fishers and Ferriers (paying rent to the crown) in the highest and lowest cubles, may Ferry any sort of goods whatsoever in their own boats, within their cubles, for their most advantage.

(2) That Fishers and Ferriers in the middle cuble (paying Ferry Rents) may only ferry in the said cuble, for their Necessaries and no further, excepting the said Thomas Braithwaite.

(3) That Thomas Braithwaite hath due and right,

Mallard with Belle Isle and the Troutbeck valley behind.

to ferry and carry over all and every the said cubles both horse and man and all sorts of goods and commodities whatsoever to his best advantage, paying his accustomed rent.

Braithwaite had assumed the ferry rights to all parts of the lake. He built a new boat in 1699 and intended to raise fares from 1d return, to re-compensate his outlay. Ferry users objected, and forty-five residents brought an action to halt the rise. Their 'Articles of Agreement' stated;

Wheras time out of mind itt hath beene ussed and Accustomed that the pties to these presents and all others who have had occasion from time to time to passe repasse and travell over Windermer Watter att the fferry boate on the Kings hyeway there have time beyond the memory of man used and Accustomed to pay onely one penny and noe more ffor their soe passing and repassing or goeing and returneing over the said fferry-boat to the ferryman in respects of his pay; And now Thomas Braithwaite the fferry man there having Lately built a new fferry boat Refuseth to receive the said Accustomed pay Intending to exact upon us and other his maisties subjects in raiseing the accustomed pay of the said ferry'.

Even by 1699 the ferry was perceived as ancient. The Braithwaites retained the ferry until 1707, when two boats were transferred from Thomas Braithwaite to the new lessee, William Rawlinson of Graythwaite, for £140. Later the same year he sold the rights back, at a profit of £30, to William Braithwaite of Satterhowe. A clause of the sale was on no account should the boats be sold to any party from the Westmorland shore. George Braithwaite, of Harrowslack, threatened to withdraw the ferry in 1725 over a dispute with others encroaching on his rights. A jury enquired;

If any fishers ferrier or ferriers in the lowest or middle cuble aforesaid may by the custome ferry any men or goods cattles wares or merchandise therein or elsewhere in upon or across the said water save their own respective person or persons goods cattle wares and merchandise and in that their respective fishing boats and allso in their peculiar low or midle cuble and not elsewhere. If any Fishers or Ferriers in the said high cuble may by the custome ferry any person or persons cattle goods wares and merchandise or other persons save within that cuble and in their own respective fishing boats.

The jury found that only George Braithwaite could ferry across more than one Cubble. In 1726, Braithwaite was claiming sole ferriage rights over the whole lake which led the Backbarrow Iron Company, who needed to transport charcoal along the lake, to complain of his 'bustle about the boats'. An agreement of 1731 found that fishermen possessed no ferry rights, except regarding their own goods, nor had they the right to allow another person to ferry. If any fisherman paid part of the ferry rent, he should have the right of ferrying in proportion to the rent paid. The Braithwaite's had complained about persistent flouting of the laws by other boatmen operating unlicensed ferries in competition.

The Braithwaite family maintained the ferry rights until the 1770s when they sold them to the new owner of Belle Isle, Thomas English. By 1786 (probably 1781 when English sold the island) they were back in Braithwaite hands, but were sold again in 1788 to John Christian Curwen, now owner of Belle Isle. Thence the ferry rights were leased from the Curwen family. From 1789 the ferryman was George Robinson and in 1792 his son-in-law Thomas Blairmire took over the inn and crossing until 1810. The lease of the ferry and the Ferry Inn went together, but not the roles. The landlord often employed a boatman; between 1789 and 1870 there were ten different proprietors of the inn.

Charles Farish's poem 'The Minstrels *of Winandermere*', of 1811 gives a good description of the year-round operation of the ferry;

The Great-boat shall be heard to go,
Thro' the cold night, from shore to shore,
While freezing ice and melting snow
Press heavy on the restless oar.

Nor yet the boatman's task be done,-
He dips his hand into the tide,
And heaves huge ice-boards, one by one,
Heaping a wall on either side.

Winning his way across the lake,
With battering maul and iron crow;
The ice still closing in his wake,
In one the knotting fragments grow.

And when these arts will serve no more,
With hawser and with rustic sleight
He slides the ponderous boat ashore;
The kneeling camel ships her freight.

Farish was a regular user and knew George Robinson – ferryman between 1789 and 1792 – on a personal basis. On one occasion he noted how *'George, the ferryman, unmoored the smaller of his boats to make the crossing to Bowness-bay'.* Robinson and other boatmen carried passengers between Bowness and the Ferry Inn, whilst the larger boat was retained for the Nab crossing. In 1800 John Curwen was requested by magistrates to remove a notice demanding tolls from those crossing in a vessel other than the ferry, illustrating how jealously the rights were guarded. Since 1793 or earlier anyone could ferry for profit on the lake.

William Green's 'Guide to the Lakes' dated 1819 states; *The Ferry-house is the property of J.C Curwen Esq., who has greatly enlarged and rendered it a very commodious and comfortable inn, and it is but justice in speaking of its situation, to observe that, for delicate, soft, and reposed scenery, it has scarcely its equal; abrupt objects rarely strike the eye – all is stillness and harmony......*

.....There are two large boats kept at the Ferry-house, for the conveyance from point to point of gentleman's carriages, post-chaises, carts, horses,

cattle, men, women and children. A miscellaneous cargo, in picturesque assemblage, is highly in contrast to the quiet of the surrounding scenery.

A little over a decade later, the 1832 'A Guide to the Lakes and Mountains of Cumberland' mentions the fares; *Here post-horses, a car, and boats are kept. Carriages and horses can cross by the ferry-boat. The charges made for conveyance are, Passengers, 2d. each; Post-chaise, 3s.; Gentleman's Chariot, 3s. 6d.; Carriage, 4s., besides a gratuity to the ferryman. No charge, however, is made for the return of vehicles the same day.*

The service crossed as required so passengers crossing from the east waited at Ferry Nab and shouted for the ferryman. but a late nineteenth century guidebook noted; *…halloo as you will, and in whatever weather, he will be sure to keep you waiting till he has what he considers a sufficient boat-load to bring from the other side.*

Wordsworth likened shouting for the ferry to the screech of owls in 'The Waggoner';

*The jolly bird hath learned his cheer
Upon the banks of Windermere;
Where a tribe of them make merry,
Mocking the Man that keeps the ferry;
Hallooing from an open throat,
Like travellers shouting for a boat.*

There were three sheltered landings on the Westmorland side; one faced north, one west, and one south. The north facing landing was used in later years when the row ferry assisted the steam ferries.

Thomas Cloudsdale operated the broad beamed square ended boats between 1831 and 1838, with strict maintenance requirements specified in his rental agreement. He had to *'at all times….keep in good Order and Repair the Boats for conveying Passengers over Windermere Water and….once in every year paint pitch coak and put in repair the Little Boat and the Great Boat every two years'.*

The ferry came with the lease of the inn, but was clearly the main money earner. Cloudsdale paid annual charges of £15 for the Inn, £40 for land near Round Table, and £75 for the ferry. In 1843 the ferry, according to James Gibson, ran from 5 am until 10 pm and fares were unchanged from 1832.

Crier of Claife

The legend of the Crier of Claife is mentioned by Harriet Martineau in her 1855 'A Description of the English Lakes'; *It was about the time of the Reformation, one stormy night, when a party of travellers were making merry at the Ferry-house, — then a humble tavern, — that a call for the boat was heard from the Nab. A quiet, sober boatman obeyed the call, though the night was wild and fearful. When he ought to be returning, the tavern guests stepped out upon the shore, to see whom he would bring. He returned alone, ghastly and dumb with horror. Next morning, he was in a high fever; and in a few days he died,* without having been prevailed upon to say what he had seen at the Nab. *For weeks after, there were shouts, yells, and howlings at the Nab, on every stormy night; and no boatman would attend to any call after dark. The Reformation had not penetrated the region; and the monk from Furness who dwelt on one of the islands of the lake, was applied to exorcise the Nab. On Christmas day, he assembled all the inhabitants on Chapel Island, and performed in their presence services which should for ever confine the ghost to the quarry in the wood behind the Ferry, now called the Crier of Claife. Some say that the priest conducted the people to the quarry and laid the ghost, — then and there. — Laid though it be, nobody goes there at night.*

The Ferry Inn was not in existence during the Reformation so some artistic license should be allowed!

A steamer pier was built at the Ferry Inn in 1845 to accommodate *Lady of the Lake*. With the arrival of the railway at Birthwaite two years later, horse drawn coach services provided timetabled services around the lakes. Adapted rowing boats with a stern ramp for loading wheeled cargo and livestock were built for the Nab Ferry. *Mary Anne* at the Steamboat Museum dates from around 1870. She is nearly 40 feet long by 11¼ wide, and needed four men to handle her. A similar boat lies sunk behind the Ferry House in Mitchell Wyke.

Harriet Martineau left us a description of the last oar ferries; *Meantime, the heavy, roomy ferryboat is ready; the horse is taken out of the car; and both are shipped. Two or three or half a dozen people take advantage of the passage; the rowers with their ponderous oars, are on the bench; and the great machine is presently afloat.*

The Little Boat and Great Boat were moored on the western shore along the wall opposite Crow Holme. Sometimes a reserve boat was moored in deeper water just off Crow Holme. In May 1867 the Cumberland Pacquet mentioned new tenant Richard Howe's plans to improve the Inn and the ferry; *Among the additions which he purposes to make, is an apparatus for the management of the ferry. The plan is to have a drum at each side of the lake, around which will revolve a sunken wire cord, and to which will be attached two boats; the drums to be turned by a pony stationed at the Ferry. By these means the boats will be able to pass backwards and forwards in half the time, and a better and more punctual system of communication will be maintained.* This novel idea never came to fruition.

The First Steam Chain Ferry

In May 1870 Geoffrey Dixon entered into a twenty-one year contract with the Curwens to operate the ferry and *'maintain a steam ferryboat in lieu of the row-boat used'* at an annual rent of £100. In August the rowing boat was still in use but by 12th November 1870 the Westmorland Gazette reported on the steam vessel; *This beautiful, but hitherto inconvenient, crossing place on Windermere Lake has now been greatly changed for the better. The steamers and chains which have taken the place of the old lumbering row boat, completes the crossing and return in much less time than the old boat took to go one way. The men employed are also prompt and obliging, so much so that they hurry across the lake on hearing the first intimation of a passenger.*

Mr George Dixon of Balla Wray designed this first mechanical ferry which, although nameless, will be referred to as the *1870 Ferry.* A flat bottomed barge with a steam engine and boiler on one side and ramps which nearly touched the water when it crossed. On the south side were stored the anchor, lifeboat and ballast to counteract the camber, later replaced by ballast inside the hull. Originally pulling itself across using a single chain – later a wire – that snapped more than once, leaving the ferry on Ramp Holme, and another time on Belle Isle. When this happened the anchor was dropped and passengers rowed ashore in the lifeboat. A second guide wire was added later.

On 25th March 1871, the paper gave a more detailed description; *The new steam boat which has been placed upon the Ferry, at Windermere, is a very great improvement upon the clumsy passage boats by which the voyage was formerly made. The motive power consists of a small, neat engine, of 7-horsepower; a chain is fastened at each side of the lake, and laid down across the bed of the lake. This chain is made to pass round a wheel in the steam boat, by the revolution of which the boat is propelled. The chain, however, will speedily be supplanted by a wire rope, which is looked upon as much stronger and less liable to be snapped by sudden strains. Horses and conveyances can now be taken across with much greater ease, and without the trouble of being unyoked.*

The arrival of steam created a more reliable service which could be timetabled for the first time.

Since 1845 steamers travelling between Newby Bridge and Bowness had called at the Ferry Inn five minutes from Bowness, in either direction, taking a share of the trade to Bowness thus annoying the ferrymen. The Kendal Mercury published a letter on this topic in June 1851; *The landlord of the Ferry Inn has no legal right whatever to charge any person anything for landing or leaving there in a boat, from or to Ambleside Bowness, or other parts of the lake, otherwise than actually in the Ferry route, that is crossing the lake from the Ferry Nab to the Inn, or vice-versa. I had myself occasion to cross the lake from Bowness Bay to the Ferry Inn, a fortnight ago, which I did in a Bowness boat, rowed by a Bowness boatman, and on reaching the Ferry Inn landing place, besides the boatman's fare, the sum also of 2d. was demanded of me for the landlord of the Ferry Inn for toll. This I declined in paying, and as I am in some degree conversant with the law pertaining to Ferries, I may observe that I was legally justified in refusing to pay this mite, and I would respectfully advise others, who may be similarly treated as myself, to follow my example.*

The letter was simply signed 'W'.

The Curwens owned land each side of the crossing and constructed the steamer pier around 1845, when the steamers landed on their own accord, not by right of access. A new pier replaced the decrepit old one in 1870. The landowners prohibited steamers from calling for a short time to force use of the chain ferry, but in May 1872 the steamers returned.

In January 1877 Geoffrey Dixon raised a case against the Curwens seeking an injunction against the steamer company to restrict a competing ferry service between the Ferry Inn and Bowness. The court queried whether this was competition, as the chain ferry crossed to the road to Bowness, whereas steamers sailed direct to Bowness village. Luckily for the steamer company the verdict was in their favour; *The lake is a public highway, and the existence of a ferry across it from a certain point on one side to a point on the other does not preclude the Queen's subjects from the use of the highway and oblige them on all occasions, to their own inconvenience, to pass from one terminus of the ferry to the other.*

When the steam ferry was out of service, the steam launch *Powerful,* owned by Mr G H Pattinson, pulled the old row ferry *Mary Anne* for a passenger-only service. *Mary Anne* remained on standby until the 1940s when she was acquired by the Curwens of Belle Isle to transport sheep to Harrowslack farm, north of Ferry House, where a small stone landing is still visible today. She eventually sank between Belle Isle and the western shore, but was raised by divers in 1978 and is now at the Windermere Steamboat Museum.

The Ferry Inn was demolished and the larger Ferry Hotel built by Pattinson on the site, opening in 1880. The first landlord was Bruce Logan, who took over the lease of the ferry. Adverts for his hotel announced in large letters that '*THE STEAM FERRY PLIES CONSTANTLY ACROSS THE LAKE'.* However this took its toll on the boat which was overhauled in early 1882. It is probable that *Powerful* and *Mary Anne* maintained the service, and the *1870 Ferry* was back in service on 18th February. In August 1894 a rod connecting the drive wheels to the engines broke, causing the wheel to come adrift, and *Mary Anne* returned for the week that it took to locate and refit the part. Coaches made the journey via Ambleside, due to the increased size of vehicles since inception of the steam ferry. Logan also introduced *Esperance* on the crossing between Bowness and the Ferry Hotel.

Frederick Fowkes of Hawkshead wrote to the Westmorland Gazette in May 1895 suggesting that the service should be taken over by the local authority; *If the ferry is to remain in private hands no one would wish any change in the present proprietor, who is universally respected, but my contention is the Ferry is a portion of the highway and should be acquired by the public authorities, who are the owners of the roads of approach and worked by them for the public.*

Two years later after further correspondence, a public meeting was held in Hawkshead. Fowkes raised concerns about charging for bicycles and the '*way in which the ferry was carried on'.* The meeting also highlighted the lack of reserve steamboat. His opinions were not the unanimous views of the western shore

Opposite: **Silverholme**, alone on the lake, with Wetherlam behind the wooded fell of Claife Heights.

communities. Mr Rutherford of Far Sawrey wrote to the Westmorland Gazette in February 1898; *I notice that Mr Fowkes still perseveres in his attack upon the Ferry across Windermere. So long as the Ferry remains in the hands of a landlord and his tenant as at present, I am obliged to make use of it oftener than suits me. But should Mr. Fowkes unfortunately succeed in getting it transferred to the hands of county or district authorities, I know well that, whatever the tariff charged, I shall suffer heavily in the way of increased rates and no longer have to pay for my own belongings, but shall have, in fact, to contribute largely towards the transit of all the big coaches and rich men's carriages that pass. So much for the alleged over-charges on the Ferry. As to the latest allegations that it is dangerous, it is simply too ridiculous except in so far as there is always a danger where wind and waves are concerned.*

The ferry remained in private hands but by the end of the first decade of the twentieth century, the *1870 ferry* had completed nearly forty years of service through some of the coldest winters in recent record. A new vessel, nicknamed the 'Iron Duke' by locals and here referred to as the *1915 Ferry*, was ordered by Bruce Logan as yard number 527 from Alley and MacLellan Limited of Polmadie. The Westmorland Gazette of 9th January 1915 implied the new boat was well needed;

The old ferryboat on Windermere, chiefly remarkable for the lustre of its fittings and the lopsidedness of its gait is about to be superannuated. No one within living memory has done full justice to that ferryboat. … if it is indeed true that a new and well founded vessel is to take the place of the old, despised and rejected machine, one cannot but wonder what will become of the lady.

The new boat was transported in sections to Windermere for assembly but the Scottish labour proved unreliable. Once paid some would head to local inns for two to three days, returning when their money ran out, and the ferry was found one day washed up on Belle Isle in an incomplete state.

Once completed, the new ferry ran alongside the *1870 Ferry* until Logan was satisfied it was fit for purpose and there is an image of the two ferries running alongside each other in 1915 probably using one cable each.

At 74 feet long including the ramps, and 18 feet wide, the new boat could carry four cars. There was also no lopsidedness as the Cochrane boiler was on one side of the vessel while the steam engines were on the other. The 12 horsepower engines burned five hundredweight of coal daily and the new vessel used one drive wheel compared to the three on the *1870 Ferry*. The ferrymen were Jim Coward and John Atkinson. The Westmorland Gazette described the new ferry;

(It) is a larger and more up-to-date steam ferry-boat with cabin accommodation, which is giving in every satisfaction. The new boat, which has been registered with Lloyd's in Class 'A' for ferry purposes… ……has its engines on the one side counter-balanced by a boiler of the Cochrane type on the opposite side, so ensuring a level keel; and the hull is divided into five water-tight compartments by cross bulkheads. The boat is capable when the need arises, of carrying four motor cars at one crossing.

For many years Hawkshead carriers would gather at Ferry House for the first ferry at 7 am, to reach Kendal as early as possible. They would return for one of the final runs, not getting back to Hawkshead until 8 or 9 pm. William Knipe and Jackson Atkinson served Kendal three times a week, and Coniston daily. They used two-wheeled carts and could carry up to a ton of coal at a time.

From the 1st March 1920 the ferry service was leased jointly by Westmorland and Lancashire County Councils, although the rights remained in the hands of the Curwen family. The Councils raised fares to create a profit, which greatly annoyed residents on the Sawrey side of the lake. They also upgraded the slipways from shingle banks to metalled roads abolishing the job of raking the gravel smooth after the vessel berthed. The ferry made a profit of £278.10s 4d in the year ending 31st March 1932, rising the following year to £330.3s 10d.

Every few years the ferry was taken off for overhaul and in September 1934 the following notice was displayed in the Westmorland Gazette; *NOTICE IS HEREBY GIVEN that the Steam Ferry Boat will be laid up for annual overhaul from Monday, 8th October, 1934, to Monday, 22nd October, 1934 inclusive. During this period no vehicular traffic will be carried, but a temporary service will be run for pedestrians and cyclists.*

In 1938, long serving ferryman John Atkinson retired after twenty-six years service. The Westmorland Gazette celebrated his long service in the edition published on 5th November; *One would hardly designate John as the Charon of Windermere, though during his career he ferried many departed souls across the narrow stretch of water separating the shores of Westmorland and Lancashire. But he also conveyed many thousands of people still living who cherish his courtesy and genial 'crack' en voyage. The ferry boat was, and still is, a bitter-sweet sort of experience. There seems to be something human about its works. When one just caught the ferry as it was moving off the shingle one could have cried out with joy and fallen on old John's neck. But if one just missed the boat and had to wait ten minutes while it crossed and another ten minutes while it came back, the least one can say about one's feelings was that they were slightly 'mixed'. The Ferry crossing could doubtless tell some spicy stories. A Gretna Green couple more than once crossed by it. An enterprising motorist, thinking that because steam would carry the ferryboat across, petrol ought to carry his combination across, changed his mind and his gears very quickly when he got up to his neck. Another story is told of an individual doing record time down the long hill from Far Sawrey, and taking a flying leap on to the boat as it was three yards from the shore. 'My word, that was a near thing,' he pantingly remarked. 'Why, we're just coming in,' replied John.*

1938 was the first recorded time that the ferry really struggled with long queues of holiday traffic, despite continuous running. In 1948 the Councils purchased the

lease rights to the ferry, and set about installing a larger vessel. *Drake* was the third cable ferry and was built in sections by the Lytham Shipbuilding and Engineering Company as yard number 903, the final boat constructed there. Named after Lancashire County Council Surveyor James Drake – a pioneer of the UK's motorway network – her seven sections were transported by rail to Lakeside between 10th and 23rd June 1954, for assembly on the slipway. She was launched on 12th July and then towed to Ferry Nab where cables were connected and she started her trials, carrying a 90 ton load on her first trip to check stability.

Built of steel at a total cost of £29,825, she was ninety five feet long including the ramps, thirty feet wide, and could carry ten cars or four coaches. Her total weight was seventy tons and her arrival allowed the 1915 ferry to be sold for scrap, valued at £53. Oddly *Drake* commenced service as a steam powered vessel, even though eighteen years earlier the LMS were building oil powered vessels.

The cables and anchor blocks were replaced in 1957, as the old set had been in constant use for seventy years. In 1960 the two cylinder steam engines were replaced with Leyland diesels providing 320 horsepower. These were more fuel efficient, burning one gallon per hour, so her five hundred gallon tank was refilled once every five weeks. The conversion saw the end of her large steam funnel, creating a more utilitarian look. Jack Bowman was ferryman, and had worked the crossing for twenty-five years by the time of the conversion. He noted a change in cargo from horse drawn transport to cars and motorcycles, and even a herd of seventy ponies.

In 1963 the lake froze from end to end but *Drake* kept running throughout the night for the duration of the freeze to keep her operational channel clear. She stopped sailing in March when during the thaw huge blocks of ice drifted down the lake causing obstructions. During the 1960s and 1970s *Drake* crossed the lake four times each way per hour during daylight hours but increasingly long queues built up on each side. And as vehicles got bigger and roads busier, *Drake*'s ten car capacity was proving insufficient. A larger vessel, capable of carrying eighteen cars and a hundred passengers, was commissioned from FL Steelcraft of Borth at a cost of £480,000. She was transported in sections to the slipway at White Cross Bay near Calgarth. *Mallard* was commissioned by Councillor C.B. Ross on 30th March 1990 before commencing service in April. *Drake* was sent to Lakeside to be scrapped after thirty-six years service. *Mallard*'s name was chosen by local school children, and she still operates the service today, still leaving vehicles behind during the summer months. Long queues seem forever the curse of the Windermere ferry.

Amey operated the ferry on behalf of the council from 2005 until May 2012, when operations were brought back under their control. The travelling public saw little change in operations.

Mallard undertakes a five-yearly major overhaul at Lakeside slipway, whilst a Bowness launch provides a replacement passenger-only service. Overhauls were undertaken in 2009 and 2014. Originally the launch cover operated the ferry route, but since 2000 this has been incorporated into the Cross-Lake Shuttle from Bowness. During the 2014 overhaul, *Mallard*'s ramp gates were moved slightly to return her to her original vehicle capacity. Despite being built to carry 18 cars, vehicle sizes have got bigger and *Mallard* filled at 15 cars. Her flotation tanks were replaced with open reversible life-rafts, similar to those carried by other passenger boats. Fears about the profitability of the service were raised in early 2014, but the county council pledged future investment of £300,000.

Mallard's crossing takes around four minutes and is timetabled to leave each side every twenty minutes giving a crossing every ten minutes. Between Easter and November a Mountain Goat minibus connects at Ferry House for Hawkshead via Sawrey, a throwback to the days when Rigg's Coaches did the same. *Mallard* operates Monday to Saturday between 6.50 am and 10.00 pm, and on Sunday between 9.50 am and 10.00 pm. In winter she finishes an hour earlier, with Christmas Day and Boxing Day off service.

General Electric Power and Traction Company

Electrically propelled boats on Windermere date back to August 1884 when Mr J. R. Bridson of Belle Isle had a launch built which was '*7 yards long, which will be driven by electricity, and used on the lake*'. Power was obtained from an electro-motor and twenty secondary batteries which were charged prior to use. She attained a speed of twelve miles an hour with a single screw twelve inches in diameter.

The General Electric Power and Traction Company was established in the late 1880s to provide passenger trips using quiet, modern electric launches. The derelict Bobbin Mill on Cunsey Beck was converted into a generator room with a dynamo fitted to a waterwheel to generate power from the stream. Wires were laid to the boathouse on the shore near Ling Holme, to charge the launches. This was one of the first times electricity had been created without burning coal.

Another boathouse was sited near Cockshott Point on the eastern shore, with a steamboat retained in case there was insufficient water in Cunsey Beck to charge the electric boats. Four boats were used for this experiment, each measuring forty feet in length and six feet six inches wide carrying up to forty passengers each '*all over the lake, from Newby Bridge to Ambleside, and from the Ferryside Hotel to the Old England*'. *Flo, Hilda, May,* and *Theo* were built by T.B. Seath & Co of Rutherglen in 1890, as yard numbers 268, 269, 270 and 271. They probably stored their charge in batteries inside the hull, and steel construction was preferred as electric boats with wooden hulls suffered timber damage caused by leaking battery acid.

In 1894 Thomas Martin mentioned the boats in his book 'Electrical Boats and Navigation'; *Another picturesque spot that has welcomed the noiseless, smooth-gliding electric launch has been Lake Windermere, with whose scenes the names of Wordsworth, Southey, Ruskin and others are so closely associated. It can easily be imagined that in such a place these launches were found preferable to steamboats. The charging station is driven by water power, an ideal source of energy in such surroundings. An old mill had been partially destroyed by fire, but as the water wheel mechanism remained intact, a Glasgow firm of boat builders conceived the happy idea of putting dynamos in the ruined building at Cockshott Point. The conditions were not such as to ensure a high efficiency for the plant, but water power is generally cheap, and a good rate of hire for the boats has been obtainable.*

Martin was misinformed in siting the dynamos in the Cockshott sheds as the only mill damaged by fire was at Cunsey.

An article in the Manchester Courier dated the 30th September 1891 mentioned '*Two electric launches that have been plying on Lake Windermere are also going to run from Manchester to Barton as soon as that section* (of the Manchester Ship Canal) *is completed'*. The two vessels were probably from Cunsey. The other two boats may have continued on the lake, but the General Electric Power and Traction Company Limited ceased trading on 21st November 1894. The demise was due to heavy operating losses and the falling price of copper; the launch operations were one arm of a company whose main focus was on manufacturing electrical equipment.

Storrs Hall Electric Boats

A few electric launches were operated by the Storrs Hall Hotel for guests in the early 1900s. In 1893 the Troutbeck Bridge electricity works was established by George Pattinson and Frederick Fowkes, producing some of the first electric street lighting in Britain. Pattinson also built a hydro electric generator at Storrs Hall to provide power to neighbouring residences. In 1900 he built a small dock – still in existence – for three small electric launches and a number of steam vessels. *Shamrock*, *Rose* and *Thistle* were charged by the generator and stored their charge in banks of batteries down the sides of the vessel. John Atkinson, later skipper of the chain ferry, was employed by Mr Townson of the Storrs Estate to run the electric and steam launches but they had a limited life spans due to acid leakage from batteries damaging their wooden hulls.

The Windermere Submarine

One of the most interesting passenger vessels on the lake was launched from Lakeside in 1997. A twenty-five ton Mergo Submarine from Finland was craned into the lake and driven onto the steamer slipway to complete preparations for lake service. Owned by Paul and Jane Whitfield, previous operators of a submarine

on Loch Ness, the *Windermere* could carry ten passengers. Alan Whitfield was the pilot and the intention was to run hour-long cruises at around half a knot. She was capable of diving to depths of 300 feet, although the deepest part of Windermere is only 220 feet, and around Lakeside is between twenty and a hundred feet deep. Limited visibility posed a few problems but it was hoped to locate wrecks to explore.

A press release issued before the season commenced stated; *Sonar equipment, cameras, and scientific instrumentation, help to locate and record all unusual targets........Who knows what will be seen, as there are numerous tales of sunken wrecks and flying boat's.*

Windermere was twenty eight feet long, nearly ten feet wide and powered by two, eleven kilowatt electric motors which pushed her along at up to three knots. There was oxygen on board to keep ten people alive for ninety six hours or forty-four man days. The fare for an hour-long cruise was £49.50 and sailings commenced in August 1997. A small wreck was soon located close to Lakeside which became a focal point for the cruise, which often went up as far as YMCA.

Over 3,500 passengers were carried during the first season. With eighty passengers daily over the best weekend. Alan Whitfield hoped to expand the enterprise but these plans never came to fruition, and the venture ceased after the 1998 season. The company had only one pilot and this expensive cruise rarely sailed at its advertised capacity.

Classic Cruises

Brendan Chapman and his family purchased a boat in 1996 and set about restoring her over the winter of 2005/6, after which she was re-launched onto the lake. *Ginny* was built on the Clyde in 1936 as the *Olga* and sailed to Barrow where she was transported to the lake for use as a leisure boat. During the Second World War the vessel was equipped with a water cooled Vickers machine gun on her bow and used by the Home Guard to defend the flying boat factory at White Cross Bay. She began operating for charter from March 2010 and now plies between various hotels, including the Beech Hill, Storrs Hall, Cragwood, Lakeside and Langdale Chase as well as using various public piers around the lake. The boat has a capacity of ten and is a Silverette classic.

Silverholme being pulled into the Ambleside boathouse for maintenance.

Appendix 1

Boat builders

There is a long tradition of local boat building, from *Lady of the Lake* at Greenodd to the many launches built in Bowness. Early boats were constructed elsewhere and brought by horse and cart to the lakeshore. Often built using wooden pegs instead of nails, they were utilitarian vessels designed for fishing and carrying, not pleasure, but as the lake's popularity increased, yachting became a pastime for the rich. Many yachts – especially in the early days of the Royal Windermere Yacht Club (formed in 1860; 'Royal' from July 1887) – were built as far away as Morison of Birkenhead, Vickers in Barrow, and Hatcher's of Southampton. They included the work of designers like G. L. Watson, Herbert and Percy Crossley, and Alfred and John Sladen. Local men became expert at designing and building yachts specifically for Windermere, and Bowness saw several boatyards spring up.

In the nineteenth century William Watson and Jack Thompson built boats at Ambleside; Watson built the passage boats *Victoria* and *Prince Albert* for Gibson and White, and the barge *Elizabeth*. Richard Ashburner of Greenodd constructed the first two steamers for the lake; the *Lady of the Lake* and the *Lord of the Isles*. He later moved to Barrow In Furness, where in 1850 he partnered his brother William, who brought experience of shipyards from the Isle of Man.

Bowness developed as the home of Lake District boat building and in the 1840s James Barrow, whose yard was on the site of today's Stag's Head inn, was building rowing boats with his father William Barrow; he became one of the first Bowness yacht builders when in 1861 he built the *Ganymede* for Louis John Crossley of the Windermere Yacht Club. Robert Barrow was also involved in the business and advertised his services as a joiner and boat builder. John Balmer was also boat building here.

Tom Storey was a lifelong builder of rowing boats, launches and yachts. One such was the *Gossip*, constructed for £55 from cedar planks during World War One. Although Tom worked in his own boatshed he was assisted when required by men from Shepherds. In 1922 his boathouse caught fire with the yacht *Nancy,* rowing boats, dinghies and sails inside, and the fire spread to the adjacent Borwicks boathouse. The largest casualty of the fire was the loss of boat building tools and equipment. Storey never built another yacht, but remained in the trade and may have built a few more rowing boats. Tom died in 1952 aged ninety-seven, and some of his rowing boats are still in use. In later years, Briggs McCrone assisted him in yacht restoration.

Tom Hayton had workshops in the middle of Bowness Bay that were demolished in 1912 when the promenade was extended. He produced rowing boats, and craft of up to fifty feet in length, including the electric launches *May Queen* and *Iris* for Derwentwater's Lodore Hotel in 1904. Hayton died in the 1930s, but his son Alf continued as a boatman in summer and boat builder during the winter months.

In the early decades of the twentieth century George Walker had a small boatyard in Parsonage Bay, building and repairing yachts; to many this was simply 'George's Bay'. George also offered sailing advice and training, and his son Eddie continued trading in Parsonage Bay after his death.

The boat sheds of Hayton & Kennedy, C. H. Breaker and Brockbank were also in Bowness. Brockbank's roots went back to the mid-nineteenth century; John Brockbank's obituary in 'The Lakes Chronicle' of February 1904 noted that he moved to the area as a married man before 1851 and operated as a boat builder until 1876. His son George Brockbank, who was closely linked with the designer Alfred Sladen, was building steam launches in 1898 and also built yachts.

Collingwood recorded in his 'The Lake Counties' that *'George Brockbank has built some of the most recent racers – the Kestrel, Turtle, Mimosa, Mabel, and others. Mr Shaw also has been a very successful builder.'* Later, the Youdell & Brockbank partnership of Upper Oak Street, Windermere pioneered a construction method for rowing boats in which the oak ribs and keel were laid upside-down on a 'jig', and mahogany planks added; this reduced build time per boat from three weeks to two.

Between 1897 and 1901 Bowness builders built seventeen of the twenty-two foot class of yachts, as well as launches and rowing boats. Brockbanks later built many wooden self-drive motor boats, which are still available for hire on the lake, moving on to building Stuart Turner powered self-drives, fibreglass vessels, and the small waterbus *Venture*.

A few boatmen built their own launches, such as Mr Huddleston and his *Have a Go*. The Bowness Bay Boating Company maintained its own boats and had its own boat builders, purchasing 'The Laundry' – about a third of a mile from the lake shore in Bowness – in 1968 for rowing boat and small launch maintenance. The site is now the Beatrix Potter exhibition. Silver Badge, across the road, was used later but is now a car park. Today's rowing boats and self-drives are maintained at The Heaning around three miles from the lake on the main road to Kendal.

Bowness' most famous boat builders were Borwicks and Shepherds although the two companies started out in 1890 as one, Shepherd & Borwick. Isaac Borwick and Nathanial Shepherd worked as apprentices for John Shaw. They set up a partnership to build boats including the 1898 electric launch *Swallow*, commissioned by Manchester solicitor, William Warburton of Belle Grange. A small water-driven generator on the beck near the house charged her batteries.

On 10th February 1900 the company split to establish their own boatyards, Shepherd to the current Winander House site, and Borwick to the present Windermere Aquatic Centre site; Borwicks later owned the large blue sheds on the shoreline south of the Beech Hill Hotel. Boat builders for the two companies earned up to 7d an hour at the turn of the century.

Shepherds continued to build rowing boats, yachts and steam launches, and Nathanial's five sons, Arthur, Jack, Kenneth, Neil and Wilfred followed him into the family business. In their first independent years, Shepherds built sleek, streamlined steam launches such as *Osprey* (1902), *Shamrock* (1906) and *Swallow* (1911), and the first locally built motorboat in 1902. Unreliable, this was usually seen accompanied by a rowing boat full of engineers ready to fix it – reaching Ambleside was a newsworthy event. In the boom year of 1907, twenty sailing boats were built for export to Spain.

Business in the heyday of boat building was steady and the firm employed around thirty people. Percy Crossley designed a unique seventeen-foot yacht class – known as the Windermere 17s – the first in 1904 at a cost of £100. The firm built many of these yachts including *Viva III* designed by Percy Crossley, and *Nomad* designed by Herbert Crossley. They were constructed quickly with the keel laid down in November and the hull launched the following April; during 1934 and 1935 Shepherds built seven of these yachts for Royal Windermere Yacht Club members. Shepherds also built other sailing yachts such as Flying Fifteens, Firefly's and GP 14's.

By 1953 Shepherds had constructed 277 vessels – nearly six a year – the largest of which was the 1938 *Princess Margaret Rose,* still trading for the Keswick on Derwentwater Launch Company. In 1955 Shepherds built the first double skinned yacht for Windermere, the David Boyd design *Delene*. Eventually Wilfred was the only Shepherd left and he appointed 1929 apprentice Briggs McCrone as manager. Wilfred retired in the early 1960s and McCrone, who became a director, ran the company. The company continued building boats, including the

Constabulary's launch, but although the company is still in existence construction has now ceased.

Isaac Borwick formed Borwicks & Sons with his sons John, a master yacht builder and draughtsman, George, who handled administration, and Arthur who developed the engineering department. They built vessels from rowing boats to motor launches and yachts, and from 1920 onwards, small hydroplanes capable of reaching speeds of up to eighty miles per hour. One craft for Norman Buckley achieved speeds of 120 mph on Windermere. In 1910 Borwicks offered *'motor boats supplied complete for £50'*. The firm built the first self-drives and cabin cruisers for the lake, but is most associated with motor launches, many of which are still in existence.

During the First World War Borwicks built pinnaces for the Admiralty, and developed as float builders for planes trialled in the years prior to the 1920s. They also built a few complete planes and Arthur Borwick lost two fingers when swinging a propeller blade for one of these early aircraft. Their association with water speed record attempts, began with building the 4,000 horsepower vessel *Miss England II* for Henry Segrave, the first to achieve 100 mph. Henry Segrave died in her during a record attempt on Windermere in 1930, but Borwicks restored *Miss England II* and Kay Don piloted her to more records in America.

Although Borwicks built three yachts in 1934 for the Royal Windermere Yacht Club, their main focus was on motor launches. During the Second World War the company built lifeboats for the Merchant Navy and around thirty tenders for the R.A.F. to access seaplanes. A few small barges were built after the war, going as far afield as Malta, but these were limited to forty-five feet to ease transport. They also designed a map of the lake on rollers inside a small box with a viewing window, so that the appropriate part of the lake could be viewed.

Borwicks built their last pleasure launch in the late 1940s but continued to construct yachts and private boats, including the Windermere 17 *Rhythm* in 1959. The focus shifted to storage, repairs and restoration, but in 1955 following the lead of Shepherds, Borwicks were commissioned to construct double skinned yachts for members of the Royal Windermere Yacht Club. They closed when their boathouses were demolished in 1973-75 to make way for the Aquatic building. The Aquarius building was built at the other end of the bay, near the piers for the railway steamers, which necessitated demolition of many more boathouses.

In the heyday of boat building, boathouses stretched from Cockshot Point to Myley Birk – the beach alongside Glebe Road in Bowness Bay. Arthur Ransome based *Rio* on Bowness in 'Swallowdale';

…Swallow and her convoy were moving in between Long Island and the shore towards the little town of Rio, with its clout of blue smoke drifting from it in the sunlight. All along this nearer side of Rio Bay were the building yards, where rowing boats were built, and little ships like Swallow, and racing yachts, besides motor-boats for the people who did not know how to manage sails. There were boathouses and little docks. There were sheds a few yards back from the water, with railway lines running down into the lake, and wheeled carriages resting on the railway lines to carry boats down into the water and to bring them up out of it. On one of these carriages was a sailing yacht, with its mast high above the roof of the sheds, and its sails neatly furled under its sail-covers, its varnishing and painting bright under the sun, ready at any moment to go sliding down into the water and become a thing alive as all ships are when they are afloat.

The Borwick & Sons builders plate on **Sunflower II**, dating from 1950.

Appendix 2

Private Steam on Windermere

As Windermere developed, many wealthy industrialists with spare time, money and enthusiasm became resident around the shore. They commissioned an unrivalled fleet of small steam vessels, many of which survive in the Steamboat Museum, and every year enthusiasts bring their own launches for Windermere Steam Week.

Manchester businessman Charles Fildes had *Fairy Queen*, the first private paddle steamer built around 1850. Clinker built, with large paddle wheels just aft of the engine, she was fitted with a large white funnel. When not in use the boiler was placed in his narrow gauge locomotive *Lavinia* to run round his garden in Sawrey. His brother Alfred owned *Dolly* built around 1850 for use on Windermere and now the world's oldest working mechanically powered boat. In the early 1890s she moved to Ullswater, and sank on 21st February 1895. Divers discovered *Dolly* in Ullswater in 1962, but it took a while to appreciate her historic value. She was raised and handed over to the Steamboat Museum for restoration. In surprisingly good condition despite her lengthy ducking, she was re-launched on Windermere on 18th September 1965 and is now kept at the Museum. The Fildes family also owned *Cuckoo*, *Bijou*, *Merlin*, *Firefly*, *Kittiwake*, and *Mary Jane*.

The boats of Colonel Ridehalgh were in a luxurious class of their own. A keen sailor, Ridehalgh was a founding member of the Windermere Yacht Club and owned several vessels including two steamboats. His first was the *Fairy Queen* built in 1859 by T.B Seath & Co. Trialled on the Clyde, she sailed to Parkhead, near Holker Hall arriving in April 1860 for transfer to a special wagon for an eventful nine-day journey to the lake. The boat weighed in at thirty tons, was sixty-five feet long and needed twenty-five horses to pull her. At Bigland Scar the wagon sank into soft ground and the steamer was left until fresh horses could be brought the next day. At Cark a wheel was repaired, but the load sank again at Staveley Meadows and was left over the weekend. She was launched onto the lake the following week. Colonel Ridehalgh used *Fairy Queen* regularly and the steamer enjoyed celebrity status. She was an innovative vessel and in 1863 was fitted with apparatus to create her own gas for lighting. Hunt's Yachting Magazine highlighted the importance;

A STEAMER LIGHTED WITH GAS

THE beautiful iron steam yacht "Fairy Queen" has arrived in Bowness Bay, Windermere, brilliantly lighted up with gas. This yacht which was built for Captain Ridehalgh by, by Mr. T. B. Seath, of Glasgow, in 1860, has during the three years she has been on the lake, undergone several improvements and ingenious contrivances by her owner. Two years ago Messrs. Sharp, Stuart, and Co. of the Atlas Works, Manchester fixed on board one of Giffard's injectors for supplying the boiler with water...........

..........In February last the yacht's engines were fitted with Ramsbottom's pistons, same as are used on the London and North Western Railway, and up to the present time have given great satisfaction. And the last improvement is lighting the yacht with gas. We believe this is the first vessel that has ever manufactured her own on board. The gas can be kept burning for any length of time. The light which is clear and white, is produced by passing a current of air through a small box containing a chemical compound. Its cost is about the same, or rather cheaper than the ordinary gas. The current of air is produced by a new patent hydraulic blower turned by clock work and a weight. The cost of the apparatus for buildings

would be from £15 and upwards, it is exceedingly simple, and takes up very little room, the whole being contained in a space about 2 feet square. The Patentees of this excellent invention are Messrs. Trachsel and Clayton of Manchester. The novelty of gas lighting in Bowness drew together a great number of people to witness it, many of whom the owner, J. G. M. Ridehalgh, Esq., very kindly took on board and showed them all the improvements.

Fairy Queen assisted in the launching of *Rothay* and *Swan* (I), and was sometimes used for public excursions from Bowness. Her logbook for early 1879 records a number of journeys between Bowness and Fell Foot, taking between 36 and 43 minutes. On the evening of March 14th she took 1½ hours, with her log book noting *'Very dark. Snowing'*. *Fairy Queen* was sold in 1879.

The larger *Britannia*, another Seath product costing £12,000 – more than any other steamer on the lake – replaced her. Britannia was conveyed in sections by rail to Lakeside prior to launch by Miss Ridehalgh on 24th June 1879. She was 102 feet long by twelve feet wide with a depth of seven feet six inches, and a draught of three and a half feet. She had a clipper stem, two masts, and a raked copper funnel just aft of centre. Fitted with a counter-stern, she also had steam nozzles – primitive bow thrusters – to assist manoeuvrability in narrow waters. Her engines were built by Plenty & Son and provided 100 horsepower. Like *Fairy Queen* she was lighted by gas that was generated on board. Large for a private steamer, the Board of Trade certified her for 122 passengers when Colonel Ridehalgh and his wife were entertaining.

On 21st June 1887 she moored in Bowness Bay to celebrate Queen Victoria's jubilee, firing a twenty-one gun salute whilst the Windermere Volunteers returned fire from the shore. This was her third salute of the day; the first at Lakeside was followed by another at 2 pm at Waterhead, where the Ambleside Volunteers responded. After her Bowness salute *Britannia* made a tour of the lake from Ambleside to Fell Foot, firing shots at random to entertain spectators. Henry Schneider provided refreshments for volunteers, and bonfires and fireworks lit up the night sky. As the parties continued *Britannia* returned to Bowness Bay again at 2 am and proceeded to open fire, *'awaking the echoes in a remarkable manner, the sound reverberating like thunder from one side of the Lake to the other for about twenty seconds'*.

Britannia was used as a spectator and press launch during the Windermere regattas, affording a better view than could be obtained from ashore. She was purchased by the FR in 1908 for £350 and used for private charters. Withdrawn in 1915 she was scrapped in 1919.

In May 1869 Seath & Co built the small steamer *Esperance* for Henry Schneider of Belsfield, Bowness. She was also transported by rail to Lakeside, after the track had been singled under bridges to allow greater clearance. Weighing in at seventeen tonnes she was sixty-five feet long with a maximum breadth of ten feet. Her hull was built of Low Moor iron and the rivets were countersunk to leave a smooth finish. The bow was heavily raked so ice posed no problem to her, and she was the first twin-screw vessel on Lloyds Register. Her engines were compound with a single cylinder block and two sets of pistons in the shape of an inverted 'V' connected to each shaft.

Schneider boarded Esperance at Bowness to begin his commute to Barrow in Furness, preceded by his butler, and breakfasting on board before taking his private train from Lakeside. His secretary met him in his private carriage on the morning train with the post to be read on his way to work. Schneider and Rev. Thomas Staniforth disagreed over the building of a grammar school in Barrow and their feud was never resolved. Staniforth inherited the Storrs estate in 1848, and henceforth

Schneider required the *Esperance* to sail along the western shoreline to keep well away from Storrs.

Esperance was laid up for four years on the Lady Slip previously used by *Lady of the Lake* after Schneider's death in 1887. Purchased by Bruce Logan of the Ferry Hotel, she operated an hourly service to Bowness at a fare of 2d under engineer George Stuart. On Sundays she sailed with hotel guests to Wray Castle boathouse for services at Wray Church; other churchgoers rowed across from Low Wood or Ambleside. She also catered for private functions, in April 1903 conveying guests to Belle Isle for a wedding. She was known to carry passengers on her roof if space was short.

Bruce Logan kept hunting hounds on Crow Holme and allegedly when his bitch had puppies she would swim across to the hotel from the island to keep a check on them. He used *Esperance* to transport his dogs to go hunting, and she operated from the hotel until the outbreak of World War One. Her engines were removed following post-war conversion into a houseboat. Arthur Ransome modelled the houseboat in his books on her, and she was later used in this capacity in the 1970s film version of *Swallows and Amazons*. By 1941 she lay sunk in twenty feet of water near Blake Holme but T C Pattinson decided to raise and restore her. He moved *Esperance* to Rayrigg Bay where she was placed on a floating mooring until work could be done. In 1956 George Pattinson installed a pair of four cylinder Ford petrol engines, providing forty-nine horsepower, and she returned to active use when the Queen visited the lake in August 1956. Retaining her original steam funnel, she was equipped with steam making apparatus and is now kept at the Steamboat Museum.

Most steam launches on Windermere were simpler, and the 1860s saw an influx of small launches, one of which was the *Linnet*. She was owned by Mr Bryans of Belfield with engines supplied, like the larger *Britannia,* by Plenty and Son of Newbury. Another was the *Wavecrest*, which was forty five feet long, eight feet wide and capable of eight miles an hour. There are few references to her, but in 1871 she was listed for sale in the Westmorland Gazette.

Not all the names and images of other launches survive. Mr White of the Swan Hotel owned *Cygnet* – built by Robert Rodger of Port Glasgow and launched in May 1870. On September 7th 1871 the Ulverston Advertiser reported that the Allithwaite Choir enjoyed an excursion aboard her. David MacIver MP owned the steam launch *Wagtail*, launched in 1872, and paddle steamer *Dodo* of 1880. The latter was built at Wanlass Howe, Waterhead, her name reflecting the outmoded, declining paddle steamer. MacIver's brother Robert had a steamer called *Maru* built by Brockbank's in 1894, which carried Kaiser Wilhelm II in 1895 and passed to his son upon his death in 1901. *Glow Worm* resembled a miniature *Esperance* and was owned by Joseph Bridson, who resided on Belle Isle from 1880 to 1885. He kept her on the Esperance pier in Bowness.

William Inman, founder of the Inman Shipping line in Liverpool, owned *Wyvern*. Built by by T.B Seath & Co in 1872, she was sold in 1875 to the Ullswater Steam Navigation Company. While working out how to move her to Ullswater, she sank in Mitchell Wyke on the 24th February 1876. The cost of raising and restoring her proved prohibitive. After raising she was sold to a Barrow contractor, Mr Hunter and towed by the *Raven* to Lakeside in August. She was last noted in London in the late 1880s. Mr Inman also owned the *Eagle* and several sailing yachts.

The late 1880s saw steam launches being used for more than just pleasure. G H Pattinson owned the *Jubilee*, *Wraith*, *Powerful*, and *Iris* amongst others. The last two transported materials and men for his construction business, and towed timber from the Bark House near Belle Grange, to Lakeside. When the steam ferry was out of service, *Powerful* often towed the old row-ferry *Mary Anne*. They also supplied the lake-side residences of Graythwaite Hall and Pullwood. A contemporary was the *Banshee*, a beautiful launch with a clipper bow complete with a bowsprit, two masts and a spacious aft cabin, owned by Sir William Bower Forwood.

Alfred Sladen, one of the greatest designers of yachts and launches, moved to the area in the late 1880s. He designed and built the twenty-seven foot launch *Bat* in 1891 for personal use. In 1902 Isaac Storey and Jack Kitchen steered *Bat* around the north basin by radio from the top of Queen Adelaide's hill, while a stoker kept the fires hot. The local paper recorded: *A new and potentially terrible engine of war is now being developed by its inventor. It is designed to enable a vessel loaded with explosives to be safely conducted into the midst of a hostile fleet primed to do its work at the proper time… A steam launch, its tiller controlled by electrical machinery, put out on the lake with no hand touching the tiller. Standing by another electrical machine on the shore, Mr. Storey steered the launch port or starboard as he willed, directing it in safety in and out of a fleet of sloops and steam launches at their moorings. The apparent miracle was made possible by an adaptation of the principle of wireless telegraphy, its adaptation to this particular work being the secret of the inventor.*

Alfred Sladen had the *Elfin* built in 1895. Built for speed, she was capable of twenty-five miles an hour and was powered by a high-pressure boiler that produced 240 horsepower. She often carried Mr Sladen to his sailing yacht at the start line of racing. Her finest hour came in Queen Victoria's 1897 Diamond Jubilee when her engine was uncoupled and connected to a generator to provide electricity to light Bowness. In November 1898 *Elfin* is said to have sailed up the River Brathay to Brathay Bridge during severe flooding. She was scrapped in 1926.

1896 saw the arrival of two of the finest steamers for the lake. Alfred Sladen's *Grebe*, built for his brother Mortimer by Forrestt and Sons of Wyvenhoe, was built in numbered sections like the *Tern* and assembled at Windermere. She had a triple expansion Sissons engine that generated a speed of eighteen miles an hour. The propeller was made from corrugated brass to increase surface area and speed, but the extra weight of the prop counteracted any benefit. *Grebe* survives at the Windermere Steamboat Museum as *Otto* – renamed in 1899 by her later owner Dr W. Whitehead in memory of Otto Burchardt, an early member of the Royal Windermere Yacht Club who died in 1895. Dr Whitehead also owned the steam yacht *Firefly* as well as the yachts *Esperanza* and *Mabel*.

The 1896 *Lily* was designed for the comfort of the Howarth family, who lived at Langdale Chase, south of Low Wood. Built of teak with carpeted saloons with leather seats, she even boasted a toilet. She remained with the Howarths until 1919 then passed to the Cowburns. George Pattinson acquired her for restoration in the 1960s as *Branksome*. In 1966 she carried the Duke of Edinburgh on a short cruise to the Royal Windermere Yacht Club. Royalty boarded again in 1977 when Prince Charles opened the Steamboat Museum and was conveyed to the Yacht Club to greet members, before heading on a tour around the islands. Princess Anne boarded in 1992 after opening the Westmorland General Hospital in Kendal. She sailed aboard the steam launch *Satis* before sounding *Branksome's* steam horn to start a race for the Royal Windermere Yacht Club. Princess Anne was again aboard the *Satis* in 2004.

A few of the private steamers employed a 'Windermere Kettle' – a coiled copper pipe containing high pressure steam from the boiler was placed in a copper urn filled with water, boiling a gallon of water in ten seconds.

The last years of the 19th century and the first decade of the 1900s saw the building of a new design of very narrow steam launches with a sleek, streamlined appearance. The *Kittiwake* was built in 1898,

Osprey in 1902, *Shamrock* in 1906, *Water Viper* in 1907, and *Swallow* in 1911. *Waterlily* of 1903 was very similar, but this Shepherds boat spent her career on Derwentwater. The 1907 build *Satanella*, was capable of twenty-three miles an hour thanks to quadruple expansion engine and very large boiler, although she burned forty gallons of paraffin per hour.

In 1925 Sir George Mellor commissioned the steam launch *Annie Mellor* (I) from Borwicks for his private use. Fitted with a toilet, she was one of the finest boats on the lake. The Prince of Wales visited the lake in 1927, travelling from Waterhead to Bowness in the motor launch *Badger*, which was followed by his entourage in the *Annie Mellor* (I). By 1935 she was replaced by the larger *Annie Mellor* (II). *Annie Mellor* (I) was sold to Derwentwater to become the *Lady Derwentwater*. *Annie Mellor* (II) followed her in the early 1950s, retaining her name. Both still operate on Derwentwater having been converted to diesel engines.

Private steam on Windermere is still a common sight. Centenarian vessels resident on the lake include *Columbine*, *Grebe*, *Janet*, *Shamrock*, *Souvenir D'antan*, and the delightful *Wisp*. More modern launches complement the veterans including the *Mosquito* – a replica of the *Elfin* and capable of seventeen miles per hour – and the *Grayling*, built in 1999. 'Steam Week' provides and annual reunion for these and many other steamers. Smaller launches can be seen around the lake meeting up at places like the Windermere Motor Boat Racing Club, the Royal Windermere Yacht Club, the Steamboat Museum, and Waterhead.

Two men who did more than anyone for steam on Windermere were Cooper Pattinson and George Pattinson, who collected a miscellany of boats – yachts, motorboats, steamboats, and rowing boats. Their collection became one of the finest in the country and in the mid-1970s George went into partnership with the National Maritime Museum to form the Windermere Nautical Trust. The Trust's aim is to preserve the collection and prevent it being dispersed. This culminated in the opening of a dedicated steamboat museum at Rayrigg Wyke north of Bowness. Opened in May 1977, it houses a wide array of vessels dating from the Victorian era to the late twentieth century including the *Dolly*, *Esperance*, *Raven*, *Kittiwake*, *Swallow*, and *Lady Elizabeth*. Motor launches are well represented by *Penelope II*, and one of the first motorboats from 1898. Many vessels mentioned in the narrative are preserved at the museum including non-powered craft such as *Mary Anne*, *Elizabeth*, and the yacht *Margaret*, dating from 1780 which was used in the race against the *Peggy* in 1796.

As of mid-2014 the museum was undergoing a major, £13.4 million refurbishment with the intention of re-opening early in 2016. The museum's collection of 40 vessels will be displayed, and it is hoped once again for a refurbished *Osprey* to offer cruises from the museum around the islands in the locality. The new museum will also house a viewable workshop where visitors will be able to see vessels under restoration. A wet dock and slipway will allow vessels to be viewed in, and out, of the water and a new café will provide refreshment. When re-opened the museum will be a major draw and a 'must do' for anyone with even a slight interest in boating heritage and the Lake District.

Appendix 3

Dredging on Windermere

Dredging was one of the last primary industries to survive on Windermere. The lakebed was long a source of building materials, becoming a commercial venture in the later eighteenth century. Sand and gravel was deposited south of the steamer piers in Bowness, and in the 1890s a dedicated wharf was constructed which also received shipments of timber. George Pattinson was lessee of the rights to take sand in 1898, but he sublet these rights to T. Walker who used barges propelled by a lug-sail and oars, but also kept a steam launch for towing them. The Bowness wharf closed in 1921 as a new site was developed at Rayrigg Wyke.

Pattinson later introduced steam launches *Iris* and *Powerful* to tow the barges into position over the gravel beds. One of the barges was the *Elizabeth* from Coniston. Dredging was a laborious two-man process, one with a twelve-foot pole with a hessian sack fitted around an iron ring on the end, held by rope by a second man at the other end of the barge. The sack was lowered to the lakebed and pulled along by rope before being winched into the hold.

The Pattinsons introduced the first mechanical dredgers in the 1930s; these were limited to working outside 100 feet from the shoreline at a working depth of around forty to fifty feet, primarily on the eastern side of the north basin. In 1949 the Windermere Sand and Gravel Company received powers from the Windermere Urban District Council to dredge from the Middle Cubble, permitting them to remove: '*sand, clay, stone, shingle, silloe*'.

The company introduced a new dredging machine in 1964, comprising two pontoons, each forty-eight feet in length and eight feet wide, with a two-foot gap between them; mounted across the rear was an NCK 205 excavator with a clamshell type bucket. The dredging unit was towed by a steel tug, and secured using a two and a half ton anchor. A more sophisticated machine was bought in 1967 to dredge to depths of 60 feet, using a pipe to pump material up from the lakebed. This was deposited into the barge with the heaviest sinking to the bottom, whilst water drained over the side.

Spoil from the lakebed was dumped into two converted canal barges reinforced with steel plate, each with a capacity of forty-five tons, although limited to thirty by the depth of the channel to the sand wharf, where they were towed by the steel tug. Here an excavator emptied material from the barges into a hopper. This separated wood and stone over four inches across, which it sent to waste, from the more valuable sandy gravel, which was taken by conveyor belt to a washing barrel. This produced sand, half-inch ballast, a three quarter inch aggregate, and one and a half inch composite material. Apparently one barge lies abandoned deep under the surface near the mouth of Trout Beck.

Dredging ceased in 1975, to much relief as it had long been suspected that removal of shingle beds was detrimental to the many fish spawning in these areas. Swan Holme, a small reedy island, was removed by excavation from the mouth of the River Brathay and is now a crater 50 feet deep. Millerground Bay was a favourite feeding place for perch, but the protecting underwater hillock has long been removed. The washing of stone at Rayrigg created large quantities of silt that drifted into the lake, settling on the lakebed and smothering plants, thereby driving fish and marine life away.

Two years later the sand wharf re-opened as the Windermere Steam Boat Museum.

Appendix 4

Early Aviation on Windermere

The first decade of the twentieth century saw pioneers racing to produce a plane capable of taking off and landing on water, with experiments at Barrow's Cavendish Dock and on Windermere. Oscar Gnosspelius of Silver Holme, Graythwaite was the first to attempt to fly from the lake in a plane built by Borwicks in 1910. Fitted with twin floats and known as the *Gnosspelius Hydro-Monoplane No.1*, Oscar changed the design to a single float, testing them behind a motorboat to see how they dragged across the water surface. Neither version took off, being underpowered by a twenty horsepower Avaston engine. On November 18th 1911, Royal Naval Commander Oliver Schwann flew his thirty-five horsepower Avro bi-plane from Cavendish Dock, rising to around twenty feet before crashing into the water and capsizing.

Gnosspelius was not deterred and produced the *Gnosspelius Hydro-Monoplane No.2,* fitted with a fifty horsepower engine in 1911. He held trials on the lake, retiring to make adjustments in the sheds. On 25th November, whilst Gnosspelius' plane was taxiing between Cockshot Point and the ferry, it lurched forwards and flipped into the lake damaging a wing and propeller. After modification the aircraft took off on 14th February 1912, the first locally built floatplane to take off from water.

Captain Edward William Wakefield, a barrister from Kendal was another Windermere pioneer. A childhood love of flying was rekindled in October 1909 when he visited the Blackpool aviation meeting – also attended by Gnosspelius. They saw both flying machines and unfortunate accidents. Whilst these *'were to be expected and quite unavoidable'*, Wakefield later asked *'In that case, why fall on the land and get hurt, when there is plenty of nice soft water to fall into?'* Henceforth he championed the idea of flying from water to reduce risk to machine and pilot. The propellers, which could drag the nose of the machine into the water, hindered water take-off, but Wakefield was undeterred and looked at converting a second hand machine. After the success of Glen Curtis who flew from water in San Diego on 26th January 1911, he approached A. V. Roe & Co of Manchester to build a similar aircraft. He also visited Henri Fabre, the first man to take off from water on 28th March 1910 near Marseilles.

Wakefield's aircraft was an Avro Curtis bi-plane with a seven cylinder Gnome rotary engine producing fifty horsepower. It was tested with a traditional undercarriage at Brooklands airstrip on 19th June 1911. Whilst there, Wakefield met Herbert Stanley Adams, a Rolls Royce engineer, and asked him to become his test pilot at Windermere. Adams and *Waterbird* arrived at Windermere in July 1911. Borwicks fitted a single central float, based on that used by Curtis in America, amended by cutting hydroplane steps into it to force air between the float and the water to aid take-off. *Waterbird* was kept in a hangar on Wakefield's land at Hill of Oaks.

On the same day as Gnosspelius' failed attempt, Adams taxied to the middle of the lake and faced north. On his second attempt he took off, and aided by a northerly wind he flew to the ferry and back, a total distance of about eight miles – the first successful water take-off and landing from anywhere in the British Empire. Adams flew *Waterbird* the entire length of the lake on 7th December at speeds of up to forty mph. In the thirty-eight days from 25th November over sixty flights were made, and slight modifications were made to improve efficiency after studying planes at Brooklands Aerodrome.

In January 1912 Captain Wakefield formed the Lakes Flying Company with Adams and the Earl of Lonsdale, building workshops and hangars at Cockshot, next to the workshops of Borwicks. They began building a larger version of *Waterbird,* but on the night of 29th/30th March the sheds were wrecked during a storm and both *Waterbird* and her successor irreparably damaged. The Cockshot hangars were repaired and rebuilt. Some saw the storm as a blessing. The 'Lake District Hydroaeroplane Protest Committee' was established on 5th January 1912, with Beatrix Potter and Canon Rawnsley at the helm. They opposed flying from the lake, and organised a 10,000-signature petition. A public inquiry in April found in favour of Wakefield, partly due to support from First Lord of the Admiralty Winston Churchill and the need for planes for military purposes.

Borwicks salvaged the engine and propeller from the damaged aircraft to build *Waterhen* – identical to the *Waterbird* at thirty-six and a half feet long with a rudder area of nine and a half square feet, and a propeller just behind the pilot. The first pilot on the inaugural flight on 30th April 1912 was Adams, and in July 1915 her single float was replaced with twin floats. Two months later she received a Gnome engine, providing eighty horsepower. She had an extra seat positioned behind the pilot to permit use for passenger flights and in her first seven months made nearly 250 flights taking around 100 passengers. Gnosspelius became an aircraft designer for the Company, putting his new monoplane at their disposal. Borwicks became experts at building floats, and the Admiralty sent Deperdussin monoplanes to Windermere for conversion to water use.

In early 1912 the Lakes Flying Company extended its remit to training pilots, with a course of lessons costing between £40-£75, while a passenger flight cost £2, available daily except Sundays. Passenger flights were not restricted to leaving from specific piers, as noted in July 1913: *'A hydro-aeroplane of the Lakes Flying Company made several ascents with passengers on Monday, and in one of these flights, made from the Ferry Hotel in the forenoon … started from the pier near where the ferry-boat lands'*. Another 1912 product was the *Seabird,* constructed at Hill of Oaks from the remains of a 1911 Avro Duigan tractor biplane, making her first flight on 28th August 1912. Fitted with a fifty horsepower Gnome engine she originally had a central float that was substituted for twin floats over the winter of 1914-15. She had a comparatively long career, lasting until written-off on 3rd June 1915.

Their first student to gain a pilot license was Lieutenant Trotter, who ordered a two-seater hydro-biplane designed by Gnosspelius. The *Gnosspelius Hydro-Biplane* was launched on 8th September 1913, and took her first flight on 20th September. Trotter landed heavily, damaging the propeller and chassis, but after repairs and a float change the plane only flew a few more times until her final flight on 11th November 1913.

The Northern Aircraft Company (NAC) was formed in February 1914 with Rowland Ding as general manager and pilot. Following the outbreak of war, passenger flights and pilot training were stopped and Gnosspelius and Adams joined the Royal Naval Air Service (RNAS), Adams as a sub lieutenant. From September 1914 Ding replaced Adams as a pilot for the Lakes Flying Company, and arranged a takeover by the Northern Aircraft Company Limited, including the three planes *Waterhen*, *Seabird*, and a monoplane under construction, as well as a hydroplane boat capable of fifty miles per hour. The NAC appointed two instructors and expanded the Hill of Oaks complex. They finished the *NAC Monoplane* in January 1915, to a Gnosspelius design. She was capable of climbing to 3,000 ft. The NAC also built a two-seater pusher bi-plane seaplane known as *PB.1.* with a sixty horsepower water cooled Green four cylinder engine. After conversion to an air-cooled eighty horsepower Gnome seven-cylinder engine she became *PB.2*.

In October *Waterhen,* flown by chief trainer John Lankester-Parker, made a quick landing on Esthwaite Water becoming the first flight to land on another body of water. A pilot at eighteen, Lankester-Parker was turned down for war service as he had childhood polio, but he was to become involved with the Short Sunderland Flying Boat factory at White Cross Bay during the Second World War.

The first plane to land on Coniston Water was *Blackburn Type 1*, built as a land based aircraft in August 1913. Purchased by the Northern Aircraft Company in 1915 she was converted for use from water by Blackburns, her original builders. Designed for quick conversion back to a land plane she was known as a Land Sea Monoplane. Lankester-Parker flew her to Coniston Water on Saturday 18th March 1916, tying up at Waterhead Hotel pier for lunch with his passenger before the return flight. On 1st April she capsized off Bowness and was written off.

The Northern Aircraft Company trained pilots for the RNAS from December 1915. The RNAS gradually introduced more planes to the fleet including Sopwiths and F.B.A. Flying Boats, before assuming total control in May 1916. They focussed on the Hill of Oaks site and in June renamed it RNAS Hill of Oaks. Lankester-Parker and Ding remained as instructors. But this did not last long. Flight Lieutenant Trotter was killed in an FBA Flying boat, which broke up in mid-air on the approach to landing in September 1916. The last instructional flight was on 13th January 1917, with the last aircraft leaving on 27th February, and the site officially closed in June. Nothing remains at either Cockshot or Hill of Oaks today.

Howard Pixton resurrected the Cockshot hangars in 1919 and used two Avro 504K seaplanes for pleasure flights from Windermere. He operated charters, and from 4th August 1919 introduced daily flights from Cockshot to Douglas Harbour, Isle of Man with copies of the 'Daily News' delivered to Windermere by the early train. Pixton was the last of the early aviators, but this was not the end of an association between aircraft and the lake. During the Second World War Short Sunderland Flying Boats were produced at White Cross Bay.

On 25th November 2011, a century after *Waterbird*'s first successful flight the Royal Naval Historic Flight charity commemoration plans were scuppered by the weather, but a successful flypast took place on 23rd July 2012 with a Sea Fury in attendance.

Berry Castle (III) at Totnes. She would later become **Lady Wakefield**.

Launch of the submarine **Windermere** at Lakeside in 1997.

Appendix 5

Other Lake services

Boating (strictly 'of sorts') is to be had on almost every lake…
– Baddeley's Guide

None of the other lakes in Cumbria have seen scheduled passenger services, but many saw boats of one sort or another for hire. Grasmere, Buttermere, Crummock Water and Loweswater maintain the tradition of rowing boats available for hire.

'The Penny Magazine of the Society for the Diffusion of Useful Knowledge' told travellers how to visit Scale Force near Buttermere: *'The usual way of visiting it is by boat from Scale Hill or Buttermere: there is however a footpath…'*. This suggests that as early as 1837 there were boats for hire, even on one of the more remote lakes. Fishing was probably the primary reason for hire, although a guide could likely be procured for an accompanied tour. By 1890 Baedeker advised tourists *'to go by boat to the mouth of the glen (fare 1s each, there and back)'*.

The same guide suggested that the best way to see Wastwater *'is perhaps to hire a boat, and go all the way by water (1s. per hour.; with boatman 2s. 6d per hour.; to the foot of the lake and back 5s.)'*.

Esthwaite Water has also had a fleet of rowing boats for over sixty years. They are still available for hire, but mainly for fishermen.

Baedeker's 1890 Guide notes that Grasmere possessed a *'Ferry near the Prince of Wales Hotel'*, presumably to reach the island. June Allonby hired 16 rowing boats on Grasmere for many years, maintaining them herself throughout the winter. She ran a ferry service for a local farmer, whereby her husband would row one boat of sheep to the lake's island for summer grazing, whilst towing a second.

In the Kentmere valley the diatomite works, based at the south end of Kentmere Tarn employed 4 boats from the 1950s until 1980. A tug boat towed a floating grab-dredger barge around the tarn. Diatomite was lifted with the grabber and dropped into the two waiting hopper barges. They were then towed to the south end of the tarn and unloaded at a specially constructed wharf.

Boating on the other lakes is permitted, with the exception of Thirlmere and Haweswater, both of which are reservoirs with limited access to preserve water quality.

FLEET LIST

Key:
##	Vessel on the National Historic Ships Register
PS	Paddle Steamer
SS	Single Screw
TS	Twin Screw
hp	Horsepower
ihp	Indicated horsepower
nhp	Nominal horsepower

Furness Railway: cross-bay vessels

Name	Built	Acquired	Disposed of	Broken up	Tons	Length ft	Breadth ft	Draught ft	Engine/ Propulsion	Builder
Helvellyn	1842	1847	1868	Unknown	153	131.1	16.5	8.3	75hp side lever steam with tubular boiler / PS	Wm. Craig & Co

Built for the Lochgoil and Lochlong Steamboat Company as Lochlong. Chartered for use on Morecambe Bay in March 1847, she was purchased by the FR in December 1848. She was displaced in 1868.

Name	Built	Acquired	Disposed of	Broken up	Tons	Length ft	Breadth ft	Draught ft	Engine/ Propulsion	Builder
Walney (I)	1868	1868	1897	1906	200	146.5	20.5	10.1	100hp side lever 2 cylinder steam / PS	McNab & Co, Greenock.

Designed by Douglas Hebson of Liverpool for the Fleetwood service. Operated to the end of the 1869 season when she became a Barrow tug, and the Fleetwood service was withdrawn. Sold to Charles W Duncan of Middlesbrough in 1897 for excursions to Scarborough.

Name	Built	Acquired	Disposed of	Broken up	Tons	Length ft	Breadth ft	Draught ft	Engine/ Propulsion	Builder
Furness	1898	1898	1937	1937	225	128.8	23.6	11.1	2 x 2 cylinder compound steam / TS	J.P. Rennoldson, South Shields

Primarily used as a tug around Barrow, and regularly on the cross bay services in 1902 to supplement Lady Evelyn. Remained at Barrow for her whole career passing to the LMS in 1923.

Name	Built	Acquired	Disposed of	Broken up	Tons	Length ft	Breadth ft	Draught ft	Engine/ Propulsion	Builder
Lady Evelyn	1900	1900	1918	1940	295/324*	170/200*	24.1	8.3	2 cylinder compound diagonal steam / PS	J. Scott & Co., Kirkcaldy

*After 1904. Built for the cross bay route and delivered via the north of Scotland and Oban. Originally equipped with 2 masts and a front well deck, but lengthened in 1904 by Vickers Son & Maxim of Barrow. Re-emerged with 2 decks and 1 mast. Operated until the end of the 1914 season and laid up until 1916 at Barrow. Requisitioned and used as a minesweeper. Returned in June 1918 and sold to W. H. Tucker for use on the Bristol Channel. Sold to P & A Campbell in 1921 and renamed Brighton Belle. Moved to the South Coast from 1923 until 1936 then returned to the Bristol Channel. Paddle boxes renewed in 1937. Requisitioned and sunk at Dunkirk on 28th May 1940. All crew were rescued by the Medway Queen.

Name	Built	Acquired	Disposed of	Broken up	Tons	Length ft	Breadth ft	Draught ft	Engine/ Propulsion	Builder
Lady Margaret	1895	1903	1908	1923	369	210	25	8.7	2 cylinder compound diagonal steam / PS	A. McMillan & Co, Dumbarton

Built for the Lady Margaret Steamship Company of Penarth and purchased by P & A Campbell in 1896 for use on Bristol Channel services. Purchased by FR in 1903 to aid Lady Evelyn entering service on the 20th May 1903. Sold in March 1908 to the Admiralty for £14,000 and used as a tender until 1923. In Admiralty service she was known as Liberty (1908), Wanderer (1913), and Roamer (1919).

Name	Built	Acquired	Disposed of	Broken up	Tons	Length ft	Breadth ft	Draught ft	Engine/ Propulsion	Builder
Walney (II)	1904	1904	1950	1952	204	120	21.1*	10	2 cylinder simple lever steam tug / PS	J.P. Rennoldson, South Shields

*35ft over paddle boxes. Primarily a tug around Barrow, used regularly on cross-bay services. Remained at Barrow until the LMS sent her to Troon around 1930. She was transferred to the Docks & Inland Waterways Executive in 1950.

Name	Built	Acquired	Disposed of	Broken up	Tons	Length ft	Breadth ft	Draught ft	Engine/ Propulsion	Builder
Philomel	1889	1908	1913	1913	564	236	27.1	9.5	2 cylinder compound diagonal steam / PS	J. Scott & Co., Kirkcaldy

Built for the General Steam Navigation Company for routes from London to East Anglia and the Kent coast. Sold to the FR in April 1908 for £5,250 and entered service on 1st June after restoration. Withdrawn at the end of the 1909 season, laid up and listed for sale in 1910, finally leaving Barrow in 1913.

Name	Built	Acquired	Disposed of	Broken up	Tons	Length ft	Breadth ft	Draught ft	Engine/ Propulsion	Builder
Lady Moyra	1905	1910	1919	1940	562	245	29	9.7	2 cylinder compound diagonal steam / PS	John Brown & Co., Clydebank

Built as the Gwalia for the Barry Railway Company sailing between Barry, Cardiff and Ilfracombe. Sold to the FR in 1910. She could carry 1,015 passengers made the cross-bay trip in 45 minutes. Requisitioned in 1915 she returned to Barrow and was sold to W. H. Tucker in 1919 for the Bristol Channel. Sold to P & A Campbell in July 1922 who renamed her Brighton Queen. Moved to the South Coast in 1933, remaining until 1939 and converted into a minesweeper. Sunk at Dunkirk on 31st May 1940 on her 2nd trip to evacuate troops.

Name	Built	Acquired	Disposed of	Broken up	Tons	Length ft	Breadth ft	Draught ft	Engine/ Propulsion	Builder
Robina*	1914	1922	1922	1953	306	159.4	26.2	8.9	Triple expansion steam / TS	Ardrossan Dry dock & Shipbuilding Company

*Never owned by the FR, chartered in 1922. Built for excursions for the New Morecambe Central Pier Company. Chartered in 1919 to the Blackpool Passenger Steamboat Company for cruises from Blackpool, occasionally to Barrow. In 1919 chartered to W. H. Tucker for the Bristol Channel alongside Lady Evelyn and Lady Moyra. Registered to William & Pratt Cordingley, Pudsey in 1922 then chartered to the FR for 2 daily sailings between Fleetwood and Barrow but lasted one season. From1925 to1942 she worked in Ireland for Wm T. McCalla of Belfast, and from 1940, the Ulster Steam Tender Company. Managed by the Caledonian Steam Packet from 1942 whilst in Admiralty service on the Clyde. Purchased by Coast Lines of Falmouth in 1946 for excursions, but sub-chartered to subsidiary David MacBrayne, for services to Loch Goil and Islay. In 1948 sailed on charter between Guernsey and Sark for the Island Shipping Company Limited.

Coniston

Key;

CL	Coniston Launch 1992 – Present
CR	Coniston Railway Company 1859 – 1862
FR	FR Company 1862 – 1923
LMS	London Midland Scottish Railway 1923 – 1948
NT	National Trust 1980 – Present
SLK	Sealink 1982
##	Vessel on the National Historic Ships Register
PS	Paddle Steamer
SS	Single Screw
TS	Twin Screw
hp	Horsepower
ihp	Indicated horsepower
nhp	Nominal horsepower

Name	Built	Acquired	Disposed of	Broken up	Tons	Length ft	Breadth ft	Draught ft	Engine/ Propulsion	Builder
Princess Royal / Queen of the Lakes (Sladen)	1850	1855	1855	unknown	?	?	?	?	Non-condensing steam-locomotive type boiler/ SS	Isaac Boulton

Built for the North Staffordshire Railway services on Rudyard Lake. Also at Hull, Manchester then Hollingworth Lake in 1853, operated by James Sladen. Came to Coniston appearing under different names in various adverts. Operated for a few weeks in July 1855. Taken back to Hollingworth Lake by Sladen and may have been the vessel launched on that lake on 29th April 1856.

Name	Built	Acquired	Disposed of	Broken up	Tons	Length ft	Breadth ft	Draught ft	Engine/ Propulsion	Builder
Gondola ## (CR / FR / LMS / SLK / NT)	1859	1859	1936	Still operational	42*+	84	13.6	4.6	2 cylinder steam-locomotive type boiler at 80lb/sq.in. 1923: re-boilered, to 100lb/sq.in. 1980: 2 cylinder steam-locomotive boiler to 150lb/sq.in. / SS	Jones, Quiggin & Co., Liverpool

* Brass plaque on board states her tonnage as launched was 25 80/100. +In 1859 her tonnage was 70 72/94 Thames Tonnage. Built of steel to carry 225 passengers. Served on the lake until 1936 when laid up until after the Second World War. Engines removed and sold, Converted into a houseboat. Sank 1963. Raised 1977 and restored by National Trust. Re-entered service in 1980, rebuilt by staff at Vickers. Only steam powered public vessel operating scheduled services in the Lakes. Passenger capacity is now 86.

Name	Built	Acquired	Disposed of	Broken up	Tons	Length ft	Breadth ft	Draught ft	Engine/ Propulsion	Builder
Lady of the Lake (FR / LMS)	1908	1908	1939	1950	76	97.5	15	4	2 x 2 cylinder simple non condensing steam-locomotive boiler at 120lb/sq.in.	J.L. Thornycroft, Southampton

Built to replace Gondola but ended up complementing her sailings. Similar in design to the Tern on Windermere and could carry 400 passengers. Operated alone from 1936 until 1939.

Name	Built	Acquired	Disposed of	Broken up	Tons	Length ft	Breadth ft	Draught ft	Engine/ Propulsion	Builder
Queen of the Lake	?	c1956	c1959	?	?	?	?	?	Diesel / SS	?

Revival of services on the lake trialled in the late 1950s using an open motor launch but did not last more than a couple of seasons.

Name	Built	Acquired	Disposed of	Broken up	Tons	Length ft	Breadth ft	Draught ft	Engine/ Propulsion	Builder
Ruskin ## (CL)	1922	1992	2013	Off lake	7	40	9.6	3	Single cylinder Thorneycroft, then a 2.5 litre BMC, a 4 cylinder Perkins, a 2 litre Phoenix diesel. In 2005 ST74 electric motor with a 144dc battery bank. / SS	Chester Boat Company

Built as Raglan II for the Chester Boat Company she served on the River Dee until the outbreak of World War Two. Renamed HMS Ariel and worked on the Dee as a minesweeper. The Chester Boat Company continued to use her on the Dee until they were taken over in 1982 by Bithells Boats. Bought by Coniston Launch in 1992 and converted into a traditional Lakeland Launch. Diesel until 2005 when solar panels and motor installed. Withdrawn after 2011 season and laid up at Pier Cottage. In 2013 sold to Pennine Cruisers for their Leeds and Liverpool Canal operations.

Name	Built	Acquired	Disposed of	Broken up	Tons	Length ft	Breadth ft	Draught ft	Engine/ Propulsion	Builder
Iris (CL)	1904	1994	1994	Laid up Derwent-water	7	45	8	2.6	Wooden electric launch converted to diesel (petrol / paraffin engine for a time?) / SS	Tom Hayton, Bowness

Operated on Derwentwater as an electric launch then converted to a motor boat and spent time on Windermere after the Second World War. By the late 1970s returned to Derwentwater, but chartered in 1994 to Coniston Launch for one season who renamed her Ransome. Modified as the piers were lower than those at Derwentwater. Taken back to Derwentwater at the end of 1994 and operated for a few more seasons before being laid up on the Isthmus.

Name	Built	Acquired	Disposed of	Broken up	Tons	Length ft	Breadth ft	Draught ft	Engine/ Propulsion	Builder
Ransome ## (CL)	1923	1994	2011	Off lake	7	40	11.3	2.9	Commodore diesel, replaced by Ford FSD 425. 2004 –Solomon Technologies ST74 electric motor with a 144dc battery bank. / SS	Clemens A W, Portsmouth

Built as The Empress in 1923 for use around Plymouth. Requisitioned to work ports on the south coast before ending up on the Thames in 1946. Refitted at Windsor in the early 1950s working for French Bros as Monarch I until the 1970s. Worked for J&G French from Shepperton. Brought to Coniston in 1994 and converted from diesel to solar in 2004. Withdrawn after 2010 season and sold in 2011 to the Avon where she was converted into a houseboat for holidays.

Campbell (CL)	1976	2010	Still operational		8.25	40	12	3	1 x Yanmar 4LH-TE 110hp 4 cylinder turbo diesel / SS	Unknown

Built in 1976 as Exonia (II) for service on the Starcross ferry from Exmouth. Acquired by D & P Faithfull of Portsmouth in 1999 and in 2010 brought to Hawkshead to be heavily modified, before beginning her lakes career in 2011. Usually found on the Red (Northern) Cruise.

Marianne (CL)	1988	2013/02	2013/10	Off lake	10	32	10.6	3	1 x Ford diesel / SS	Windsor Marina

Built as a charter boat and operated by French Brothers on the Thames as Windsor Minstrel. Used usually for private functions, including charters to take the Queen Mother to Windsor races. In 2010 she was sold to Avon Leisure Cruises Limited who renamed her Avon Spirit, and used her for cruises on the river Avon at Evesham from 2010 before coming to Coniston and being renamed Marianne in 2013. Limited to 12 passengers and used mainly for charters. Sold back to the Thames later the same year.

Cygnet (CL)	1965	2013	Still operational		10	43	12.3	3	1 x Scania DS11 325hp Diesel / SS	Voe Shipyard, Holland

Cygnet was one of 4 tenders to the Ms Kungsholm IV (Later renamed Sea Princess). Operated on canals near Manchester in the 1980s before service on the River Bann at Coleraine in 1985, named Cygnet. Sold in1995 for trips on the River Tawe, and in 2000 then purchased by Cardiff Cats Limited for a waterbus service between Cardiff and Penarth. Cygnet arrived at Coniston on the 13th June 2013, and commenced service on the 1st August inaugurating the Wild Cat Island Cruise. Overhauled before the start of the 2014 season.

+ Thames Tonnage is a system developed in 1855 by the Royal Thames Yacht Club for measuring small vessels and yachts. Thames tonnage is calculated by subtracting the beam from the length of the boat, then multiplying the figure by the beam squared and dividing the total by 188.

Derwentwater

Key;

AML	Ambleside Motor Launch Company 1940s – 1968
BBBC	Bowness Bay Boating Company 1934 – 1993 (Ltd from 1968)
CL	Coniston Launch 1992 – Present
KDMLC	Keswick on Derwentwater Motor Launch Company Ltd 1933 – Present
KELC	Keswick Electric Launch Company c1904 – c1930
##	Vessel on the National Historic Ships Register
PS	Paddle Steamer
SS	Single Screw
TS	Twin Screw

Name	Built	Acquired	Disposed of	Broken up	Tons	Length ft	Breadth ft	Draught ft	Engine/ Propulsion	Builder
Spec	?	1848	1848	?	?	?	?	?	Passage boat	?

Early passage boat started in June 1848 but lasted one week. Likely remained on the lake as a hire boat.

Name	Built	Acquired	Disposed of	Broken up	Tons	Length ft	Breadth ft	Draught ft	Engine/ Propulsion	Builder
Passage Boat	?	1848	c1896	?	?	?	?	?	Passage Boat	?

Cheaper passage boat undercutting the original, probably remaining in service after The Steamer was introduced.

Name	Built	Acquired	Disposed of	Broken up	Tons	Length ft	Breadth ft	Draught ft	Engine/ Propulsion	Builder
The Steamer	1850	1850	c1898	?	?	?	?	?	Passage boat / SS	?

Oddly named passage boat probably operated during the summer until the larger launches were introduced.

Name	Built	Acquired	Disposed of	Broken up	Tons	Length ft	Breadth ft	Draught ft	Engine/ Propulsion	Builder
Lorna Doone	?	c1898	c1930	c1930	?	?	?	?	Wooden steam launch / SS	?

Ex herring boat built in the late nineteenth century. Possibly the steam launch brought to the Lodore Hotel by Mr Ceasari in March 1898 from Ullswater. Coal fired, she could carry up to 53 passengers and was latterly operated by Mr Hodgson who sold her to Whitehaven owners. Beached on the Isthmus but later sank, and after raising was broken up.

Name	Built	Acquired	Disposed of	Broken up	Tons	Length ft	Breadth ft	Draught ft	Engine/ Propulsion	Builder
Derwent	?	c1900	c1940	?	?	?	?	?	Wooden steam launch, later converted to motor launch. / SS	?

Derwent could carry 23 passengers. Possibly the launch referred to as being purchased in 1904 to rival the arrival of the electric boats at Lodore.

Name	Built	Acquired	Disposed of	Broken up	Tons	Length ft	Breadth ft	Draught ft	Engine/ Propulsion	Builder
Waterlily	1903	1903	c1995	c1995	?	?	?	?	Wooden launch. Steam to begin with. Diesel for most of career / SS	Shepherds of Bowness

Steam launch later converted to diesel and incorporated into the KDMLC in 1933. A traditional Lakeland launch with an open bow and a cabin aft. Withdrawn in anticipation of a total rebuild in the late 1980s which never happened – burned in the mid 1990s.

Name	Built	Acquired	Disposed of	Broken up	Tons	Length ft	Breadth ft	Draught ft	Engine/ Propulsion	Builder
May Queen	1904	1904	c1993	c1999	7	45	8	2.6	Electric launch converted to diesel. May have had a petrol /paraffin engine for a time / SS	Tom Hayton, Bowness

Operated by the Keswick Electric Launch Company between the Lodore and Derwent hotels, Brandlehow, and Keswick landings. Converted to a motor launch, and then incorporated into the KDMLC in 1933. Different from traditional Lakeland launch design as cabin was placed mid-way along the hull giving her a distinctive appearance. Withdrawn from service around 1993 and burned as she was deemed unsuitable for further use. She was latterly on the National Historic Ships Register.

Name									
Iris	1904	1904	Laid up at The Isthmus	7	45	8	2.6	Wooden electric launch converted to diesel (petrol /paraffin engine for a time?) / SS	Tom Hayton, Bowness

Teak built vessel operated from the Lodore Hotel to Brandlehow, Portinscale and Keswick as an electric launch. Originally had her cabin mid-ships, like the May Queen and was still used by the hotel in the 1920s. Converted to a motor vessel and incorporated into the KDMLC in 1933. Went to Windermere after the Second World War for the AML, and later the BBBC. Cabin moved aft at some point. Returned to Derwentwater by the late 1970s, but chartered in 1994 to CL for one season and renamed Ransome. Modified as the piers were lower than those at Derwentwater. Returned at the end of 1994, and operated for a few more seasons before being laid up.

Doris	?	c1920	c1940	?	?	?	?	?	Wooden motor launch / SS	?

Small motor launch operated by the owner of the Honister House hotel. She operated from around the end of the First World War.

Water Nymph	?	c1910	c1940	?	?	?	?	?	Wooden motor launch / SS	?

Small motor launch for around 20 passengers. She had a blue hull for a time.

Swan	?	c1910	c1940	?	?	?	?	?	Wooden motor launch / SS	?

Small motor launch which operated on Derwentwater.

Dolly	?	c1910	c1940	?	?	?	?	?	Wooden motor launch / SS	?

Small motor launch which operated on Derwentwater.

May-flower	?	c1910	c1940	?	?	?	?	?	Wooden motor launch / SS	?

Small motor launch which operated on Derwentwater for only a year. Possibly on loan from Windermere.

Ino	?	c1910	c1940	?	?	?	?	?	Wooden motor launch / SS	?

Small 12 seater wooden launch.

Trojan	?	c1910	c1940	?	?	?	?	?	Wooden motor launch / SS	?

One of the smallest wooden launches on the lake, Trojan could only carry 8 passengers on Derwentwater.

Lady ## Derwent-water	1925	1935	Still operational	12.5	60	12	3	Wooden launch. Originally steam on Windermere. Diesel on Derwentwater / TS	Borwick & Sons, Bowness

Built for Sir George Mellor as Annie Mellor (I) after his sister. Fitted with a toilet and used as a day boat on Windermere. In 1935 sold to the KDMLC and dragged there by 2 teams of horses. Converted to a motor launch and renamed Lady Derwentwater. Originally built with 4 windows and an open stern. From the 1980s operated with 6 windows and from 2010 with 5. Around 2008 her canoe stern was replaced with a square transom.

Unknown Motor Boat	?	c1920	c1970	?	?	?	?	?	Diesel motor launch / SS	?

Operated by the Mitchell family and later by Mr Newby, between Portinscale and the Keswick Foreshore before the KDMLC called at Nichol End. The motor launch took over from a succession of rowing boats which had been plying the route since 1860.

Annie Mellor (II) ##	1935	c1950	Still operational	13.5	63	13	3	Wooden launch. Initially steam then converted to diesel on Derwentwater / TS	Borwick & Sons, Bowness

Built for Sir George Mellor, Annie Mellor (II) was a replacement for his first boat that had been sold to Derwentwater. Used on Windermere until around 1950 then sold to the KDMLC. Converted for passenger use and refurbished between 2005 and 2007.

Princess Margaret Rose ##	1938	1938	Still operational	12.5	60	12	3	Diesel wooden launch / SS	Shepherds of Bowness

Only vessel built specifically for KDMLC. Largest boat built by Shepherds at the time and transported to Derwentwater by traction engine.

Lakeland Mist	1954	1998	Still operational	19	60	12	3	Diesel Dutch style waterbus / SS	Holland

Built as the Prinses Juliana for service in Amsterdam, purchased by Cruise Loch Lomond in 1990 and renamed Lomond Mist. In 1998 purchased by the Keswick on Derwentwater Motor Launch Company Ltd. Saloon removed around 2000 and a wooden deckhouse installed.

Lakeland Star	1978	2004	2011	Off lake	27	63	19	5	Twin engined catamaran / TS	?

Built as Twin Star II in 1978 for the Ford Dagenham ferry. Closed in 2003 and purchased by the KDMLC. Sailed to Workington before being transported by lorry to the lake in 2004. Painted blue, red and white for her first season but then black and brown. Draught too deep for Derwentwater so sold in 2011 to the Dartmouth Steam Railway and Riverboat Co. and renamed Kingswear Princess for the River Dart.

Ullswater

The Ullswater Steam Navigation Company operated the boats until 1904, when they changed their name to the Ullswater Navigation and Transit Company Limited.

Key;

##	Vessel on the National Historic Ships Register
PS	Paddle Steamer
SS	Single Screw
TS	Twin Screw
2SCSA	2 stroke, compression-ignition, single acting marine diesel engine
4SCSA	4 stroke, compression-ignition, single acting marine diesel engine
D	Diesel
hp	Horsepower
ihp	Indicated horsepower
nhp	Nominal horsepower

Name	Built	Acquired	Disposed of	Broken up	Tons	Length ft	Breadth ft	Draught ft	Engine/ Propulsion	Builder
Enterprise	1859	1859	c1880	c1880	46*	80	14	2.5	Condensing steam / PS	Jones, Quiggin & Co., Liverpool

*In 1859 her tonnage was 76 61/94 Thames Tonnage.+ First steamer on the lake and the only paddle vessel. Built of iron with a straight stern, and a wheel at the bow to aid manoeuvres. Her tall funnel was black with a broad white band around the middle. Remained in service after the Lady of the Lake was introduced, but probably withdrawn soon after. Her engines were provided by R.M. Lawrence & Co, Liverpool.

Name	Built	Acquired	Disposed of	Broken up	Tons	Length ft	Breadth ft	Draught ft	Engine/ Propulsion	Builder
Wyvern	1872	1875	1876	c1890	38	79	11.5	3	2 cylinder 14nhp simple non condensing steam / SS	T.B. Seath & Co, Rutherglen, Glasgow

William Inman, founder of the Inman Shipping line in Liverpool, owned Wyvern as a private vessel. She was sold in 1875 to the Ullswater Steam Navigation Company. While working out how to move her to Ullswater, she sank in Mitchell Wyke, Windermere, on the 24th February 1876. The cost of raising and restoring her proved prohibitive and she never made it to Ullswater, probably due to the difficulties in transporting her there. After raising she was sold to a Barrow contractor, Mr Joseph Hunter. Her fate remains unknown, although she was noted in London in the late 1880s. Her engines were provided by A Campell & Son, Glasgow.

Name	Built	Acquired	Disposed of	Broken up	Tons	Length ft	Breadth ft	Draught ft	Engine/ Propulsion	Builder
Lady of the Lake ##	1877	1877	Still operational		43	97	14.7	2.4	2 x 2 cylinder 34hp simple non condensing steam; 1903 – Re-boiled; 1934 – 2 x 6 cylinder 150hp 2SCSA Crossley D; 1978 – 2 x Kelvin 115hp D; 2005– 2 x Cummins 180hp D / TS	T.B. Seath & Co, Rutherglen, Glasgow

First screw steamer on the lake. Built in sections at the lake-side and one of the oldest ships in regular working service. Sunk in 1881, and again in 1950. Both times she was raised and restored. She spent 1965 – 1979 laid up after a fire. As built had 10 windows but later extended to 12 when she received a wheelhouse just forward of the funnel. After conversion to a motor ship she appeared with 8. After overhaul in early 2014 she gained a saloon extension and now has 9 windows with her wheelhouse and funnel moved 4 feet aft, and deck extended forward. Now licensed for 200 passengers. Usually operates on the roster that leaves Glenridding at 10.30 am during the summer months. Electricity now provided by Yanmar generator supplying 240 volts.

Name	Built	Acquired	Disposed of	Broken up	Tons	Length ft	Breadth ft	Draught ft	Engine/ Propulsion	Builder
Raven ##	1889	1889	Still operational		63	112.3	15	2.9	2 x 2 cylinder 100hp non condensing simple steam 1935 – 2 x 4 cylinder 142hp 4SCSA National Gas and Oil Engineering Co D. 1964 – 2 x Thorneycroft AEC T590 150hp D. 2004 – 2 x Cummins 155hp D / TS	T.B. Seath & Co, Rutherglen, Glasgow

Built after Thomas Cook complained about the absence of a service while Lady of the Lake was being repaired, Raven remains the largest steamer on Ullswater. Carried royalty on more than one occasion and operated alone between 1965 and 1979. Now mainly operates on the roster that leaves Glenridding at 9.45 am during the summer months. As built she had 11 windows, but she now has 12. Now licensed for 246 passengers. Electricity now provided by Yanmar generator supplying 240 volts.

Name	Built	Acquired	Disposed of	Broken up	Tons	Length ft	Breadth ft	Draught ft	Engine/ Propulsion	Builder
Cygnet	1879	1955	1957	1964	50	100	14	3.5	2 x 2 cylinder 13.5nhp compound steam. 1924 – 2 x 8 cylinder 60nhp 4SCSA paraffin / TS	Barrow Shipbuilding Co

Built for the Furness Railway's Windermere services, she sailed her last Windermere season in 1953 and was sold to Lake District Estates Company Limited, who sold her in 1955 to Sir Wavell Wakefield, who had a controlling interest in the Ullswater steamers. Cygnet was to move to Ullswater and was painted in the new company's colours at Lakeside. She received a new funnel in 1956, but she never made it to Ullswater, probably due to difficulties in transporting her to Ullswater. The intended route was via road through Kendal and Shap. She was sold in 1957 to Lake Windermere Properties Limited for conversion into a houseboat. Moored near Lakeside, she sank on 17th May 1962, became a total loss and was broken up in 1964.

Name	Built	Acquired	Disposed of	Broken up	Tons	Length ft	Breadth ft	Draught ft	Engine/ Propulsion	Builder
Lady Dorothy	1967	2001	Still operational		14	50	12	4	1 x 180hp Leyland D 1 x Perkins D / SS	C.P. Wilson

Built for the Channel Islands, and entered service in May 1968 sailing mainly between Guernsey and Herm. Sold in March 2001 and sailed to Poole from where she was brought to Ullswater by road. After restoration by Frank Howard, she was launched onto the lake on the 5th November 2001. Mainly operates during the winter, and when not in use can be seen on a mooring in St Patrick's Bay, or at the inner berth at Glenridding pier.

Lady Wakefield ##	1949	2005	Still operational	45	67	16.5	3	2 x Glennifer D 2 x Gardner 6LXB D / TS	Philip & Son, Dartmouth

Built as Berry Castle (III) for the River Dart Steamboat Company, and sold in 1972 to Fareham, then Rochester where she was renamed Golden Cormorant. Purchased by Dart Pleasure Company in 1977, renamed Totnes Castle (III) and moved back to the Dart. Operated by Plymouth Boat Cruises from 1985 to May 2005 when she came to Ullswater via Whitehaven. After restoration was officially re-launched in April 2007 by HRH Princess Alexandra.

Western Belle ##	1935	2010	Still operational	63	70	15.3	3.6	2 x 6 cylinder Atlantic D; 1965 – 2 x Gardner 6 cylinder 6LXB D; 2010 2 x 6 cylinder Ford Sabre 2725E 130hp D / TS	Fellows & Company, Great Yarmouth

Built for the Millbrook Steamboat and Trading Company for excursions along the River Tamar, and on the Plymouth to Millbrook ferry. Continued until 1985 apart from a brief charter to British Rail in 1955. In 1985 moved to River Dart when the Dart Pleasure Craft Company purchased the Millbrook Company. Sold in 2000 for the River Thames where she was operated by Chris Cruises from 2005 to 2008. Purchased for use on Ullswater and after a marathon coastal journey to Maryport she remained there for a year – remaining unharmed when a tidal surge breached the lock gate of marina – before heading under her own power to Mersey Heritage at McTay's, Bromborough yard for a total refurbishment. Entered service in late 2010, after launch by Jane Hasell McCosh of Dalemain House.

+ Thames Tonnage is a system developed in 1855 by the Royal Thames Yacht Club for measuring small vessels and yachts. Thames tonnage is calculated by subtracting the beam from the length of the boat, then multiplying the figure by the beam squared and dividing the total by 188.

Windermere

Windermere has 4 fleet lists; the steamers, Nab ferries, waterbuses and wooden launches. As there are vessels in each list which are currently in service on the lake, to avoid confusion a list of the current fleet follows; Tern, Teal (II), Swan (II), Mallard, Miss Cumbria, Miss Cumbria II, Miss Cumbria III, Miss Cumbria IV, Miss Lakeland, Miss Lakeland II, Miss Westmorland, Silverholme, Venture, Muriel II, Sunflower II, Queen of the Lake, and Princess of the Lake. Cygnet is retained as a works boat for Windermere Lake Cruises.

Key;

AML	Ambleside Motor Launch Company 1940s – 1968
BBBC	Bowness Bay Boating Company 1934 – 1993 (Ltd from 1968)
BR	British Railways 1948 – 1963
BRB	British Railways Board 1963 – 1970
FR	FR Company 1869 – 1923
G	James Gibson 1837 – 1841
G&W	Gibson & White 1841 – 1846
KDMLC	Keswick on Derwentwater Motor Launch Company Ltd 1933 – Present
LMS	London Midland & Scottish Railway 1923 – 1948
SC	Sea Containers 1984 – 1993
SLK	Sealink Windermere 1970 – 1984
WISBC	Windermere Iron Steamboat Company 1848 – 1858
WLC	Windermere Lake Cruises 1993 – Present
WML	Windermere Motor Launch Company 1913 – 1934
WSYC	Windermere Steam Yacht Company 1845 – 1858
WUSYC	Windermere United Steam Yacht Company 1858 – 1869
##	Vessel on the National Historic Ships Register
PS	Paddle Steamer
SS	Single Screw
TS	Twin Screw
2SCSA	2 stroke, compression-ignition, single acting marine diesel engine
4SCSA	4 stroke, compression-ignition, single acting marine diesel engine
D	Diesel
hp	Horsepower
ihp	Indicated horsepower
nhp	Nominal horsepower

Miss Cumbria being built at Molenaars. (Howson)

Passage Boats and Steamers

Name	Built	Acquired	Disposed of	Broken up	Tons	Length ft	Breadth ft	Draught ft	Engine/ Propulsion	Builder
Passage Boat (I) (G)	?	1837	c1844	?	?	?	?	?	Large rowing boat, possibly with auxiliary sail	Unknown – William Watson, Ambleside?

First passage boat on Windermere introduced by James Gibson in 1837 to ply between Ambleside and Bowness. In 1840 he extended the service to Newby Bridge. Probably displaced by the Victoria and Prince of Wales.

Passage Boat (II) (G&W)	?	1841	c1844	?	?	?	?	?	Large rowing boat, possibly with auxiliary sail	Unknown – William Watson, Ambleside?

In 1841 Thomas White introduced a second boat to double the frequency of sailings on the lake. Probably displaced by the Victoria and Prince of Wales.

Victoria (G&W)	1844	1844	1846	?	?	?	?	?	Large rowing boat, possibly with auxiliary sail	William Watson, Ambleside

Launched in May 1844 Victoria was a lavishly fitted out passage boat, and was probably identical to the Prince of Wales. Remained in service after the Lady of the Lake was introduced and had a successful year in 1845. Withdrawn at the end of the 1846 season after the Lord of the Isles arrived.

Prince of Wales (G&W)	1844	1844	1846	?	?	?	?	?	Large rowing boat, possibly with auxiliary sail	William Watson, Ambleside

Launched in May 1844 Prince of Wales was a lavishly fitted out passage boat, and was probably identical to the Victoria. Remained in service after the Lady of the Lake was introduced and had a successful year in 1845. Withdrawn at the end of the 1846 season after the Lord of the Isles arrived.

Lady of the Lake (WSYC/ WUSBC)	1845	1845	c1865	c1865	49	80	11.6	1.3	Steam providing 20nhp / PS	Richard Ashburner, Greenodd

The first steamboat introduced to Windermere, launched from Newby Bridge, was a success despite initial outcry from the local gentry. She had a successful career even though she had to have major work carried out twice. She was probably withdrawn at the end of the 1865 season and broken up shortly after. Whilst in service she could carry around 200 passengers at a speed of 9 mph.

Lord of the Isles (WSYC)	1846	1846	1850	1850	52	80	15.5	2.5	Twin steam each providing 16hp / PS	Richard Ashburner, Greenodd

After the success of the Lady of the Lake, the WSYC ordered another, similar but slightly larger steamer, from the same builders, which was launched at Newby Bridge. Unfortunately she had a pitifully short career and was destroyed by fire in 1850. She was never replaced by the WSYC.

Firefly (WISBC/ WUSBC)	1849	1849	1879	1879	50	75	11.5	3	Twin steam / PS	McConochie & Claude, Liverpool

First iron steamer for Windermere launched from Low Wood and capable of 12 mph. A long and successful career, despite initial teething problems with the timetable. She remained in service until replaced by the twins launched in 1879 although by the end of her career was unreliable.

Dragonfly (WISBC/ WUSBC)	1850	1851	c1885	c1885	80	95	16.5	3.3	Twin steam providing 50ihp / PS	McConochie & Claude, Liverpool

The Dragonfly was a considerably larger version of the Firefly and could carry 250 passengers. The first double ended, as well as the longest, steamer on the lake at the time. Launched from Low Wood and remained in service until the mid-1880s, latterly as a spare vessel. Unreliable towards the end of her career.

Rothay (WUSBC/ FR)	1866	1866	1891	1891	100	105	15	3	Twin steam / PS	Lune Iron Shipbuilding Co

Rothay was the final fully non-railway steamer built for the lake, as well as being the last paddle steamer and the last vessel built to navigate the confines of the River Leven. Too large to turn at Newby Bridge so she was equipped with 2 bows, and a rudder at each end. Displaced by the Tern.

Esperance ## (Ferry Hotel)	1869	1891	1914	Museum	17	65	10	4.5	Steam -Twin single cylinder compound. 1956 – 2 x 4 cylinder Ford. Now 2 x Vosper Thorneycroft petrol / TS	T.B. Seath & Co, Rutherglen, Glasgow

A private steam launch used by Henry Schneider to commute to work. Used for a public ferry between Bowness and the Ferry Hotel, operating an hourly service, between 1891 and 1914. On Sundays she conveyed passengers to church at Wray. Later became a houseboat, and was sunk by 1941. Raised ad restored by G. Pattinson, she was once again plying the lake in August 1956. She is currently at the Windermere Steamboat Museum.

Swan (I) (FR / LMS)	1869	1869	1938	1938	120	147	17	3.3	2 x 2 cylinder 20nhp simple non condensing steam / TS	T.B. Seath & Co, Rutherglen, Glasgow

Swan (I) was the first twin screw railway steamer built for Windermere and her design became standard for the next few vessels. She was involved in a number of incidents including sinking and grounding and had a very long career, not being displaced until the Swan (II) was launched.

Raven ## (FR / LMS / Vickers)	1871	1871	1927	Museum	41	71	14.9	4	1 x 5nhp single cylinder steam / SS	T.B. Seath & Co, Rutherglen, Glasgow

The FR's only non-passenger steamer was a barge designed to carry cargo around the lake, departing Lakeside 3 times weekly for piers around the lake, many for private residences. Withdrawn in 1922 but remained in the LMS fleet as a work barge. Sold in 1927 to Vickers Sons and Maxim who kept her on the lake as a barge and also used her for testing mine laying equipment. Sold to ship breakers in the late 1950s, but saved by George Pattinson of the Windermere Steamboat Museum where she is still kept.

Cygnet (FR/LMS/BR)	1879	1879	1955	1964	50	100	14	3.5	2 x 2 cylinder 13.5nhp compound steam. 1924 – 2 x 8 cylinder 60nhp 4SCSA paraffin / TS	Barrow Shipbuilding Co

The first of the twins was launched on the 22nd May – the first steel railway steamer. A popular vessel retained by the LMS. Earmarked for conversion to oil, in 1924. This caused bad vibrations so she was only used when necessary. Operated the 1947 season due to coal shortages but her last sailing season was 1953 when she was offered for sale. Purchased in 1955 by Sir Wavell Wakefield, of the Ullswater steamers, she was painted in their colours, receiving a new funnel, but never left Windermere. She was then sold again and became a houseboat but sank on 17th May 1962. Raised and broken up in 1964.

Teal (I) (FR / LMS)	1879	1879	1926	1927	50	100	14	3.5	2 x 2 cylinder 13.5nhp compound steam / TS	Barrow Shipbuilding Co

Second of the twins was launched on the 5th June, after trials in Barrow. Had early bridge controls with direct communications with the engines. When the LMS took over she was kept in service before being laid up in 1927. Scrapped in 1928.

Name	Built	Acquired	Disposed of	Broken up	Tons	Length	Breadth	Draught	Engine/Propulsion	Builder
Britannia (FR)	1879	1908	1919	1919	49	102	12	3.5	2 x 50hp steam engines / TS	T.B. Seath & Co, Rutherglen,

Built in 1879 for £12000 for Colonel Ridehalgh of Fell Foot, for use as a private yacht; after his death, his wife continued to use and charter the steamer. The FR purchased her for £350 in 1908 as a director's yacht, and for charters. She was laid up during the First World War and broken up in 1919.

Name	Built	Acquired	Disposed of	Broken up	Tons	Length	Breadth	Draught	Engine/Propulsion	Builder
Tern ## (FR / LMS / BR / BRB / SLK / SC / WLC)	1891	1891	Still operational		120	145	18	4	2 x 2 cylinder 20nhp simple non condensing steam loco boiler; 1958 – 2 x 6 cylinder 150hp Gleniffer D; 1997 – 2 x 6 cylinder 160hp Cummins N855M D / TS	Forrestt & Son, Wyvenhoe, Essex

Oldest vessel in regular working service on WIndermere, Tern, could carry 633 passengers as built. Later modifications and safety regulations reduced this to 250, but now licensed for 350 passengers. After conversion to diesel in the 1950s received a squat motor funnel, but in 1991 was given a dummy steam funnel on her centenary year. Wheelhouse was also moved forward in the same year. Fitted with bow thruster in December 1997. Now mainly operates on the summer roster which departs Lakeside at 10.20 am. Electricity now provided by a set of Perkins generators.

Name	Built	Acquired	Disposed of	Broken up	Tons	Length	Breadth	Draught	Engine/Propulsion	Builder
Swift (LMS / BR / BRB / SLK / SC / WLC)	1900	1900	1981	1998	203	150	21	4	2 x 2 cylinder 63.5nhp compound steam engines; 1957 – 2 x 6 cylinder 150hp Gleniffer D / TS	T.B. Seath & Co, Rutherglen,

The longest vessel built for the lake services, and the last to be built by the famed T.B. Seath & Co. for Windermere. Converted from steam to diesel in the late 1950s, she made her last voyage for Sealink in 1981 and was converted into a museum at Lakeside in 1989. Eventually broken up in September 1998.

Name	Built	Acquired	Disposed of	Broken up	Tons	Length	Breadth	Draught	Engine/Propulsion	Builder
Teal (II) ## (LMS / BR / BRB / SLK / SC / WLC)	1936	1936	Still operational		251	142	25	4	2 x 4 stroke 8 cylinder 160hp Gleniffer 4SCSA; 1993 – 2 x 6 cylinder 160hp Kelvin TA6 D / TS	Vickers Armstrong, Barrow

Largest (in tonnage) passenger vessel built for the lake when launched. Originally carried 867 passengers, but current passenger compliment is 533. In 1956 she carried royalty on a trip from Ambleside to Bowness and Royalty returned in 2013 to cruise between Bowness and Brockhole. Has seen a few modifications including the widening of her saloon and the addition of bow thrusters. Passenger complement is now 533. Electricity now provided by a Perkins generator with a Cummins set as spare.

Name	Built	Acquired	Disposed of	Broken up	Tons	Length	Breadth	Draught	Engine/Propulsion	Builder
Swan (II) ## (LMS / BR / BRB / SLK / SC / WLC)	1938	1938	Still operational		251	142	25	4	2 x 4 stroke 8 cylinder 160hp Gleniffer 4SCSA: 1996 – 2 x 6 cylinder 160hp Cummins N855M D/ TS	Vickers Armstrong, Barrow

Final large passenger vessel built for the LMS Windermere services. As built she could carry 820 passengers. Later modified, including widening of her saloon and the addition of bow thrusters. Her passenger compliment has been reduced to 533. Electricity now provided by a Perkins generator with a Cummins set as spare.

Windermere Nab Ferries

A succession of rowing ferries were used on the crossing prior to the Mary Anne coming into service, from as early as 1438, if not earlier. In 1699 a new large boat was built, and by at least 1707 there were 2 boats. In the 1830s there was a Little Boat and a Great Boat in use, one presumably capable of conveying a horse and cart. Mary Anne probably replaced the Great Boat.

Name	Built	Acquired	Disposed of	Broken up	Tons	Length (with ramps) ft	Breadth ft	Draught ft	Engine/Propulsion	Builder
Mary Anne ##	c1870	c1870	c1940	Museum	?	39.5	11.25	2	Large rowing ferry propelled by long sweeps	Unknown

Last rowing ferry built for the crossing with a stern ramp for the loading of horses and carriages, remaining as a standby until the 1940s when used to service Belle Isle, including moving sheep from Harrowslack, eventually sinking near the island. Recovered and placed in the Windermere Steamboat Museum in 1978.

Name	Built	Acquired	Disposed of	Broken up	Tons	Length	Breadth	Draught	Engine/Propulsion	Builder
1870 Ferry	1870	1870	1915	c1915	?	?	?	?	7hp steam engine	Locally built, overseen by George Dixon

First steam ferry on the route had a very lopsided gait as the engines and boiler were both on one side. Originally had just one cable, and 3 guide wheels all on one side, but later an extra cable was added. She could carry 2 sets of horses and coaches.

Name	Built	Acquired	Disposed of	Broken up	Tons	Length	Breadth	Draught	Engine/Propulsion	Builder
1915 Ferry	1915	1915	1954	c1954	?	74	18	2	12hp steam engines, with Cochrane boiler	Alley & MacLellan Ltd, Polmadie

Built at Ferry Nab by workmen sent from Scotland, she could carry around 4 vehicles on the crossing. Overcame the lopsided gait of her predecessor as her engines were on the opposite side to her boiler.

Name	Built	Acquired	Disposed of	Broken up	Tons	Length	Breadth	Draught	Engine/Propulsion	Builder
Drake	1954	1954	1990	1990	70	95	30	2	2 cylinder steam engine. 1960 – Twin Leyland 160hp diesel engines	Lytham Shipbuilding and Engineering Company

Final steam ferry originally had a very large funnel, which was removed in 1960 when the Leyland diesels were installed. Could carry about 10 cars.

Name	Built	Acquired	Disposed of	Broken up	Tons	Length	Breadth	Draught	Engine/Propulsion	Builder
Mallard	1990	1990	Still operational		150	87	36	2	1990 – Twin Perkins diesels 2014 – Twin Perkins diesels.	Fl Steelcraft, Borth

Sections of Mallard were transported from Wales to Calgarth slip where she was constructed prior to being towed down the lake to the Nab. Carries 18 cars and up to 100 passengers and receives an overhaul at the Lakeside slipway every 5 years. Her last one was undertaken in 2014.

Windermere Waterbuses

All the Windermere waterbuses were operated by the Bowness Bay Boating Company (BBBC), and from 24th May 1993 by Windermere Lake Cruises (WLC).

Name	Built	Acquired	Disposed of	Broken up	Tons	Length ft	Breadth ft	Draught ft	Engine/ Propulsion	Builder
Venture	1966	1966	Still operational		8	34.7	12.5	2.9	1 x Tempest diesel. Shaft drive / SS	Youdell & Brockbank, Windermere

Originally based in Bowness. She still operates as a reserve vessel for the Windermere fleet and can usually be found tied up at Lakeside. Due to her small size she is suitable for deputising for the wooden launches as she can easily access the small piers at Fell Foot and Wray Castle etc.

Name	Built	Acquired	Disposed of	Broken up	Tons	Length ft	Breadth ft	Draught ft	Engine/ Propulsion	Builder
Wynander	1971	1971	1998	Off lake	10.5	45	11	4.5	1 x Tempest diesel. V drive unit / SS	Cheverton Workboats, Isle of White

She operated for BBBC until 1996 then laid up at Lakeside until late 1998 when sold to Mullen's Cruises of Balloch. After refit started service on the Loch in 1999, renamed the Lomond Monarch. In 2002 Mullen's Cruises was purchased by Sweeny's, who renamed her Glen Falloch. Operated mainly in peak season and spent time laid up in Balloch boatyard. In service again in 2012 for the Balloch-Balmaha waterbus link; resumed in 2013. No Balloch – Balmaha service in 2014, but she occasionally saw service on other routes, and offering trips from Loch Lomond Shores.

Name	Built	Acquired	Disposed of	Broken up	Tons	Length ft	Breadth ft	Draught ft	Engine/ Propulsion	Builder
Belle Isle	1972	1972	1998	Off lake	10.5	45	11	4.5	1 x Tempest diesel. V drive unit / SS	Cheverton Workboats, Isle of White

Late in her career on Windermere had rear deck enclosed. Served on the lake until 1996 then laid up at Lakeside until 1998 when sold to Mullen's Cruises of Balloch. After refit started service on the Loch in 1999, renamed the the Lomond Maid (II) displacing the Lomond Maid (I). In 2002 Mullen's Cruises was purchased by Sweeny's, who sold Lomond Maid (II) to Wear Cruises Limited under the name of Brokaela. Sold in 2005 to River Escapes Limited on the Tyne, who renamed her Coventina, for cruises on the River Tyne from a base near the Gateshead Millennium Bridge.

Name	Built	Acquired	Disposed of	Broken up	Tons	Length ft	Breadth ft	Draught ft	Engine/ Propulsion	Builder
Ladyholme	1934	1973	1990	Off lake	20	39	10	4.5	1 x diesel. Shaft drive / SS	Molenaars Scheepswerf, Zaandam

Dutch style waterbus served in Ireland as the Harbour Princess before coming to Windermere in 1973 to be renamed and painted red for a period. Mainly based from Ambleside and sold in 1990 to Loch Lomond Sailings (later Mullen's Cruises) of Balloch, who renamed her Lomond Maid (I). Served there until 1998 when sold to operate cruises on Llyn Trawsfynydd, as Mared. In 2005 – 2006 operated on Loch Tay as Glen Lyon but returned to Llyn Trawsfynydd. In 2007 was laid up. Operated the 2009 season for 2 different operators, with little success. In November 2009 she broke free during a storm, taking part of the jetty with her, ending up ashore near the dam. Beached, and re-floated in July 2010, taken away for restoration and returned to service. Current whereabouts unknown but listed for sale in 2012 for £28,000 by an Alloa-based company, with the boat's location marked as Staffordshire.

Name	Built	Acquired	Disposed of	Broken up	Tons	Length ft	Breadth ft	Draught ft	Engine/ Propulsion	Builder
Miss Cumbria	1974	1974	Still operational		42.3	65.9	15	3.9	1 x 145hp Volvo Penta Marine diesel. Shaft drive / SS	Molenaars Scheepswerf, Zaandam

Largest waterbus on the lake when launched on 16th May 1974. Originally fitted with a well deck at the rear. In the late 1990s had her rear deck raised and inside revamped with tables being fitted in place of bus seating. In 2010 had another complete internal refit. Operates all year and is usually based in Bowness. She has a stand alone generator to power the bar.

Name	Built	Acquired	Disposed of	Broken up	Tons	Length ft	Breadth ft	Draught ft	Engine/ Propulsion	Builder
Miss Cumbria II	1977	1977	Still operational		42.3	65.9	15	3.9	1 x 145hp Volvo Penta Marine diesel. Shaft drive / SS	Molenaars Scheepswerf, Zaandam

Originally fitted with a well deck at the rear. In the late 1990s she had her rear deck raised. Operates all year and was usually based in Waterhead in summer and Bowness in winter, but following Miss Cumbria III's refit is now based in Bowness in summer and Lakeside in winter. Received extensive refit in the winter of 2013-14 gaining a bar.

Name	Built	Acquired	Disposed of	Broken up	Tons	Length ft	Breadth ft	Draught ft	Engine/ Propulsion	Builder
Miss Cumbria III	1979	1979	Still operational		42.3	65.9	15	3.9	1 x 145hp Volvo Penta Marine diesel. Shaft drive / SS	Molenaars Scheepswerf, Zaandam

Originally fitted with a well deck at the rear. In the late 1990s had her rear deck raised. Withdrawn in late 2011 and had saloon totally revamped, replacing bus style seating with tables and cushioned bench seats. She also received a bar and operates all year. For most of her career she was based in Bowness, but after receiving a bar she swapped with Miss Cumbria II and is now based in Ambleside all year.

Name	Built	Acquired	Disposed of	Broken up	Tons	Length ft	Breadth ft	Draught ft	Engine/ Propulsion	Builder
Silverholme	1969	1981	Still operational		35.6	53.1	12	4.6	1 x Volvo Penta 62hp diesel. Shaft drive / SS	Philip & Son, Dartmouth

Yard number 6089 was launched for the Manchester Ship Canal Company as Silver Arrow II, replacing an earlier Silver Arrow on the canal. Purchased in 1981 and brought to Bowness operating the first season without top deck seating, similar to Ladyholme in appearance. Top deck seating was added with a rear deck, small bar in the saloon and toilet facilities in 1982. The rear deck has since been extended again. Silverholme is now standby vessel on Pier 3 at Bowness for the fleet but is in full time use during the school holidays.

Name	Built	Acquired	Disposed of	Broken up	Tons	Length ft	Breadth ft	Draught ft	Engine/ Propulsion	Builder
Miss Lakeland	1985	1985	Still operational		46.64	62.9	15	5.2	1 x 145hp Volvo Penta Marine diesel. V drive unit / SS	Molenaars Scheepswerf, Zaandam

Largest waterbus on the lake carrying 175 passengers. First Windermere waterbus to have a wheelhouse. Operates all year round and is based from Bowness. She has a standalone generator to power the bar.

Name	Built	Acquired	Disposed of	Broken up	Tons	Length ft	Breadth ft	Draught ft	Engine/ Propulsion	Builder
Miss Westmorland	1988	1988	Still operational		46.3	60	15	5.2	1 x Volvo Penta 62hp diesel. V drive unit / SS	David Abel Boat builders, Bristol

Built in Bristol as another Miss Lakeland but never received her wheelhouse and a steering position was created downstairs. Usually found on the islands cruises operating from Bowness throughout the year. She has a belt driven generator to power the bar.

Name	Built	Acquired	Disposed of	Broken up	Tons	Length ft	Breadth ft	Draught ft	Engine/ Propulsion	Builder
Miss Cumbria IV	1988	1991	Still operational		42.3	65.9	15	3.9	1 x Gardner 127hp diesel. Shaft drive / SS	Molenaars Scheepswerf, Zaandam

Built as Sir William Wallace for Clyde Marine Motoring Company Limited. Operated on the Clyde for the Glasgow Garden festival with sister Robert the Bruce then offered summer cruises from Glasgow to Govan, Renfrew, Clydebank, Newshot Isle and the Erskine Bridge. In April 1991 she headed for Bowness and had top deck fitted before being renamed Miss Cumbria IV and commencing service, on the 20th May. She has bow thrusters as well as power steering. In May 2014 her rear deck was extended by 18 inches to better facilitate carriage of bikes. Operates all year and is based in Bowness. She has a hydraulically driven generator to power the bar.

| Miss Lakeland II | 1992 | 1992 | Still operational | 43 | 66.7 | 15 | 5.2 | 1 x 145hp Volvo Penta Marine diesel. Shaft drive / SS | Molenaars Scheepswerf, Zaandam |

Last waterbus built for the lake as an improved Miss Lakeland. Has a smaller wheelhouse, but a larger rear deck and is fitted with power steering. A hydraulically driven generator powers the bar. Received new flooring and tables in early 2011 and now operates all year, based at Waterhead.

Windermere Smaller Launches

The following is a list of launches we have been able to gather, and it also shows which yard built them, which company operated them, and what happened when their public service was over. For many of the boats not all the information is available but what could be discovered has been added. Inevitably there will be vessels missed off, but the history of these vessels is very vague at best. If a name is followed by a number in brackets, e.g. (II), it means the vessel is the second of the name. If the 'II' is not in brackets, the 'II' was part of the actual name of the vessel. ## means that the vessel is on the National Historic Ships Register.

Many of the launches were built by the Bowness based boat builders, either Borwicks or Shepherds and unfortunately many of the names of the pleasure launches have not survived history but a potted history has been gathered. Every vessel in the following list was built from wood with the exception of the Windermere Submarine and the 4 steel vessels operated by the General Electric Traction and Power Company; Flo, Hilda, May, and Theo. All were single screw except for the submarine.

Name	Approximate Dates of use on Windermere	Builder	Operating Company
August Moon	1920s – c1976	Borwick & Sons, Bowness	Individual boatman / BBBC
	Operated from Bowness but was burned at Ambleside around 1976.		
Bee	1930s – 1950s	Probably Borwick & Sons, Bowness	AML
	Scrapped before amalgamation with the BBBC in the late 1960s.		
Cygnet	1870s – 1900s	?	Mr White of the Swan Hotel
	A small steam launch operating from the Swan Hotel in the later nineteenth century		
Cygnet	C1985 – Still used by WLC as a workboat.	?	SC / WLC
	Small, ex Morecambe Bay, fishing boat from Arnside, purchased by Sea Containers around 1985. Inaugurated service between Lakeside and Fell Foot, but limited to 12 passengers on the crossing. Superseded by Sunflower II, but retained as a work boat. Has an air cooled 3 cylinder Lister engine which can be crank started.		
Daphne ##	1908 – 1960s	Borwick & Sons, Bowness	Old England Hotel
	Petrol boat fitted with a new engine in 1919, receiving a Morris Navigator engine in the 1930s and a Gardner 4BCR in the 2000s. Converted to electric propulsion in 2003. Now in private hands at Preston Brook in Cheshire		
Dolly	1930s – 1960s	Borwick & Sons, Bowness?	BBBC
	Small launch with a blue hull for a time, operated from Bowness.		
Doreen	1920s – 1950s	?	Individual boatman / BBBC
	Small motor launch operating from Bowness, carrying around 12 passengers. May have been part of the BBBC fleet in the 1930s.		
Dorothy	1926 – 1960s; 2004 onwards	Borwick & Sons, Bowness	Probably BBBC
	Purpose built for Windermere operation, probably carrying around 12 passengers. Private sale to the river Thames in the 1960s and later noted on the River Hamble. Returned to the Thames in the early 2000s, returning to Windermere around 2004 after extensive restoration. Often seen out in summer powered by her original Morris Oxford Navigator engine, which was re-bored and stripped back at Scorton. An exact replica was built in Turkey in 2006; named Constance she is stored in a boathouse about 200 yards from where Dorothy is kept.		
Duchess	1920s – 1950s	?	Individual boatman / BBBC
	Small motor launch operating from Bowness carrying around 12 passengers. She became part of the BBBC in the 1930s. Probably the sister to the Duke.		
Duke	1920s – 1950s	?	Individual boatman / BBBC
	Small motor launch operating from Bowness carrying around 12 passengers. She became part of the BBBC in the 1930s. Probably the sister to the Duchess.		
Fairy Queen	1930s – 1970s	Borwick & Sons, Bowness	BBBC
	Had a 3 cylinder diesel engine with an enormous flywheel, and a white hull in most images.		
Fleurette	1930s – 1960s	Borwick & Sons, Bowness?	Langdale Chase Hotel
	Small motor launch was kept at the Langdale Chase private pier – still operating in the early 1960s.		
Flo	1890 – c1894	T.B. Seath & Co, Rutherglen, Glasgow	General Electric Traction and Power Co
	Steel electric launch operated from Cunsey boathouse. Charged up using a generator operated by a waterwheel. One of 4 sisters (others: Hilda, May, and Theo), 2 were probably sold to Manchester in 1891; 2 likely remained in service until 1894.		
Flo	1910s – 1950s	?	Individual boatman
	Small boat operating from Bowness carrying around 12 passengers. Appears on images from between the 2 World Wars.		
Formosa	1920s – 1940s	Crossfield boat builders?	William Robinson
	Built in Arnside the Formosa could accommodate up to 60 passengers and operated from Bowness.		

Ginny	1930s – Still Operational	James Silver's Yard, Rosneath	Classic Cruises
	Brendan Chapman and his family purchased the Olga in 1996 and set about restoring her in 2005/6. Built on the Clyde in 1936 and sailed to Barrow in Furness she was transported to the lake for use as a leisure boat. During the Second World War she was equipped with a water cooled Vickers machine gun on her bow and used by the Home Guard to defend the flying boat factory at White Cross Bay. She began operating for charter from March 2010 as Ginny and now plies between various hotels, including the Beech Hill, Storrs Hall, Cragwood, Lakeside and Langdale Chase as well as using various public piers around the lake. The boat has a capacity of ten and is a Silverette classic.		
Glider	1930s – 1970s	Borwick & Sons, Bowness	BBBC
	She operated from Bowness for the BBBC.		
Have a Go	1940s – 1960s Still operational on Loch Rannoch in 1975.	Joe Huddleston	Huddleston & Kellett
	Operated from Lakeside by 'Huddleston & Kellett Boat Proprietors, Lakeside' perhaps a partnership between the builder and the family who had owned Kellett's Hotel. Sold on for service on Loch Lomond and around 1975 was on Loch Rannoch, linked to the Kinloch Rannoch Hotel. The hotel is long closed, and there is no sign of the vessel.		
Hilda	1890 – c1894	T.B. Seath & Co, Rutherglen, Glasgow	General Electric Traction and Power Co
	Steel electric launch operated from Cunsey boathouse. Charged up using a generator operated by a waterwheel. One of 4 sisters (others: Flo, May, and Theo), 2 were probably sold to Manchester in 1891; 2 likely remained in service until 1894.		
Irene	1920s – 1960s	?	Individual boatman / BBBC
	Small motor launch operating from Bowness from the 1920s. She carried around 12 passengers. She may have become part of the BBBC in the 1930s, but this has not been confirmed.		
Iris	c1945 – c1975; Laid up on Derwentwater	Tom Hayton	KDMLC/AML / BBBC
	Teak built vessel operated on Derwentwater from the Lodore Hotel to Brandlehow, Portinscale and Keswick as an electric launch. Originally had her cabin mid-ships, like the May Queen and was still being used by the hotel in the 1920s. Converted to a motor vessel and incorporated into the KDMLC in 1933. Went to Windermere after the Second World War and operated for the AML, and later the BBBC. Her cabin was moved aft at some point. Returned to Derwentwater by the late 1970s, but chartered in 1994 to Coniston Launch for one season as Ransome. Modified for use there as the piers were lower than those at Derwentwater. Operated a few seasons on Derwentwater after 1994 before being laid up on the Isthmus, where she awaits a major rebuild.		
Iris	1920s – 1950s	?	Individual boatman / BBBC
	Small motor launch operating from Bowness in the 1920s. She may have become part of the BBBC in the 1930s.		
Iroquois	1920s – 1950s	?	Individual boatman / BBBC
	Small 12 passenger motor launch operated from Bowness in the 1920s. May have been in the 1930s BBBC fleet.		
Joan	1920s – 1950s		Individual boatman / BBBC
	Small 12 passenger motor launch operated from Bowness in the 1920s. May have been in the 1930s BBBC fleet.		
Kiwi	1920s – 1960s	Borwick & Sons, Bowness	BBBC
	Operated from Bowness for the BBBC.		
Lady Hamilton	1929 – 1960s	Gibbs of Trowlock Island	Probably AML
	Built in 1924 on the Thames and powered by a 10hp Gaines 'Universal' engine she was acquired by the Sandys family of Graythwaite Hall for private use on Windermere. During the Second World War she had an anti-aircraft gun mounted on the bow and was used by the Home Guard to protect White Cross Bay. After the war she was stored in a boathouse south of Graythwaite Hall before being purchased by Jack Huddleston of Ambleside in 1958. It is thought he used her for cruises from Waterhead, maybe as part of the AML. In the late 1960s (after the amalgamation with the BBBC?) she became the property of Brathay Hall and later sunk. Raised and restored in the 1980s she was restored by the Windermere Nautical Trust and is now electric. In 2009 she was launched onto the River Great Ouse in Cambridgeshire, but is now in dry storage near Henley, for sale for £75,000.		
Lotus ##	1929 – 1991	Borwick & Sons, Bowness	AML / BBBC
	She became part of the AML and remained in the combined fleet after their merger with the BBBC in 1968. Sold 1991 to Stratford upon Avon and converted to electric to operate short cruises on the River Avon.		
May	1890 – c1894	T.B. Seath & Co, Rutherglen, Glasgow	General Electric Traction and Power Co
	Steel electric launch operated from Cunsey boathouse. Charged up using a generator operated by a waterwheel. One of 4 sisters (others: Flo, Hilda, and Theo), 2 were probably sold to Manchester in 1891; 2 likely remained in service until 1894.		
Mayflower (I)	1900s – 1920s	Borwick & Sons, Bowness	Individual boatman
	Operated from Bowness. Sold to Loch Lomond, probably in the early 1920s with Sunflower (I). Noted as being much smaller than the Sunflower (I) while on Loch Lomond, probably carrying around 30 passengers. Operated for Bob Roxburgh and then the Sweeny family from the early 1930s to the 1950s. Likely disposed of before the transfer to Blair's at Balloch in 1951.		
Mayflower (II)	1912 – 1991	Borwick & Sons, Bowness	Individual boatman / WML / BBBC
	She became part of the WML in 1913 and then the BBBC in 1934. Originally carried 63 passengers but this was later reduced. Used on the Belle Isle cruise in the 1980s and between Ambleside and Brockhole. Finally sold in 1991 to Stratford upon Avon. After conversion to electric she still operates short cruises on the River Avon.		

Merlin	1910s – 1930s		William Robinson
	Originally owned by an inhabitant of Wray, William Robinson operated her from Bowness before purchasing the larger Formosa.		
Merry Maid	1920s – 1970s; still on lake	?	Individual boatman / BBBC
	Operated from Bowness by the BBBC. Still on the lake in private hands and now named Merrie Maid.		
Merry Widow	1922 – 1970s	Borwick & Sons, Bowness	Individual boatman / BBBC
	Came into the ownership of the BBBC. Sold for further use and ended up sunk on the River Thames. Rescued and later seen operating for United Motor Boats Bournemouth Boating Services on the United Ferry on the River Stour in Dorset. They fitted a dummy steam funnel to her engine box and still operate her during the summer months. She is 30 foot long and has a capacity for 30 passengers. Her current engine is a 30hp Yamaha.		
Miss Pat	1930s – 1971	Borwick & Sons, Bowness	BBBC
	Sold on to a private owner at Walney near Barrow in 1971.		
Muriel	1920s – 1950s	Borwick & Sons, Bowness?	WML / BBBC
	A launch capable of carrying 58 passengers.		
Muriel II ##	1936 – Still operational	Borwick & Sons, Bowness	BBBC / WLC
	Built to work from Bowness for the BBBC. Originally fitted with an awning over the after end of the vessel but this was replaced with a cabin to match that fitted to Sunflower II after 1950. Still works for WLC, usually on the run from Bowness to Ferry House. She received a new Volvo engine before the summer season in 2015.		
Nellie	1920s – 1950s	?	Individual boatman / BBBC
	Small motor launch operating from Bowness in the 1920s. She may have become part of the BBBC in the 1930s.		
Osprey ##	1930s – Still operational	Shepherds of Bowness	BBBC
	Built in 1902 as a private steam launch, she is 45.5 feet long with a breadth of 18 feet. Became part of the BBBC fleet and fitted with a petrol paraffin engine. She later received a diesel engine. In 1981 joined the Windermere Steamboat Museum and was fitted with a Sissons steam engine for pleasure trips from the museum. Currently undergoing a major rebuild. It is hoped she will once again offer trips on the lake when the Steamboat Museum re-opens.		
Ousel	1880s – 1920s	?	?
	A steam launch which operated from Bowness in the late nineteenth and early twentieth centuries.		
Ousel (II)	1920s – 1970s	Borwick & Sons, Bowness	BBBC
	Operated from Bowness by the BBBC. One of her distinguishing features was a large bus style wheel laid horizontal. After sale remained on the lake as the Gannet with her hull painted blue. Still on the lake in 2009 in a boathouse near Ramp Holme.		
Pastime	1930s – 1960s	Borwick & Sons, Bowness	BBBC
	Built by Borwicks and operated from Bowness by the BBBC.		
Penguin	1930s – 1970s	Borwick & Sons, Bowness	BBBC
	Built by Borwicks and operated from Bowness by the BBBC. She has a white hull in most images.		
Princess of the Lake ##	1950 – Still operational	Watercraft of Molesey	AML / BBBC / WLC
	Built for the AML and worked from Bowness for a time after the merger with the BBBC in 1968. Wheelhouse added around 1981. Still works for WLC, usually operating the 'green cruise' from Ambleside to Wray Castle and Brockhole. Originally had a Gardner 4LW engine, but is now powered by a British Leyland 504.		
Queen of the Lake ##	1949 – Still operational	Watercraft of Molesey	AML / BBBC / WLC
	Built for the AML and worked from Bowness for a time after the merger with the BBBC in 1968. Wheelhouse added around 1981. Still works for WLC, usually operating the 'green cruise' from Ambleside to Wray Castle and Brockhole. In 2012 visited the Thames to take part in Queen Elizabeth's diamond jubilee celebrations. Her engine is a rare Gardner 4LW – recent parts were sourced from South Africa, and removed from a lorry working in a diamond mine.		
Rose	1900 – c1910	?	Storrs Hall Estate
	One of 3 electric launches owned by Mr Townson, the proprietor of the Storrs estate. The others were Shamrock and Thistle. Available for guests of the hotel, charged by a small hydro-electric generator at Storrs. The charge was stored in banks of batteries along the hull. Leakage of acid deteriorated the hull and the vessel had a limited lifespan.		
Shamrock	1900 – c1910	?	Storrs Hall Estate
	One of 3 electric launches owned by Mr Townson, the proprietor of the Storrs estate. The others were Rose and Thistle. Available for guests of the hotel, charged by a small hydro-electric generator at Storrs. The charge was stored in banks of batteries along the hull. Leakage of acid deteriorated the hull and the vessel had a limited lifespan.		
Shamrock ##	1929 – 1974; still in steaming condition	Shepherds of Bowness	Individual boatman / BBBC
	Built in 1906 as a private launch for W.M. Birtwistle and operated by his boatman, Charles Ashley, she was fitted with a Sissons triple expansion steam engine. After Birtwistle's death, Mr Ashley acquired the boat in 1929 and ran it until 1934 when his son William Ashley took over to hire for charters. In 1948 she received a petrol paraffin engine and was used for public cruises by the BBBC for whom William Ashley was a founder. Later received a diesel engine. Put up for sale in 1974 and in November 1976 was acquired and restored by Roger Mallinson. He has installed various types of steam engine, and in 2001 she received her 5th.		

Silver Gleam	1930s – 1970s	Borwick & Sons, Bowness?	BBBC
	A small launch which was operated from Bowness by the BBBC. She was sold to a new owner at Carnforth and placed on the Lancaster Canal. It is believed she has since been scrapped after being badly damaged.		
Spray	1925 – 1991; still operational on River Avon	Borwick & Sons, Bowness	AML / BBBC
	Became part of the AML and remained in the combined fleet after the merger with the BBBC in 1968. Sold in 1991 to Stratford upon Avon and after conversion to electric power still operates short cruises on the River Avon.		
Sunflower (I)	1913– c1920	Borwick & Sons, Bowness	WML
	Operated from Bowness until sold to Loch Lomond – probably in the early 1920s with Mayflower (I) – to Bob Roxburgh and then the Sweeny Family from the early 1930s. Later passed to Blair's, and in 1951 the Lynn family. Joined by Sunflower II (ex Sunflower (II) of Windermere) and fitted with a forward cabin to protect from the short sharp waves on the loch. Renamed Lomond Breeze, but disposed of in 1973.		
Sunflower (II)	1920s – 1940s	Borwick & Sons, Bowness	WML / BBBC
	Operated from Bowness for the WML in the early 1930s and could carry 63 passengers. A 'Sunflower II' from Windermere was operated from Balloch by Blair in 1950, so it is likely to be this vessel. In 1951 Blair's was bought out by Lynn's and Sunflower II was fitted with a forward cabin to protect from the short sharp waves on the loch. Renamed Lomond Gael' but disposed of in 1973.		
Sunflower II ##	1950 – Still operational	Borwick & Sons, Bowness	BBBC / WLC
	Built for BBBC in 1950, and one of the last launches to be built by Borwicks. Still works for WLC, usually on the run from Lakeside to Fell Foot and is fitted with a diesel engine. In 2013 introduced a service for cyclists between Brockhole and Wray Castle at weekends between May and September and daily during the holidays. This was extended to include Bark Barn in 2014. Her role at Fell Foot was covered by Venture. She received a new Volvo engine before the summer season in 2015.		
Theo	1890 – c1894	T.B. Seath & Co, Rutherglen, Glasgow	General Electric Traction and Power Co
	Steel electric launch operated from Cunsey boathouse. Charged up using a generator operated by a waterwheel. One of 4 sisters (others: Flo, Hilda, and May), 2 were probably sold to Manchester in 1891; 2 likely remained in service until 1894.		
Thistle	1900 – c1910	?	Storrs Hall Estate
	One of 3 electric launches owned by Mr Townson, the proprietor of the Storrs estate. The others were Shamrock and Rose. Available for guests of the hotel, charged by a small hydro-electric generator at Storrs. The charge was stored in banks of batteries along the hull. Leakage of acid deteriorated the hull and the vessel had a limited lifespan.		
Waterlily	1926 – 1973; still operational on Loch Awe	Borwick & Sons, Bowness	Individual boatman / BBBC
	Operated from Bowness with a capacity of 39 passengers and distinguishable by her blue roof. Sold in 1973 to W E Gott of Gunthorpe for the River Trent. In 1979 the Trentside Café in Gunthorpe operated her as 'Water Lily Cruises'. Purchased in 1984 by Avril and Harry Watson of Renfrew and converted to steam with a Sisson replica non-condensing compound engine. On 9th August 1986 in service on Loch Awe as Lady Rowena. Sank in 2001 but was raised and after refurbishment re-entered service in 2003. Sank again and was sold to the Ardnaseig Steam Packet renamed Lady Gertrude and operates for guests on Loch Awe.		
Windermere	1997 – 1998	Finland	Paul and Jane Whitfield
	A Mergo Tourist Submarine weighing 24 tons, able to work at a depth of 300 ft but usually between 20 – 100 ft. Carried 10 passengers on hour-long cruises from Lakeside for the 1997 and 1998 seasons. The vessel was removed from the lake in late 1998.		

Bibliography

Anon, 1822, An account of the principle pleasure tours in England and Wales.

Anon, 1853, Keswick and its neighbourhood, a handbook for the use of visitors.

Michael Andrews, 2003, The Furness Railway in and around Barrow.

Michael Andrew and Geoff Holme, 2005, The Coniston Railway.

Baedecker's Guide, 1890/ 1937, Great Britain,

A G Banks, 1984, H W Schneider of Barrow and Bowness.

Robert Beale, 2011, Steamers of the Lakes Vol.1: Windermere.

Robert Beale, 2011, Steamers of the Lakes Vol.2: Coniston, Derwentwater, Ullswater.

A R Bennett, 1927, The Chronicles of Boulton's Sidings.

Michael Berry and Reid Yuen, 2002, A Sunlit Intimate Gift… A tribute to the tri-centenary of the Low Wood Hotel 1702 – 2002.

Anon, 1853, Black's picturesque guide to the English Lakes.

Harold D Bowtell, 1989, Rails through Lakeland, an illustrated history of the Cockermouth, Keswick and Penrith Railway.

John R. Broughton, 2008, The Furness Railway,

Alan Brown, 2000, Loch Lomond Passenger Steamers 1818 – 1989.

Arthur Brydson, 1911, Sidelights on mediaeval Windermere.

Joseph Budworth, 1792, A Fortnight's Ramble to The Lakes.

Alastair Cameron, 1996, Slate from Coniston.

William Collingwood, 1902, The Ancient Ironworks of Coniston Lake.

William Collingwood, 1906, Coniston Tales.

William Collingwood, 1906, The Book of Coniston.

Bill Curtis, 1986, Fleetwood – a town is born.

Ken Davies, 1984, English Lakeland Steamers,

Ken Davies, 2001, Lakeland Pleasure Craft.

Duckworth and Langmuir, 1968, Railway and Other Steamers.

Duckworth and Langmuir, 1990, Clyde River and Other Steamers.

Alfred Fell, 1908, The early iron industry of Furness and District.

J. Fleming and P. L. Nock, c1975, A Cruise on Windermere.

J. Fleming and P. L. Nock, c1988, A Pictorial Souvenir of Windermere.

J. Fleming and P. L. Nock, C1995, Windermere – Ten Miles of Magic.

J. Fleming, 2010, Cruise on Windermere – Souvenir Commentary.

William Ford, 1843, Description of Scenery in the Lake District.

William B. Forwood and Isaac Storey, 1905, Windermere and the Royal Windermere Yacht Club.

James Gibson, 1843, A Guide to the Scenery of Windermere.

Leslie R Gilpin, 2008, The Ulverstone & Lancaster Railway.

David Glover, 2014, The Quarries of Lakeland.

William Green, 1819, The Tourists New Guide, Containing a Description of the Lakes, Mountains and scenery, in Cumberland, Westmorland and Lancashire, with some account of their bordering towns and villages.

Christopher Gregory, 2000, The Extractive Industries of Kentmere.

Alan Hankinson, 1989, The Regatta Men.

Barbara Hall, 1960, The Royal Windermere Yacht Club 1860 – 1960.

Nathanial Hawthorne, 1870, English Note Books.

Eric Holland, 1987, Coniston Copper.

Irvine Hunt, 1975, Fenty's Album.

Irvine Hunt, 1979, Old Lakeland Transport.

Anon, 1863, Hunts Yachting Magazine, Volume the twelfth.

Ian Jones, 2010, RWYC 2010.

David Joy, 1967, Main Line over Shap.

David Joy, 1983, A Regional History of the Railways of Great Britain: Vol 14: The Lake Counties.

Allan King, 2011, Wings on Windermere.

Charlotte Kipling, 1972, The Commercial Fisheries of Windermere (Transactions of Cumberland & Westmorland Antiquarian & Archaeological Society, Volume LXXVII).

Richard Kirkman and Peter van Zeller, 1988, Rails round the Cumbrian Coast.

The Lakeside & Haverthwaite Railway, 2013, Visitors Guide.

Leigh, 1832, Leighs Guide to the Lakes of Westmoreland, Cumberland and Lancashire,

Walter Lees, c1955, Lake Windermere by a Local Boatman.

Charles MacKay, 1846, The scenery and poetry of the English Lakes, a summer ramble.

John Marsh, 1985, Life in Old Lakeland.

John Marsh, 1987, Windermere Lake & Town in Times Past.

John Marsh and John Garbutt, 1994, The Lake Counties of one hundred years ago.

J D Marshall, 1958, Furness & The Industrial Revolution.

J D Marshall and M Davies-Shiel, 1969, The Industrial Archaeology of the Lake Counties.

John Marshall and John K Walton, 1981, The Lake Counties from 1830 to the mid-twentieth century.

Thomas Martin, 1894, Electrical Boats and Navigation.

Harriet Martineau, 1855, Guide to Windermere.

Harriet Martineau, 1855, A complete guide to the English Lakes.

Harriet Martineau, 1885, The English Lake District.

Robin Martakies, 2007, The History of the Windermere Steamers.

Diana R. Matthews, 1982, Lake Festivals on Windermere.

Diana R. Matthews, 1988, Lake Windermere's Golden Jubilee.

Julian Mellentin, 1980, Kendal & Windermere Railway.

J Melville & J L Hobbs, 1951, Early Railway History in Furness.

Peter Morison, Peter Nock, 1992, Comedy of Boating: Memoirs of a Lake District Launch Driver.

Ian L. Muir, 2011, The Ferry Inn on Windermere.

Findlay Muirhead, 1930, Great Britain.

Jonathan Otley, 1834, A Description of the English Lakes (5th Edition).

Peter Nock, 1989, Tales and Legends of Windermere.

K J Norman, 1994, The Furness Railway.

John Wilson Parker, 2002, An Atlas of the English Lakes.

Joseph Palmer, 1798, Windermere: A Poem.

George H. Pattinson, 1977, Windermere Steamboat Museum (and later editions).

George H. Pattinson and Gerry Jackson, 1979, Salvage of Steam Launch Dolly.

George H. Pattinson, 1982, The Great Age of Steam on Windermere.

Herman Ludolph Prior, 1865, Ascents and passes in the Lake District.

Herman Ludolph Prior, 1881, Pedestrian and general guide to the Lake District.

H I Quayle and S C Jenkins, 1977, The Lakeside & Haverthwaite Railway.

Brian Reed, 1969, Crewe to Carlisle.

John Robinson, 1833, Views of the Lakes in the North of England .

William Rollinson, 1996, The Lake District Life and Traditions.

Dick Smith, 2002, The Kendal & Windermere Railway.

Leonard Smith, 2009, Kendal's Port, A Maritime History of the Creek of Milnthorpe.

James Stockdale, 1872, Annales Caermoelenses, or, Annals of Cartmel.

Ian Charles Sumner, 2010, In Search of the Picturesque: The English Photographs of John Wheeley Gough Gutch 1856 – 1859.

Henry Swainson Cowper, 1899, Hawkshead: The Northernmost Parish of Lancashire.

George Tattershall, 1836, The Lakes of England.

Christopher D. Taylor, 1983, A Portrait of Windermere.

M A Tedstone, 2005, The Barry Railway Steamers.

The National Trust, 1987, Steam Yacht Gondola (and 2007 edition).

Ian Tyler, 1992, Greenside: A Tale of Lakeland Miners.

Ian Tyler, 1995, Seathwaite Wad and the Mines of the Borrowdale Valley.

Ian Tyler, 2002, The Gunpowder Mills of Cumbria.

Ian Tyler, 2005, Goldscope and the Mines of Derwent Fells.

Transactions of the Historic Society of Lancashire and Cheshire, 1867, The Two Conistons.

Ullswater Steam Navigation Company, 1903, Ullswater.

B L Thompson, 1971, The Windermere Ferry, An antiquarian essay.

W F Topham, 1869, The Lakes of England.

Oliver M Westall (ed), 1976, Windermere in the Nineteenth Century.

Robert Western, 2001, The Cockermouth, Keswick & Penrith Railway.

Robert Western, 2012, The Kendal & Windermere Railway.

Dick White, 2002, The Windermere Ferry.

Andrew White, 2006, Fast Packet Boats to Kendal.

L A Williams, 1975, Road Transport in Cumbria in the Nineteenth Century.

Anon, 1907, Letters of the Wordsworth Family

Various articles from magazines; 'BackTrack', 'Country Life', 'Cumbria', 'Flight', 'Meccano', 'Old Glory', 'Paddle Wheels', and 'Sea Breezes'.

Jones, Quiggin Co. Builders Book – Merseyside Maritime Museum Archives & Library (Reference DX/154).

Various timetables and guide books from all the boat operators, and railway companies.

Newspaper articles, notably from the 'Carlisle Patriot', 'Kendal Mercury', 'Ulverston Advertiser', and 'Westmorland Gazette'.

Acknowledgements

Countless people have provided us with the odd snippet or fact about the lakes, their history and their boats and unfortunately there will probably be some here that have been missed.

The patient Local Studies team at Kendal Library, headed by Jackie Fay put up with Robert for many hours helping with the newspaper microfilm, and researching some very niche subjects. Margaret Reid and James Arnold of the Windermere Steamboat Museum read proofs and were very encouraging, and the Merseyside Maritime Museum Archives & Library helped uncover the history of the *Enterprise* on Ullswater.

Of the various boating companies Douglas Hodgson and Darren Szafranski helped greatly with both Coniston Launch and the Keswick Launches of which they are affiliated. Greg Simpson, engineer and master of the Gondola, Dennis Whittaker and Peter Keen of the same company, along with Christian Grammar of Ullswater steamers were also forthcoming and accommodating when it came to their respective concerns. Gordon Hall assisted with information from his time at Coniston. David Fozard, John Sweeney, and Colin Dale provided information on some of the waterbuses from Windermere that went on to work elsewhere, whilst Ben Salter helped with the early history of *Cygnet* before her career started on Coniston Water. Ian Clarke of Pennine cruisers updated on *Ruskin's* new career. Derek Hinds donated information and images relating to the re-launch of *Lady of the Lake* in 1978.

As an employee of Windermere Lake Cruises, Robert had lots of help from everyone there in one way or another, but notably Peter Morison, Peter Nock, Ron Walker, John Woodburn, Keith Jackson, Philip Ridley, Tom Cowherd, Alex Williamson, Lee Howson, Nick Breakall, Brian Howson, Nick Thompson, Colin Greatorex and Russell Bowden. All photographs are from the authors' collection, except where indicated.

The Cumbrian Railways Association continues to provide stimulus for Richard's long-standing interest in the railways of the region. Peter van Zeller helped kindle this interest.

Miles Cowsill of Lily Publications has been a constant source of encouragement for the project and Ian Smith has applied his usual design wizardry to the content.

Lastly thanks is due to our families. Kim, Lewis and Alfie put up with Robert on his computer night after night and were happily dragged on field trip after field trip to all the lakes, time and time again for many years. Christina, Charley and Tom tolerated Richard's frequent disappearances to tweak the text and maps.